MW01387821

Android Programming Tutorials

by Mark L. Murphy

COMMONSWARE

Android Programming Tutorials
by Mark L. Murphy

Copyright © 2009-2011 CommonsWare, LLC. All Rights Reserved.
Printed in the United States of America.

CommonsWare books may be purchased in printed (bulk) or digital form for educational or business use. For more information, contact *direct@commonsware.com*.

Printing History:
         Sep 2011: 4th Edition   ISBN: 978-0-9816780-7-8

The CommonsWare name and logo, "Busy Coder's Guide", and related trade dress are trademarks of CommonsWare, LLC.

All other trademarks referenced in this book are trademarks of their respective firms.

The publisher and author(s) assume no responsibility for errors or omissions or for damages resulting from the use of the information contained herein.

Table of Contents

Preface

Welcome to the Book!

If you come to this book after having read its companion volumes, *The Busy Coder's Guide to Android Development*[1] and *The Busy Coder's Guide to Advanced Android Development*[2], thanks for sticking with the series! CommonsWare aims to have the most comprehensive set of Android development resources (outside of the Open Handset Alliance itself), and we appreciate your interest.

If you come to this book having learned about Android from other sources, thanks for joining the CommonsWare community!

Prerequisites

This book is a collection of tutorials, walking you through developing Android applications, from the simplest "Hello, world!" to applications using many advanced Android APIs.

Since this book only supplies tutorials, **you will want something beyond it as a reference guide**. That could be simply the Android SDK documentation, available with your SDK installation or online. It could be the other books in the CommonsWare Android series. Or, it could be another Android book – a list of currently-available Android books can be

---

[1] http://commonsware.com/Android/
[2] http://commonsware.com/AdvAndroid/

found on the Android Programming knol[3]. What you do not want to do is attempt to learn all of Android solely from these tutorials, as they will demonstrate the breadth of the Android API but not its depth.

Also, the tutorials themselves have varying depth. Early on, there is more "hand-holding" to explain every bit of what needs to be done (e.g., classes to import). As the tutorials progress, some of the simpler Java bookkeeping steps are left out of the instructions so the tutorials can focus on the Android aspects of the code.

Those wishing to use Eclipse need prior Eclipse experience – more on this below.

You can find out when new releases of this book are available via:

- The commonsguy[4] Twitter feed
- The CommonsBlog[5]
- The Warescription newsletter, which you can subscribe to off of your Warescription[6] page

Getting Help

If you have questions about the book examples, visit StackOverflow[7] and ask a question, tagged with **android** and **commonsware**.

If you have general Android developer questions, visit StackOverflow and ask a question, tagged with **android** (and any other relevant tags, such as **java**).

Using the Tutorials

Each tutorial has a main set of step-by-step instructions, plus an "Extra Credit" section. The step-by-step instructions are intended to guide you

---

3   http://knol.google.com/k/-/android-programming
4   http://twitter.com/commonsguy
5   http://commonsware.com/blog
6   http://wares.commonsware.com
7   http://stackoverflow.com

through creating or extending Android applications, including all code you need to enter and all commands you need to run. The "Extra Credit" sections, on the other hand, provide some suggested areas for experimentation beyond the base tutorial, without step-by-step instructions.

If you wish to start somewhere in the middle of the book, or if you only wish to do the "Extra Credit" work, or if you just want to examine the results without doing the tutorials directly yourself, you can download the results of each tutorial's step-by-step instructions from the book's github repository[8]. You can either clone the repository, or click the Download button in the upper-right to get the source as a ZIP file. The source code is organized by tutorial number, so you can readily find the project(s) associated with a particular tutorial from the book.

Note that while you are welcome to copy and paste code out of the book, you may wish to copy from the full source code[9] instead. A side-effect of the way the source code listings are put into this book makes them difficult to copy from some PDF viewers, for example.

The tutorials do not assume you are using Eclipse, let alone any other specific editor or debugger. The instructions included in the tutorials will speak in general terms when it comes to tools outside of those supplied by the Android SDK itself.

The tutorials include instructions for both Linux and Windows XP. OS X developers should be able to follow the Linux instructions in general, making slight alterations as needed for your platform. Windows Vista users should be able to follow the Windows XP instructions in general, tweaking the steps to deal with Vista's directory structure and revised Start menu.

If you wish to use the source code from the CommonsWare Web site, bear in mind a few things:

1. The projects are set up to be built by Ant, not by Eclipse. If you wish to use the code with Eclipse, you will need to create a suitable

---

8   https://github.com/commonsguy/cw-lunchlist
9   https://github.com/commonsguy/cw-lunchlist

Android Eclipse project and import the code and other assets – these instructions will help you load the project into a workspace.

2. You should delete build.xml, then run `android update project -p ...` (where ... is the path to a project of interest) on those projects you wish to use, so the build files are updated for your Android SDK version.

Also, please note that the tutorials are set up to work well on HVGA and larger screen sizes. Using them on QVGA or similar sizes is not recommended.

This Book and Eclipse

For building GUIs, the latest Android Developer Tools (ADT) plugin for Eclipse offers drag-and-drop manipulation of widgets and the ability to adjust widget properties via context menus and the like.

This book offers instructions for both Eclipse users and those using other IDEs or ordinary editors. These separate instructions are only for the sections involving changes to the application's GUI or related files – sections involving changing the Java code are the same.

This book does not cover Eclipse use in general, only the Android-specific features that are necessary to build the sample application. If you do not have experience with Eclipse on Java projects, you should either obtain that experience before using this book or perhaps bypass Eclipse and use a regular editor.

The first several tutorials offer detailed instructions, including screenshots of the Eclipse editing tools. Later tutorials simply provide Eclipse-specific instructions. Starting around tutorial #20, it is assumed that you have internalized the use of Eclipse, and so Eclipse-specific instructions are no longer required.

Warescription

This book will be published both in print and in digital form. The digital versions of all CommonsWare titles are available via an annual subscription – the Warescription.

The Warescription entitles you, for the duration of your subscription, to digital forms of *all* CommonsWare titles, not just the one you are reading. Presently, CommonsWare offers PDF and Kindle; other digital formats will be added based on interest and the openness of the format.

Each subscriber gets personalized editions of all editions of each title: both those mirroring printed editions and in-between updates that are only available in digital form. That way, your digital books are never out of date for long, and you can take advantage of new material as it is made available instead of having to wait for a whole new print edition. For example, when new releases of the Android SDK are made available, this book will be quickly updated to be accurate with changes in the APIs.

From time to time, subscribers will also receive access to subscriber-only online material, including not-yet-published new titles.

Also, if you own a print copy of a CommonsWare book, and it is in good clean condition with no marks or stickers, you can exchange that copy[10] for a free four-month Warescription.

If you are interested in a Warescription, visit the Warescription section of the CommonsWare Web site[11].

What's New

For those of you who have a Warescription, or otherwise have been keeping up with this book, here is what is new in this version:

- The tutorials all have Eclipse-specific instructions, as mentioned earlier in this preface

---

10 http://commonsware.com/trade-in.html
11 http://commonsware.com/warescription.html

- Minor improvements were made to the LunchList UI, such as better support for the soft keyboard

- The tutorials were lightly tested on Android 3.1

About the "Further Reading" Sections

Each tutorial has, at the end, a section named "Further Reading". Here, we list places to go learn more about the theory behind the techniques illustrated in the preceding tutorial. Bear in mind, however, that the Internet is fluid, so links may not necessarily work. And, of course, there is no good way to link to other books. Hence, the "Further Reading" section describes where you can find material, but actually getting there may require a few additional clicks on your part. We apologize for the inconvenience.

Errata and Book Bug Bounty

Books updated as frequently as CommonsWare's inevitably have bugs. Flaws. Errors. Even the occasional gaffe, just to keep things interesting. You will find a list of the known bugs on the errata page[12] on the CommonsWare Web site.

But, there are probably even more problems. If you find one, please let us know!

Be the first to report a unique concrete problem in the current digital edition, and we'll give you a coupon for a six-month Warescription as a bounty for helping us deliver a better product. You can use that coupon to get a new Warescription, renew an existing Warescription, or give the coupon to a friend, colleague, or some random person you meet on the subway.

By "concrete" problem, we mean things like:

- Typographical errors

---

12 http://commonsware.com/AndTutorials/errata

- Sample applications that do not work as advertised, in the environment described in the book

- Factual errors that cannot be open to interpretation

By "unique", we mean ones not yet reported. Each book has an errata page on the CommonsWare Web site; most known problems will be listed there. One coupon is given per email containing valid bug reports.

NOTE: Books with version numbers lower than 0.9 are ineligible for the bounty program, as they are in various stages of completion. We appreciate bug reports, though, if you choose to share them with us.

We appreciate hearing about "softer" issues as well, such as:

- Places where you think we are in error, but where we feel our interpretation is reasonable

- Places where you think we could add sample applications, or expand upon the existing material

- Samples that do not work due to "shifting sands" of the underlying environment (e.g., changed APIs with new releases of an SDK)

However, those "softer" issues do not qualify for the formal bounty program.

Be sure to check the book's errata page[13], though, to see if your issue has already been reported.

Questions about the bug bounty, or problems you wish to report for bounty consideration, should be sent to CommonsWare[14].

---

13 http://commonsware.com/AndTutorials/errata
14 mailto:bounty@commonsware.com

Source Code License

The source code samples shown in this book are available for download from the book's GitHub repository[15]. All of the Android projects are licensed under the Apache 2.0 License[16], in case you have the desire to reuse any of it.

Creative Commons and the Four-to-Free (42F) Guarantee

Each CommonsWare book edition will be available for use under the Creative Commons Attribution-Noncommercial-ShareAlike 3.0[17] license as of the fourth anniversary of its publication date, or when 4,000 copies of the edition have been sold, whichever comes first. That means that, once four years have elapsed (perhaps sooner!), you can use this prose for non-commercial purposes. That is our Four-to-Free Guarantee to our readers and the broader community. For the purposes of this guarantee, new Warescriptions and renewals will be counted as sales of this edition, starting from the time the edition is published.

This edition of this book will be available under the aforementioned Creative Commons license on June 1, 2015. Of course, watch the CommonsWare Web site, as this edition might be relicensed sooner based on sales.

For more details on the Creative Commons Attribution-Noncommercial-ShareAlike 3.0 license, visit the Creative Commons Web site.

Note that future editions of this book will become free on later dates, each four years from the publication of that edition or based on sales of that specific edition. Releasing one edition under the Creative Commons license does not automatically release *all* editions under that license.

---

15 http://github.com/commonsguy/cw-andtutorials
16 http://www.apache.org/licenses/LICENSE-2.0.html
17 http://creativecommons.org/licenses/by-nc-sa/3.0/

Lifecycle of a CommonsWare Book

CommonsWare books generally go through a series of stages.

First are the pre-release editions. These will have version numbers below 0.9 (e.g., 0.2). These editions are incomplete, often times having but a few chapters to go along with outlines and notes. However, we make them available to those on the Warescription so they can get early access to the material.

Release candidates are editions with version numbers ending in ".9" (0.9, 1.9, etc.). These editions should be complete. Once again, they are made available to those on the Warescription so they get early access to the material and can file bug reports (and receive bounties in return!).

Major editions are those with version numbers ending in ".0" (1.0, 2.0, etc.). These will be first published digitally for the Warescription members, but will shortly thereafter be available in print from booksellers worldwide.

Versions between a major edition and the next release candidate (e.g., 1.1, 1.2) will contain bug fixes plus new material. Each of these editions should also be complete, in that you will not see any "TBD" (to be done) markers or the like. However, these editions may have bugs, and so bug reports are eligible for the bounty program, as with release candidates and major releases.

A book usually will progress fairly rapidly through the pre-release editions to the first release candidate and Version 1.0 – often times, only a few months. Depending on the book's scope, it may go through another cycle of significant improvement (versions 1.1 through 2.0), though this may take several months to a year or more. Eventually, though, the book will go into more of a "maintenance mode", only getting updates to fix bugs and deal with major ecosystem events – for example, a new release of the Android SDK will necessitate an update to all Android books.

Roster of Tutorials

Here is what you can expect in going through the tutorials in this book:

1. We start off with a simple throwaway project, just to make sure you have the development tools all set up properly.

2. We then begin creating `LunchList`, an application to track restaurants where you might wish to go for lunch. In this tutorial, we set up a simple form to collect basic information about a restaurant, such as a name and address.

3. We expand the form to add radio buttons for the type of restaurant (e.g., takeout).

4. Instead of tracking just a single restaurant, we add support for a list of restaurants – but each restaurant shows up in the list only showing its name.

5. We extend the list to show the name and address of each restaurant, plus an icon for the restaurant type.

6. To give us more room, we split the UI into two tabs, one for the list of restaurants, and one for the detail form for a restaurant.

7. We experiment with an options menu (the kind that appears when you press the MENU button on a phone) and display a pop-up message.

8. We learn how to start a background thread and coordinate communications between the background thread and the main ("UI") thread.

9. We learn how to find out when the activity is going off-screen, stopping and restarting our background thread as needed.

10. We create a separate UI description for what the tabs should look like when the phone is held in a landscape orientation.

11. We finally add database support, so your restaurant data persists from run to run of the application.

12. We eliminate the tabs and split the UI into two separate screens ("activities"), one for the list of restaurants, and one for the detail form to add or edit a restaurant.

13. We establish a shared preference – and an activity to configure it – to allow the user to specify the sort order of the restaurants in the list.

14. We re-establish the landscape version of our UI (lost when we eliminated the tabs in Tutorial 12) and experiment with how to handle the orientation changing during execution of our application.

15. We retrieve an RSS feed for our restaurant and display its results in a separate activity

16. We move the RSS fetch-and-parse logic to a service

17. We give the user the ability to record the GPS coordinates of a restaurant

18. Given those GPS coordinates, we give the user the ability to display where the restaurant is on a map

19. We add an option for the user to have a "lunchtime alarm" that will let them know when it is time for lunch

20. We extend the alarm to either pop up an activity (as before) or display a status bar icon

21. We create an app widget, to allow users to pick a random restaurant right from the home screen

22. We embellish the app widget on Android 3.x devices, to show the list of restaurants right on the home screen, instead of just a single restaurant.

23. We add support for the Android 3.x action bar to the app, plus move all of its business logic into fragments, using the Android Compatibility Library.

24. We leverage the fragments from the previous tutorial to allow the user to see both the restaurants and the details of a selected restaurant on the screen at one time, for large screen devices (e.g., tablets) held in the landscape orientation.

25. We add online help, by adding HTML to the project and displaying it in a dedicated activity.

26. We test the application using the Test Monkey.

27. We add ringtone support to our lunchtime alarms, with a user-selected ringtone.

28. We track the phone number of the restaurant and allow the user to call that phone number from the app.

PART I – Core Tutorials

Your First Android Project

There are two major steps for getting started with Android:

1. You need to install the Android SDK and developer tools

2. You should build a test project to confirm that those tools are properly installed and configured

If you have already done some form of "hello, world" project with the development tools on your development machine, you can skip this tutorial.

If you have not yet installed the Android SDK and related tools, there is an appendix that covers this process. Once you have the Android SDK, it is time to make your first Android project. The good news is that this requires zero lines of code – Android's tools create a "Hello, world!" application for you as part of creating a new project. All you need to do is build it, install it, and see it come up on your emulator or device. That is what this tutorial is for.

Step #1: Create the New Project

Android's tools can create a complete skeleton project for you, with everything you need for a complete (albeit very trivial) Android application. The only real difference comes from whether you are using Eclipse or the command line. Hence, as you will see with many sections in this book, there are separate instructions for Eclipse users and everyone else – please follow the instructions that pertain to you.

Step #1: Eclipse

From the Eclipse main menu, choose File | New | Project..., and this will bring up a list of project types to choose from. Fold open the Android option and click on Android Project:

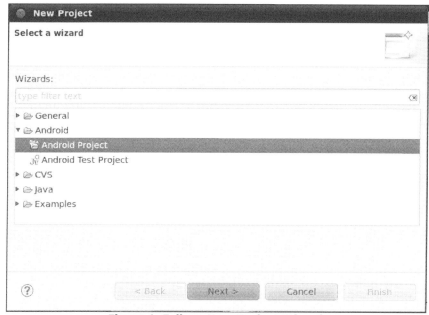

Figure 1. Eclipse New Project Wizard

Press Next to advance the wizard to the main Android project page:

Figure 2. Eclipse New Project Wizard, Android Project

Fill in the following:

- The name of the project (e.g., Now) in the "Project name" field

- The Android SDK you wish to compile against (e.g., Google APIs for Android 2.2) in the "Build Target" table

- The display name for your application (e.g., "Now Sample App") in the "Application name" field

- The name of the Java package in which this project goes (e.g., `com.commonsware.android.skeleton`) in the "Package name" field

- The name of the initial activity to create (e.g., Now) in the "Create Activity" field

- If there is a "Min SDK Version" specified in the wizard, change it to be 4.

At this point, clicking Finish will create your Eclipse project.

Step #2: Command Line

Here is a sample command that creates an Android project from the command line:

```
android create project --target "Google Inc.:Google APIs:8" --path Skeleton/Now
--activity Now --package com.commonsware.android.skeleton
```

This will create an application skeleton for you, complete with everything you need to build your first Android application: Java source code, build instructions, etc. However, you are probably going to need to customize this somewhat. Here are what those command-line switches mean:

- `--target` indicates what version of Android you are "targeting" in terms of your build process. You need to supply the ID of a target that is installed on your development machine, one you downloaded via the SDK and AVD Manager. You can find out what targets are available via the `android list targets` command. Typically, your build process will target the newest version of Android that you have available.

- `--path` indicates where you want the project files to be generated. Android will create a directory if the one you name does not exist. For example, in the command shown above, a `Skeleton/Now/` directory will be created (or used if it exists) underneath the current working directory, and the project files will be stored there.

- --activity indicates the Java class name of your first activity for this project. Do not include a package name, and the name has to meet Java class naming conventions.

- --package indicates the Java package in which your first activity will be located. This package also uniquely identifies your project on any device on which you install it, and this package also needs to be unique on the Android Market if you plan on distributing your application there. Hence, typically, you construct your package based on a domain name you own (e.g., com.commonsware.android.skeleton), to reduce the odds of an accidental package name collision with somebody else.

For your development machine, you will need to pick a suitable target, and you may wish to change the path. The activity and package you can leave alone for now.

Step #2: Build, Install, and Run the Application in Your Emulator or Device

Having a project is nice and all, but it would be even better if we could build and run it, whether on the Android emulator or your Android device. Once again, the process differs somewhat depending on whether you are using Eclipse or not.

Step #1: Eclipse

With your project selected in the Package Explorer pane, click the green "play" button in the Eclipse toolbar to run your project. The first time you do this, you will have to go through a few steps to set up a "run configuration", so Eclipse knows what you want to do.

First, in the "Run As" list, choose "Android Application":

Figure 3. Eclipse "Run As" List

If you have more than one emulator AVD or device available, you will then get an option to choose which you wish to run the application on. Otherwise, if you do not have a device plugged in, the emulator will start up with the AVD you created earlier. Then, Eclipse will install the application on your device or emulator and start it up.

Step #2: Outside of Eclipse

For developers not using Eclipse, launch an emulator (or have a device plugged in and set up for debugging), then, in your terminal, change into the Skeleton/Now directory, then run the following command:

```
ant clean install
```

The Ant-based build should emit a list of steps involved in the installation process, which look like this:

```
Buildfile: /home/some-balding-guy/projects/Skeleton/Now/build.xml
 [setup] Android SDK Tools Revision 8
 [setup] Project Target: Google APIs
 [setup] Vendor: Google Inc.
 [setup] Platform Version: 2.1-update1
```

```
[setup] API level: 7
[setup]
[setup] ------------------
[setup] Resolving library dependencies:
[setup] No library dependencies.
[setup]
[setup] ------------------
[setup]
[setup] WARNING: No minSdkVersion value set. Application will install on all
Android versions.
[setup]
[setup] Importing rules file: tools/ant/main_rules.xml

clean:
 [delete] Deleting directory /home/some-balding-guy/projects/Skeleton/Now/bin

-debug-obfuscation-check:

-set-debug-mode:

-compile-tested-if-test:

-dirs:
 [echo] Creating output directories if needed...
 [mkdir] Created dir: /home/some-balding-guy/projects/Skeleton/Now/bin
 [mkdir] Created dir: /home/some-balding-guy/projects/Skeleton/Now/gen
 [mkdir] Created dir: /home/some-balding-guy/projects/Skeleton/Now/bin/classes

-pre-build:

-resource-src:
 [echo] Generating R.java / Manifest.java from the resources...

-aidl:
 [echo] Compiling aidl files into Java classes...

-pre-compile:

compile:
 [javac] /opt/android-sdk-linux/tools/ant/main_rules.xml:361: warning:
'includeantruntime' was not set, defaulting to build.sysclasspath=last; set to
false for repeatable builds
 [javac] Compiling 2 source files to /home/some-balding-
guy/projects/Skeleton/Now/bin/classes

-post-compile:

-obfuscate:

-dex:
 [echo] Converting compiled files and external libraries into /home/some-
balding-guy/projects/Skeleton/Now/bin/classes.dex...

-package-resources:
```

```
 [echo] Packaging resources
 [aapt] Creating full resource package...

-package-debug-sign:
[apkbuilder] Creating Now-debug-unaligned.apk and signing it with a debug key...

debug:
 [echo] Running zip align on final apk...
 [echo] Debug Package: /home/some-balding-guy/projects/Skeleton/Now/bin/Now-
debug.apk

BUILD SUCCESSFUL
Total time: 4 seconds
```

Note the BUILD SUCCESSFUL at the bottom – that is how you know the application compiled successfully.

When you have a clean build, in your emulator or device, open up the application launcher, typically found at the bottom of the home screen:

Figure 4. Android emulator application launcher

Notice there is an icon for your Now application. Click on it to open it and see your first activity in action. To leave the application and return to the launcher, press the "BACK button", located to the right of the [MENU] button, and looks like an arrow pointing to the left.

A Simple Form

This tutorial is the first of several that will build up a "lunch list" application, where you can track various likely places to go to lunch. While this application may seem silly, it will give you a chance to exercise many features of the Android platform. Besides, perhaps you may even find the application to be useful someday.

Step-By-Step Instructions

Here is how you can create this application:

Step #1: Generate the Application Skeleton

First, we need to create a new project. As with many sections of this book, this one has separate instructions for people using Eclipse and people working outside of Eclipse.

Eclipse

Use the new-project wizard to create an empty Android project named LunchList, as described in the previous tutorial. This will create an application skeleton for you, complete with everything you need to build your first Android application: Java source code, build instructions, etc.

In particular:

- Choose API Level 8 with the Google APIs as your build target, so you can add a map to the application later in this book

- Also use API Level 8 as the minimum SDK version

- Name the project `LunchList`, with an initial activity also named `LunchList`

- Use `apt.tutorial` for the package name

Your Eclipse new Android project wizard window will look a bit like:

Figure 5. The Eclipse new Android project wizard, with settings for LunchList

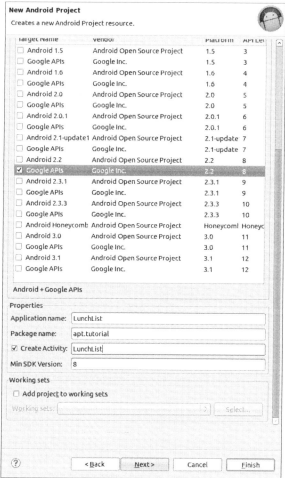

Figure 6. The Eclipse new Android project wizard, with settings for LunchList (continued)

Outside of Eclipse

If you are not using Eclipse, then inside your terminal (e.g., Command Prompt for Windows), switch to some directory where you would like the project to be created . Then, run the following command:

```
android create project --target "Google Inc.:Google APIs:8" --path ./LunchList
--activity LunchList --package apt.tutorial
```

This will create an application skeleton for you, complete with everything you need to start building the LunchList application.

Step #2: Modify the Layout

Now, we need to set up the initial user interface.

Eclipse

In the Package Explorer tab (typically on the left), find the res/layout/main.xml file in your project:

Figure 7. The Package Explorer for LunchList

Double-click on that file to open it up in Eclipse. Initially, it will appear in the GUI builder mode, where you can drag-and-drop widgets on the screen:

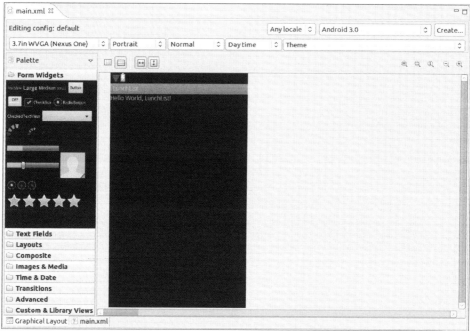

Figure 8. The LunchList main activity layout

By default, your activity's layout will have just a "hello, world" sort of TextView inside of it. We want to change this to have:

- A vertical LinearLayout, holding onto...

- ...a horizontal LinearLayout, with a TextView and EditText for capturing the name of a restaurant, and...

- ...another horizontal LinearLayout, with another TextView and EditText for getting the address of the restaurant, and...

- ...a Button labeled "Save"

First, delete the existing TextView, by clicking on it and pressing the Delete key.

Then, let's add the initial horizontal LinearLayout. In the tool palette on the left side of the graphical editor, click on the Layouts accordion button:

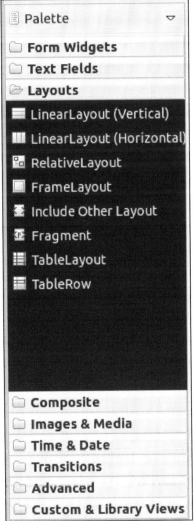

Figure 9. The graphical editor tool palette

Drag a "LinearLayout (Horizontal)" from the tool palette to anywhere in the Android screen in the editor itself:

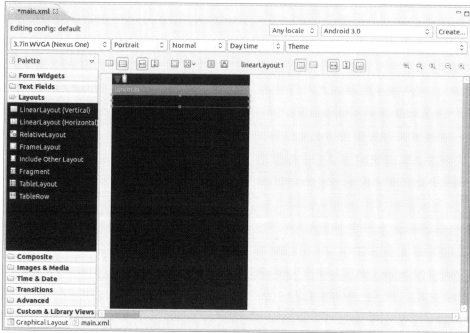

Figure 10. The LunchList main activity layout, with the added horizontal LinearLayout

Next, switch to the Form Widgets section of the tool palette:

Figure 11. The graphical editor tool palette, showing "Form Widgets"

Now, drag and drop a TextView (upper-left corner of the Form Widgets area of the tool palette) into the LinearLayout:

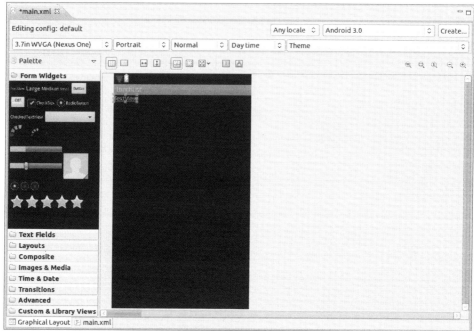

Figure 12. The LunchList main activity layout, with the added TextView

To change the text of the TextView, right-click over it and choose Properties > Text in the context menu. This brings up a dialog where you can type in the new value to be displayed. Enter Name: and click OK, which then updates the main graphical editor to match:

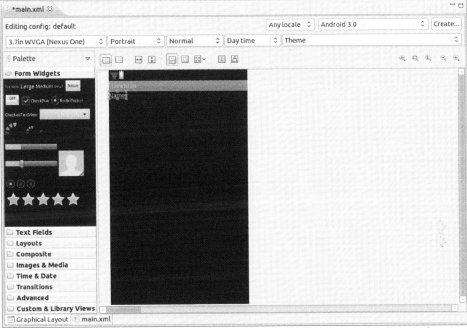

Figure 13. The LunchList main activity layout, with the revised TextView

Next, switch to the Text Fields portion of the tool palette:

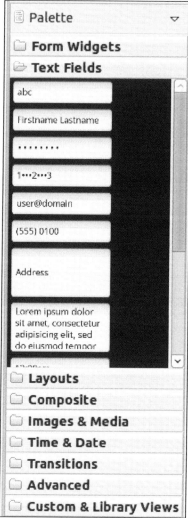

Figure 14. The graphical editor tool palette, showing "Text Fields"

Drag the top-most EditText (the one labeled "abc") into the horizontal LinearLayout to the right of your TextView:

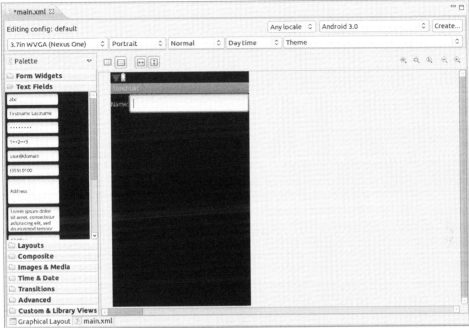

Figure 15. The LunchList main activity layout, with the added ExitText

We need to associate an ID value with this EditText, so we can refer back to it later. To do that, right-click over the EditText and choose "Edit ID..." from the context menu. In the dialog that appears, enter name and click OK.

Then, switch back to the Layouts section of the tool palette and drag a second "LinearLayout (Horizontal)" from the tool palette to anywhere in the Android screen beneath the first horizontal LinearLayout:

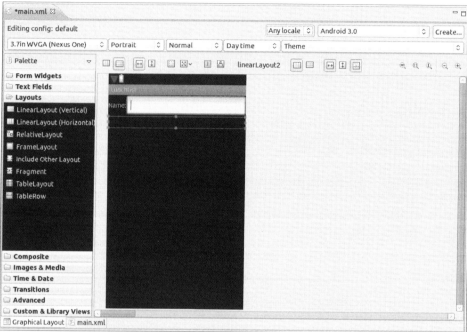

Figure 16. The LunchList main activity layout, with the second horizontal LinearLayout

Switch back to the Form Widgets section of the tool palette and drag a TextView into the second horizontal LinearLayout:

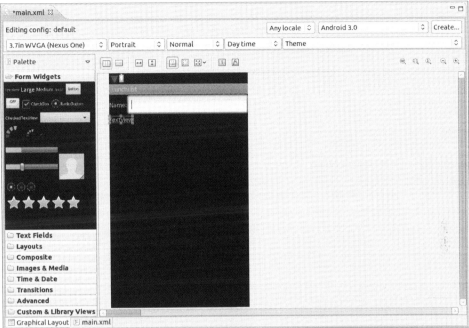

Figure 17. The LunchList main activity layout, with the second TextView

Right-click on the second TextView, choose Properties > Text from the context menu, fill in a value of Address:, and click OK, giving you this:

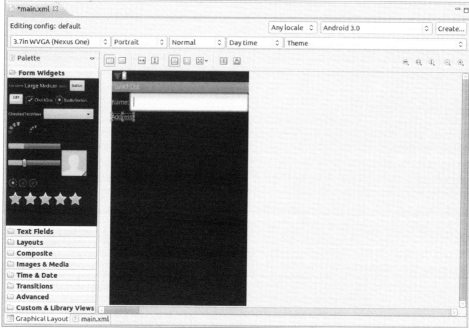

Figure 18. The LunchList main activity layout, with the modified second TextView

Now, switch back to the Text Fields portion of the tool palette and drag another EditText into the layout, to the right of your new TextView:

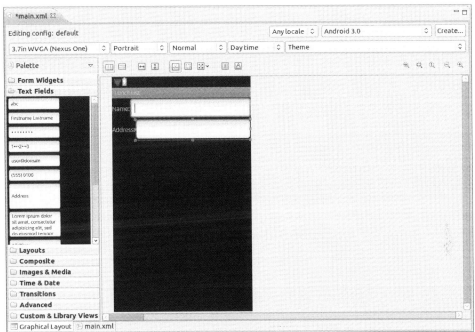

Figure 19. The LunchList main activity layout, with the second EditText

Right-click on the EditText, choose "Edit ID...", fill in a value of addr, and click OK – this assigns an android:id value to the widget.

Then, switch back to the Form Widgets portion of the tool palette, and drag a Button widget (upper-right of the palette) into the form, below the two horizontal LinearLayout widgets:

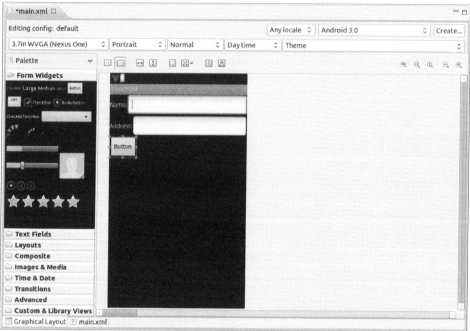

Figure 20. The LunchList main activity layout, with the Button

The Button, by default, has its width set to wrap_content, meaning that it will only take up as much space as is required by the caption. To give the user a bigger target, we can make it fill the width of the screen. To do this, with the Button widget selected (blue outline with the blue squares on the perimeter), click the "Toggle Fill Width" toolbar button above the form – it looks like a horizontal two-headed arrow. This will cause the Button to now fill the width:

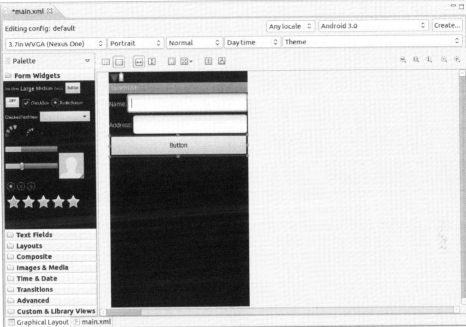

Figure 21. The LunchList main activity layout, with the resized Button

We need to adjust the caption of the Button to be something other than "Button". To do this, right-click on the Button, choose Properties > Text from the context menu, fill in a value of Save in the dialog, and click OK:

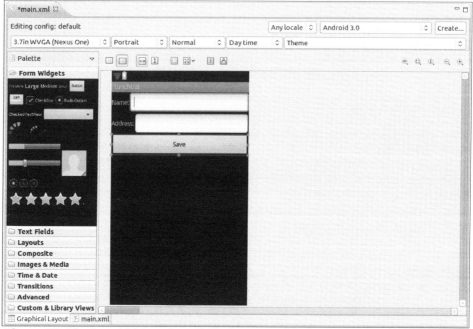

Figure 22. The LunchList main activity layout, with the newly-captioned Button

Now, we need to give the Button an ID value, so we can refer to it at runtime. To do this, right-click on the Button, choose "Edit ID..." from the context menu, enter save in the dialog, and click OK.

Finally, save this file, via the standard Eclipse save-file toolbar button, or via File|Save from the main menu, or by pressing <Ctrl>-<S>.

Outside of Eclipse

Using your text editor, open the LunchList/res/layout/main.xml file. Initially, that file will look like this:

```
<?xml version="1.0" encoding="utf-8"?>
<LinearLayout xmlns:android="http://schemas.android.com/apk/res/android"
 android:orientation="vertical"
 android:layout_width="match_parent"
 android:layout_height="match_parent"
 >
<TextView
```

```
  android:layout_width="match_parent"
  android:layout_height="wrap_content"
  android:text="Hello World, LunchList"
  />
</LinearLayout>
```

Change that layout to look like this:

```
<?xml version="1.0" encoding="utf-8"?>
<LinearLayout xmlns:android="http://schemas.android.com/apk/res/android"
  android:orientation="vertical"
  android:layout_width="match_parent"
  android:layout_height="match_parent"
  >
  <LinearLayout
    android:orientation="horizontal"
    android:layout_width="match_parent"
    android:layout_height="wrap_content"
    >
    <TextView
      android:layout_width="wrap_content"
      android:layout_height="wrap_content"
      android:text="Name:"
      />
    <EditText android:id="@+id/name"
      android:layout_width="match_parent"
      android:layout_height="wrap_content"
      />
  </LinearLayout>
  <LinearLayout
    android:orientation="horizontal"
    android:layout_width="match_parent"
    android:layout_height="wrap_content"
    >
    <TextView
      android:layout_width="wrap_content"
      android:layout_height="wrap_content"
      android:text="Address:"
      />
    <EditText android:id="@+id/addr"
      android:layout_width="match_parent"
      android:layout_height="wrap_content"
      />
  </LinearLayout>
  <Button android:id="@+id/save"
    android:layout_width="match_parent"
    android:layout_height="wrap_content"
    android:text="Save"
  />
</LinearLayout>
```

This gives us a three-row form: one row with a labeled field for the restaurant name, one with a labeled field for the restaurant address, and a big Save button.

Step #3: Support All Screen Sizes

You may want to test this application on an emulator. You may want to test it on a phone. You may want to test it on a tablet.

The layouts we use in these tutorials will work on a variety of screen sizes, but they will work better if we tell Android that we do indeed need those screen sizes. To that end, we need to modify the manifest for our project, to add a `<supports-screens>` element, declaring what sizes we support and do not.

Once again, there are separate instructions depending on whether you are using Eclipse or not.

Eclipse

In the Package Explorer tree (typically on the left), find `AndroidManifest.xml`:

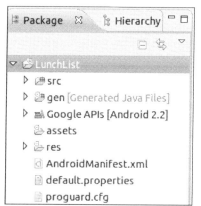

Figure 23. The Eclipse Package Manager

Double-click on that file to bring up the graphical manifest editor:

Figure 24. The LunchList manifest, in the Eclipse manifest editor

Click the Add... button to the right of the list of "Manifest Extras", which brings up an untitled dialog that resembles the following:

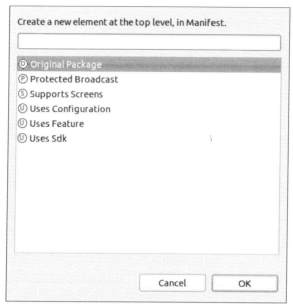

Figure 25. The Eclipse manifest extras dialog

Click on "Supports Screens", then click the OK button. This will add a "Supports Screens" entry in the "Manifest Extras" list:

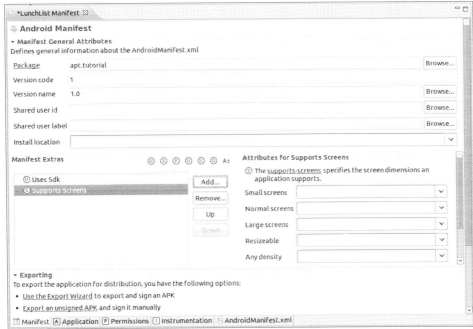

Figure 26. The LunchList manifest with the "Supports Screens" extra

In the "Attributes for Supports Screens" area to the right of the "Manifest Extras" list, change "Small Screens" to `false` and both "Normal Screens" and "Large Screens" to `true`, using the drop-down lists:

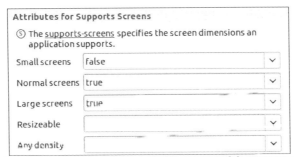

Figure 27. Attributes for Supports Screens, with proper settings

Then, save the manifest file (e.g., via <Ctrl>-<S>).

Outside of Eclipse

Open the `AndroidManifest.xml` file in the root of your project tree, and add in a `<supports-screens>` element. The resulting file should resemble:

```xml
<?xml version="1.0" encoding="utf-8"?>
<manifest android:versionCode="1"
          android:versionName="1.0"
          package="apt.tutorial"
          xmlns:android="http://schemas.android.com/apk/res/android">

  <supports-screens android:largeScreens="true"
                     android:normalScreens="true"
                     android:smallScreens="false" />
  <application android:label="@string/app_name">
    <activity android:label="@string/app_name"
              android:name=".LunchList">
      <intent-filter>
        <action android:name="android.intent.action.MAIN" />
        <category android:name="android.intent.category.LAUNCHER" />
      </intent-filter>
    </activity>
  </application>
</manifest>
```

Here, we are declaring that we support normal, and large, but not small screens. Android will not automatically scale down our UI, so our application will not run on a small-screen device (typically under 3" diagonal screen size). However, it will run well on everything bigger than that.

Step #4: Run the Application

If you are using Eclipse, you should be able to run the application (e.g., click the green "play" toolbar button). The first time you run an Android project (or any Eclipse project), you will be prompted to choose how you want to run it – choose "Android Application". If your emulator is not already running, Eclipse will auto-start it for you, then will install your application and run the initial activity. Note, though, that Eclipse cannot dismiss the "keyguard" (on phones, that's the "slide the green dot to the right" screen you get to prevent "butt-dialing" somebody), so you will have to do that yourself.

If you are not using Eclipse, compile and install the application in the emulator by running the following commands in your terminal:

```
ant clean install
```

Then, in your emulator, in the application launcher, you will see an icon for your LunchList application. Click it to bring up your form.

Regardless of whether you run the application from Eclipse or just from the emulator launcher, you should see a UI like this:

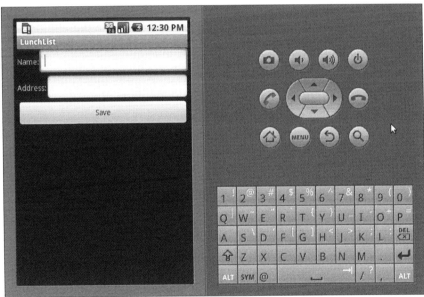

Figure 28. The first edition of LunchList

Use the directional pad (D-pad) to navigate between the fields and button. Enter some text in the fields and click the button, to see how those widgets behave. Then, click the BACK button to return to the application launcher.

Step #5: Create a Model Class

Now, we want to add a class to the project that will hold onto individual restaurants that will appear in the LunchList. Right now, we can only really work with one restaurant, but that will change in a future tutorial.

So, create a new file named LunchList/src/apt/tutorial/Restaurant.java with the following contents:

```
package apt.tutorial;

public class Restaurant {
  private String name="";
  private String address="";

  public String getName() {
    return(name);
  }

  public void setName(String name) {
    this.name=name;
  }

  public String getAddress() {
    return(address);
  }

  public void setAddress(String address) {
    this.address=address;
  }
}
```

Eclipse users can right-click over apt.tutorial in the Package Explorer and choose New > Class from the context menu to bring up the new class dialog, setting the class name to be Restaurant. Non-Eclipse users can simply create a file with the appropriate content in the appropriate location.

This is simply a rudimentary model, with private data members for the name and address, and getters and setters for each of those.

Of course, don't forget to save your changes!

Step #6: Save the Form to the Model

Finally, we want to hook up the Save button, such that when it is pressed, we update a restaurant object based on the two EditText fields. To do this, open up the LunchList/src/apt/tutorial/LunchList.java file and replace the generated Activity implementation with the one shown below:

```
package apt.tutorial;

import android.app.Activity;
import android.os.Bundle;
import android.view.View;
import android.widget.Button;
import android.widget.EditText;

public class LunchList extends Activity {
  Restaurant r=new Restaurant();

  @Override
  public void onCreate(Bundle savedInstanceState) {
    super.onCreate(savedInstanceState);
    setContentView(R.layout.main);

    Button save=(Button)findViewById(R.id.save);

    save.setOnClickListener(onSave);
  }

  private View.OnClickListener onSave=new View.OnClickListener() {
    public void onClick(View v) {
      EditText name=(EditText)findViewById(R.id.name);
      EditText address=(EditText)findViewById(R.id.addr);

      r.setName(name.getText().toString());
      r.setAddress(address.getText().toString());
    }
  };
}
```

In Eclipse, you will find the LunchList activity in the src/ tree of the Package Explorer, just like any other Java project.

Here, we:

- Create a single local restaurant instance when the activity is instantiated

- Get our `Button` from the `Activity` via `findViewById()`, then connect it to a listener to be notified when the button is clicked

- In the listener, we get our two `EditText` widgets via `findViewById()`, then retrieve their contents and put them in the restaurant

This code sample shows the use of an anonymous inner class implementation of a `View.OnClickListener`, named `onSave`. This technique is used in many places throughout this book, as it is a convenient way to organize bits of custom code that go into these various listener objects.

Then, run the `ant install` command to compile and update the emulator, or re-run the project from Eclipse. Run the application to make sure it seems like it runs without errors, though at this point we are not really using the data saved in the restaurant object just yet.

Extra Credit

Here are some things you can try beyond those step-by-step instructions:

- Try replacing the icon for your application. To do this, you will need to find a suitable 48x48 pixel image, create a `drawable/` directory inside your `res/` directory in the project, and adjust the `AndroidManifest.xml` file to contain an `android:icon = "@drawable/my_icon"` attribute in the application element, where `my_icon` is replaced by the base name of your image file.

- Try playing with the fonts for use in both the `TextView` and `EditText` widgets. The Android SDK documentation will show a number of XML attributes you can manipulate to change the color, make the text boldface, etc.

Further Reading

You can learn more about XML layouts in the "Using XML-Based Layouts" chapter of The Busy Coder's Guide to Android Development[18]. Similarly,

---

18 http://commonsware.com/Android

you can learn more about simple widgets, like fields and buttons, in the "Employing Basic Widgets" chapter of the same book, where you will also find "Working with Containers" for container classes like LinearLayout.

A Fancier Form

In this tutorial, we will switch to using a TableLayout for our restaurant data entry form, plus add a set of radio buttons to represent the type of restaurant.

Step-By-Step Instructions

First, you need to have completed the previous tutorial. If you are beginning the tutorials here, or if you wish to not use your existing work, you can download a ZIP file with all of the tutorial results, and you can copy the 02-SimpleForm edition of LunchList to use as a starting point. If you are using Eclipse, these instructions will help you load the project into a workspace.

Step #1: Switch to a TableLayout

A TableLayout will make our form a bit neater, in that the columns will line up, as opposed to the ragged look we get with the nested LinearLayout containers.

As usual, there are separate instructions for those of you using Eclipse and those of you not using Eclipse.

Eclipse

Unfortunately, at the time of this writing, Eclipse lacks much support for reorganizing existing layouts. You cannot drag and drop widgets into new containers and such very readily, let alone convert a `LinearLayout` into a `TableLayout` without deleting its contents. Hence, this is a case where we are forced to work more at the XML level.

If you double-click on the `res/layout/main.xml` resource to bring it up in the graphical editor, there are actually two sub-tabs at the bottom of the editor pane. One is "Graphical Layout", which is the drag-and-drop mode you used in the previous tutorial. The other is "main.xml":

Figure 29. The left side of the editor pane, showing the two sub-tabs at the bottom

Clicking the "main.xml" sub-tab brings up the XML source for the layout file:

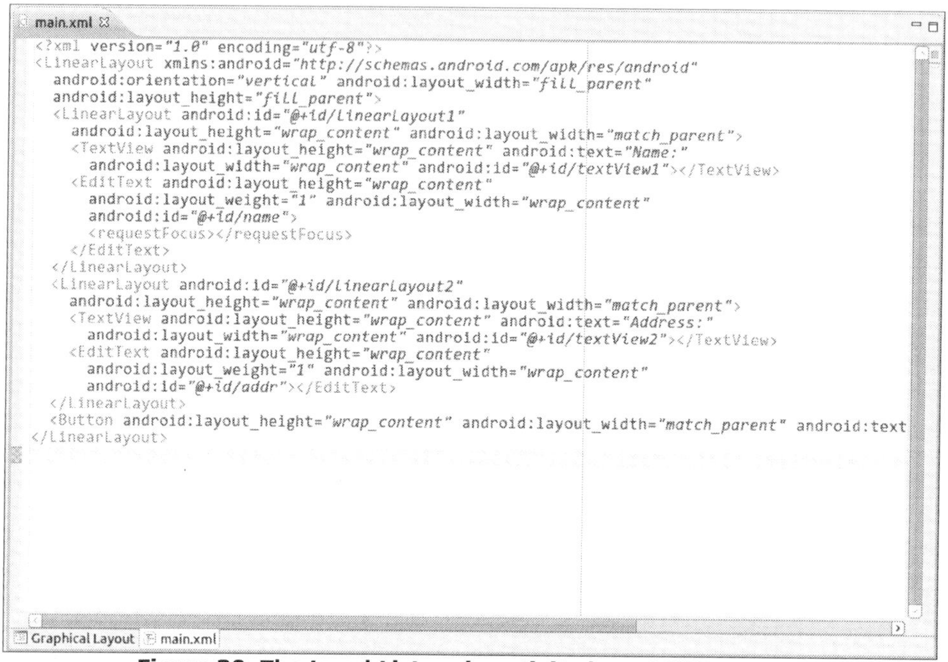

Figure 30. The LunchList main activity layout XML source

Select the whole thing and replace it with:

```xml
<?xml version="1.0" encoding="utf-8"?>
<TableLayout xmlns:android="http://schemas.android.com/apk/res/android"
  android:layout_width="match_parent"
  android:layout_height="match_parent"
  android:stretchColumns="1"
  >
  <TableRow>
    <TextView android:text="Name:" />
    <EditText android:id="@+id/name" />
  </TableRow>
  <TableRow>
    <TextView android:text="Address:" />
    <EditText android:id="@+id/addr" />
  </TableRow>
  <Button android:id="@+id/save"
    android:layout_width="match_parent"
    android:layout_height="wrap_content"
    android:text="Save"
  />
</TableLayout>
```

Notice that we replaced the three `LinearLayout` containers with a `TableLayout` and two `TableRow` containers. We also set up the `EditText` column to be stretchable.

If you switch back to the "Graphical Layout" sub-tab, you will see the preview of the modified layout:

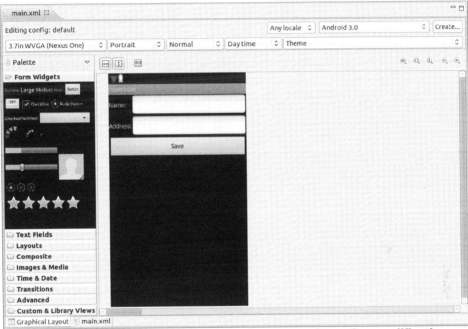

Figure 31. The LunchList main activity layout preview, after modifications

You will notice that the toolbar atop the preview itself has changed. Rather than having buttons to change the desired width (e.g., as we used for the Save button), there is now one that will add a new `TableRow` to the `TableLayout`.

At this point, you can run the modified project on your device or emulator.

Outside of Eclipse

First, open `LunchList/res/layout/main.xml` and modify its contents to look like the following:

```
<?xml version="1.0" encoding="utf-8"?>
<TableLayout xmlns:android="http://schemas.android.com/apk/res/android"
  android:layout_width="match_parent"
  android:layout_height="match_parent"
  android:stretchColumns="1"
  >
  <TableRow>
    <TextView android:text="Name:" />
    <EditText android:id="@+id/name" />
  </TableRow>
  <TableRow>
    <TextView android:text="Address:" />
    <EditText android:id="@+id/addr" />
  </TableRow>
  <Button android:id="@+id/save"
    android:layout_width="match_parent"
    android:layout_height="wrap_content"
    android:text="Save"
  />
</TableLayout>
```

Notice that we replaced the three `LinearLayout` containers with a `TableLayout` and two `TableRow` containers. We also set up the `EditText` column to be stretchable.

Recompile and reinstall the application, then run it in the emulator.

All Environments

When you run the application, you should see something like this:

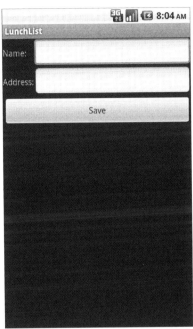

Figure 32. Using a TableLayout

Notice how the two EditText fields line up, whereas before, they appeared immediately after each label.

NOTE: At this step, or any other, when you try to run your application, you may get the following screen:

Figure 33. A "force-close" dialog

If you encounter this, first try to do a full rebuild of the project. In Eclipse, this would involve doing **Project** > **Force Clean**. At the command line, use ant clean or delete the contents of your bin/ and gen/ directories, then ant install. If the problem persists after this, then there is a bug in your code somewhere. You can use adb logcat, DDMS, or the DDMS perspective in Eclipse to see the Java stack trace associated with this crash, to help you perhaps diagnose what is going on.

Step #2: Add a RadioGroup

Next, we should add some RadioButton widgets to indicate the type of restaurant this is: one that offers take-out, one where we can sit down, or one that is only a delivery service.

As is usual with UI changes, there are separate instructions for Eclipse users and everybody else.

Eclipse

The add-row toolbar button in the graphical editor, visible when you have a TableLayout as the base layout for the activity, will add a row above the currently-selected row. So, click on the Save button, then click the add-row toolbar button. That will insert a blank row after the address row and before the Save button:

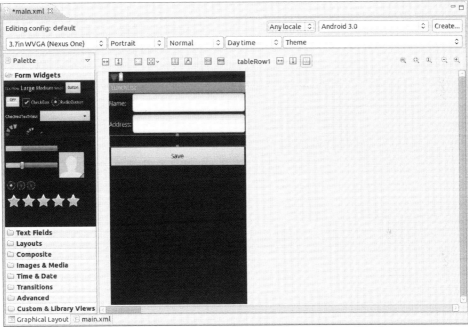

Figure 34. The LunchList main activity layout preview, with the new row

From the "Form Widgets" portion of the tool palette, drag a TextView into the row. Right-click on it, choose Properties > Text... from the context menu, and give it a caption of Type:, which will then give you the following result:

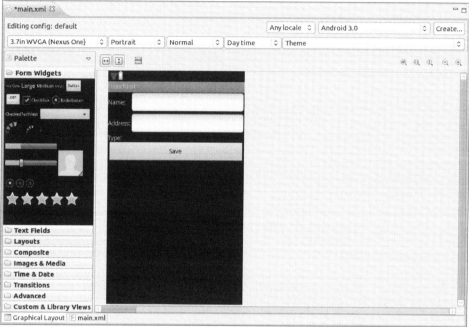

Figure 35. The LunchList main activity layout preview, with the added TextView

Next, drag a `RadioGroup` into the row. The `RadioGroup` icon is in the "Form Widgets" portion of the tool palette and looks like three radio buttons side-by-side. This will give you something that looks like this:

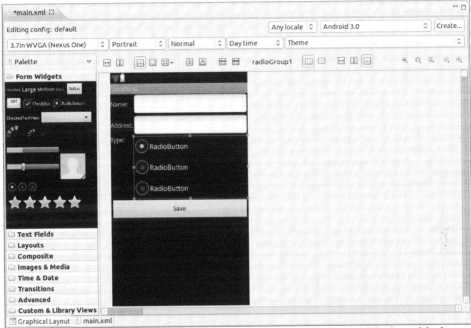

Figure 36. The LunchList main activity layout preview, with the added RadioGroup

You will note that it not only puts in the group, but adds three RadioButton widgets for us. As it turns out, that is precisely how many we need, though we could click on existing ones to delete extras, or drag other RadioButton widgets from the tool palette into the group. The RadioGroup is set to have vertical orientation, which is a good default and what we need to use here, though we could modify that via the context menu on the RadioGroup if we needed to.

However, we do need to set the android:id value for the RadioGroup. To do this, right-click on the RadioGroup (to the right of the RadioButton widgets, so you do not right-click on one of those), choose Edit ID... from the context menu, fill in a value of types, and click OK.

Also, we do need to adjust the RadioButton widgets – if nothing else, we need more useful captions. So, right-click on the top RadioButton, and choose Properties > Text... from the context menu, and give it a caption of Take-Out. Also, right-click on it, choose Edit ID... from the context menu, and give it an ID value of take_out. Repeat those steps for the other two RadioButton widgets, with Sit-Down and sit_down for the second widget's caption and ID, and Delivery and delivery for the third widget's caption and ID. This should give you:

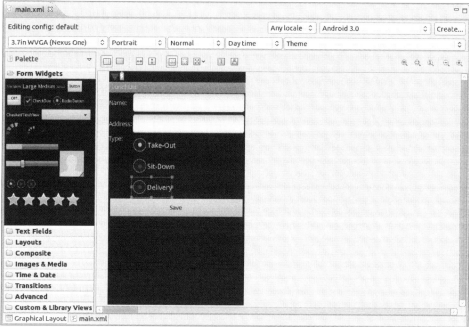

Figure 37. The LunchList main activity layout preview, with the configured RadioButton widgets

At this point, save your layout file, then run the project to see your changes in action.

Outside of Eclipse

To do this, modify LunchList/res/layout/main.xml once again, this time to look like:

```xml
<?xml version="1.0" encoding="utf-8"?>
<TableLayout xmlns:android="http://schemas.android.com/apk/res/android"
  android:layout_width="match_parent"
  android:layout_height="match_parent"
  android:stretchColumns="1"
```

```
  android:shrinkColumns="1"
  >
  <TableRow>
    <TextView android:text="Name:" />
    <EditText android:id="@+id/name" />
  </TableRow>
  <TableRow>
    <TextView android:text="Address:" />
    <EditText android:id="@+id/addr" />
  </TableRow>
  <TableRow>
    <TextView android:text="Type:" />
    <RadioGroup android:id="@+id/types">
      <RadioButton android:id="@+id/take_out"
        android:text="Take-Out"
        android:checked="true"
      />
      <RadioButton android:id="@+id/sit_down"
        android:text="Sit-Down"
      />
      <RadioButton android:id="@+id/delivery"
        android:text="Delivery"
      />
    </RadioGroup>
  </TableRow>
  <Button android:id="@+id/save"
    android:layout_width="match_parent"
    android:layout_height="wrap_content"
    android:text="Save"
  />
</TableLayout>
```

Our RadioGroup and RadioButton widgets go inside the TableLayout, so they will line up with the rest of table – you can see this once you recompile, reinstall, and run the application. Also note that we make one of the RadioButton widgets be checked at the outset.

Step #3: Update the Model

Right now, our model class has no place to hold the restaurant type. To change that, modify LunchList/src/apt/tutorial/Restaurant.java to add in a new private String type data member and a getter/setter pair, like these:

```
public String getType() {
  return(type);
}

public void setType(String type) {
```

```
    this.type=type;
  }
```

When you are done, your restaurant class should look something like this:

```
package apt.tutorial;

public class Restaurant {
  private String name="";
  private String address="";
  private String type="";

  public String getName() {
    return(name);
  }

  public void setName(String name) {
    this.name=name;
  }

  public String getAddress() {
    return(address);
  }

  public void setAddress(String address) {
    this.address=address;
  }

  public String getType() {
    return(type);
  }

  public void setType(String type) {
    this.type=type;
  }
}
```

Step #4: Save the Type to the Model

Finally, we need to wire our `RadioButton` widgets to the model, such that when the user clicks the Save button, the type is saved as well. To do this, modify the `onSave` listener object to look like this:

```
private View.OnClickListener onSave=new View.OnClickListener() {
  public void onClick(View v) {
    EditText name=(EditText)findViewById(R.id.name);
    EditText address=(EditText)findViewById(R.id.addr);

    r.setName(name.getText().toString());
```

```
    r.setAddress(address.getText().toString());

  RadioGroup types=(RadioGroup)findViewById(R.id.types);

  switch (types.getCheckedRadioButtonId()) {
    case R.id.sit_down:
      r.setType("sit_down");
      break;

    case R.id.take_out:
      r.setType("take_out");
      break;

    case R.id.delivery:
      r.setType("delivery");
      break;
  }
 }
};
```

Note that you will also need to import `android.widget.RadioGroup` for this to compile. The full activity will then look like this:

```
package apt.tutorial;

import android.app.Activity;
import android.os.Bundle;
import android.view.View;
import android.widget.Button;
import android.widget.EditText;
import android.widget.RadioGroup;

public class LunchList extends Activity {
  Restaurant r=new Restaurant();

  @Override
  public void onCreate(Bundle savedInstanceState) {
    super.onCreate(savedInstanceState);
    setContentView(R.layout.main);

    Button save=(Button)findViewById(R.id.save);

    save.setOnClickListener(onSave);
  }

  private View.OnClickListener onSave=new View.OnClickListener() {
    public void onClick(View v) {
      EditText name=(EditText)findViewById(R.id.name);
      EditText address=(EditText)findViewById(R.id.addr);

      r.setName(name.getText().toString());
      r.setAddress(address.getText().toString());
```

```
    RadioGroup types=(RadioGroup)findViewById(R.id.types);

    switch (types.getCheckedRadioButtonId()) {
      case R.id.sit_down:
        r.setType("sit_down");
        break;

      case R.id.take_out:
        r.setType("take_out");
        break;

      case R.id.delivery:
        r.setType("delivery");
        break;
    }
  }
};
}
```

Recompile, reinstall, and run the application. Confirm that you can save the restaurant data without errors.

If you are wondering what will happen if there is no selected RadioButton, the RadioGroup call to getCheckedRadioButtonId() will return -1, which will not match anything in our switch statement, and so the model will not be modified.

Extra Credit

Here are some things you can try beyond those step-by-step instructions:

- If you have an Android device, try installing the app on the device and running it there. The easiest way to do this is to shut down your emulator, plug in your device, and run ant reinstall.

- Try creating the RadioButton widgets in Java code, instead of in the layout. To do this, you will need to create the RadioButton objects themselves, configure them (e.g., supply them with text to display), then add them to the RadioGroup via addView().

- Try adding more RadioButton widgets than there are room to display on the screen. Note how the screen does not automatically scroll to show them. Then, wrap your entire layout in a ScrollView container, and see how the form can now scroll to accommodate all of your widgets.

Further Reading

You can learn more about radio buttons in the "Employing Basic Widgets" chapter of The Busy Coder's Guide to Android Development[19]. Also, you will find material on TableLayout in the "Working with Containers" chapter of the same book.

---

19 http://commonsware.com/Android

TUTORIAL 4

Adding a List

In this tutorial, we will change our model to be a list of restaurants, rather than just one. Then, we will add a ListView to view the available restaurants. This will be rather incomplete, in that we can only add a new restaurant, not edit or delete an existing one, but we will cover those steps too in a later tutorial.

Step-By-Step Instructions

First, you need to have completed the previous tutorial. If you are beginning the tutorials here, or if you wish to not use your existing work, you can download a ZIP file with all of the tutorial results, and you can copy the 03-FancierForm edition of LunchList to use as a starting point. If you are using Eclipse, these instructions will help you load the project into a workspace.

Step #1: Hold a List of Restaurants

First, if we are going to have a list of restaurants in the UI, we need a list of restaurants as our model. So, in LunchList, change:

```
Restaurant r=new Restaurant();
```

to:

```
List<Restaurant> model=new ArrayList<Restaurant>();
```

Note that you will need to import java.util.List and java.util.ArrayList as well.

Step #2: Save Adds to List

Note that the above code will not compile, because our onSave Button click handler is still set up to reference the old single restaurant model. For the time being, we will have onSave simply add a new restaurant.

All we need to do is add a local restaurant r variable and populate it:

```
private View.OnClickListener onSave=new View.OnClickListener() {
  public void onClick(View v) {
    Restaurant r=new Restaurant();
    EditText name=(EditText)findViewById(R.id.name);
    EditText address=(EditText)findViewById(R.id.addr);

    r.setName(name.getText().toString());
    r.setAddress(address.getText().toString());

    RadioGroup types=(RadioGroup)findViewById(R.id.types);

    switch (types.getCheckedRadioButtonId()) {
      case R.id.sit_down:
        r.setType("sit_down");
        break;

      case R.id.take_out:
        r.setType("take_out");
        break;

      case R.id.delivery:
        r.setType("delivery");
        break;
    }
  }
};
```

At this point, you should be able to rebuild and reinstall the application. Test it out to make sure that clicking the button does not cause any unexpected errors.

You will note that we are not adding the actual restaurant to anything – r is a local variable and so goes out of scope after onClick() returns. We will address this shortcoming later in this exercise.

Step #3: Implement toString()

To simplify the creation of our ListView, we need to have our restaurant class respond intelligently to toString(). That will be called on each restaurant as it is displayed in our list.

For the purposes of this tutorial, we will simply use the name – later tutorials will make the rows much more interesting and complex.

So, add a toString() implementation on Restaurant like this:

```
public String toString() {
  return(getName());
}
```

Recompile and ensure your application still builds.

Step #4: Add a ListView Widget

Now comes the challenging part – adding the ListView to the layout.

The challenge is in getting the layout right. Right now, while we have only the one screen to work with, we need to somehow squeeze in the list without eliminating space for anything else. In fact, ideally, the list takes up all the available space that is not being used by our current detail form.

One way to achieve that is to use a RelativeLayout as the over-arching layout for the screen. We anchor the detail form to the bottom of the screen, then have the list span the space from the top of the screen to the top of the detail form.

Unfortunately, for Eclipse users, there does not seem to be a good way to accomplish this purely via drag-and-drop, short of starting over from scratch. It is simpler to modify the XML directly.

To make this change, replace your current LunchList/res/layout/main.xml with the following:

```xml
<?xml version="1.0" encoding="utf-8"?>
<RelativeLayout xmlns:android="http://schemas.android.com/apk/res/android"
  android:layout_width="match_parent"
  android:layout_height="match_parent"
  >
  <TableLayout android:id="@+id/details"
    android:layout_width="match_parent"
    android:layout_height="wrap_content"
    android:layout_alignParentBottom="true"
    android:stretchColumns="1"
    android:shrinkColumns="1"
    >
  <TableRow>
    <TextView android:text="Name:" />
    <EditText android:id="@+id/name" />
  </TableRow>
  <TableRow>
    <TextView android:text="Address:" />
    <EditText android:id="@+id/addr" />
  </TableRow>
  <TableRow>
    <TextView android:text="Type:" />
    <RadioGroup android:id="@+id/types">
      <RadioButton android:id="@+id/take_out"
        android:text="Take-Out"
        android:checked="true"
      />
      <RadioButton android:id="@+id/sit_down"
        android:text="Sit-Down"
      />
      <RadioButton android:id="@+id/delivery"
        android:text="Delivery"
      />
    </RadioGroup>
  </TableRow>
  <Button android:id="@+id/save"
    android:layout_width="match_parent"
    android:layout_height="wrap_content"
    android:text="Save"
  />
</TableLayout>
<ListView android:id="@+id/restaurants"
  android:layout_width="match_parent"
  android:layout_height="wrap_content"
```

```
    android:layout_alignParentTop="true"
    android:layout_above="@id/details"
  />
</RelativeLayout>
```

From an XML standpoint, here we:

- Wrap the entire existing XML in a RelativeLayout element, moving our xmlns:android declaration to the new root

- Add android:layout_alignParentBottom="true" to the TableLayout, to position it on the bottom

- Add android:id="@+id/details" to the TableLayout, so we can position the ListView relative to it

- Change android:layout_height to wrap_content on the TableLayout, to leave room for the ListView

- Add the ListView element and its attributes

If you recompile and rebuild the application, then run it, you will see our form slid to the bottom, with empty space at the top:

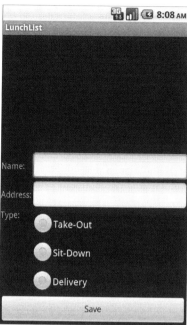

Figure 38. Adding a list to the top and sliding the form to the bottom

Step #5: Build and Attach the Adapter

The ListView will remain empty, of course, until we do something to populate it. What we want is for the list to show our running lineup of restaurant objects.

Since we have our ArrayList<Restaurant>, we can easily wrap it in an ArrayAdapter<Restaurant>. This also means, though, that when we add a restaurant, we need to add it to the ArrayAdapter via add() – the adapter will, in turn, put it in the ArrayList. Otherwise, if we add it straight to the ArrayList, the adapter will not know about the added restaurant and therefore will not display it.

Here is the new implementation of the LunchList class:

```
package apt.tutorial;

import android.app.Activity;
```

```
import android.os.Bundle;
import android.view.View;
import android.widget.ArrayAdapter;
import android.widget.Button;
import android.widget.EditText;
import android.widget.ListView;
import android.widget.RadioGroup;
import java.util.ArrayList;
import java.util.List;

public class LunchList extends Activity {
  List<Restaurant> model=new ArrayList<Restaurant>();
  ArrayAdapter<Restaurant> adapter=null;

  @Override
  public void onCreate(Bundle savedInstanceState) {
    super.onCreate(savedInstanceState);
    setContentView(R.layout.main);

    Button save=(Button)findViewById(R.id.save);

    save.setOnClickListener(onSave);

    ListView list=(ListView)findViewById(R.id.restaurants);

    adapter=new ArrayAdapter<Restaurant>(this,
                      android.R.layout.simple_list_item_1,
                      model);
    list.setAdapter(adapter);
  }

  private View.OnClickListener onSave=new View.OnClickListener() {
    public void onClick(View v) {
      Restaurant r=new Restaurant();
      EditText name=(EditText)findViewById(R.id.name);
      EditText address=(EditText)findViewById(R.id.addr);

      r.setName(name.getText().toString());
      r.setAddress(address.getText().toString());

      RadioGroup types=(RadioGroup)findViewById(R.id.types);

      switch (types.getCheckedRadioButtonId()) {
        case R.id.sit_down:
          r.setType("sit_down");
          break;

        case R.id.take_out:
          r.setType("take_out");
          break;

        case R.id.delivery:
          r.setType("delivery");
          break;
```

```
    }

    adapter.add(r);
  }
};
}
```

The magic value `android.R.layout.simple_list_item_1` is a stock layout for a list row, just displaying the text of the object in white on a black background with a reasonably large font. In later tutorials, we will change the look of our rows to suit our own designs.

If you then add a few restaurants via the form, it will look something like this:

Figure 39. Our LunchList with a few fake restaurants added

Extra Credit

Here are some things you can try beyond those step-by-step instructions:

- See what the activity looks like if you use a `Spinner` instead of a `ListView`.

- Make the address field, presently an `EditText` widget, into an `AutoCompleteTextView`, using the other addresses as values to possibly reuse (e.g., for multiple restaurants in one place, such as a food court or mall).

Further Reading

Information on `ListView` and other selection widgets can be found in the "Using Selection Widgets" chapter of The Busy Coder's Guide to Android Development[20].

---

20 http://commonsware.com/Android

Making A More Elaborate List

In this tutorial, we will update the layout of our `ListView` rows, so they show both the name and address of the restaurant, plus an icon indicating the type. Along the way, we will need to create our own custom `ListAdapter` to handle our row views and a `RestaurantHolder` to populate a row from a restaurant.

Regarding the notion of adapters and `ListAdapter`, to quote from *The Busy Coder's Guide to Android Development*:

> *In the abstract, adapters provide a common interface to mul-*
> *tiple disparate APIs. More specifically, in Android's case,*
> *adapters provide a common interface to the data model be-*
> *hind a selection-style widget, such as a listbox...Android's*
> *adapters are responsible for providing the roster of data for a*
> *selection widget plus converting individual elements of data*
> *into specific views to be displayed inside the selection widget.*

Step-By-Step Instructions

First, you need to have completed the previous tutorial. If you are beginning the tutorials here, or if you wish to not use your existing work, you can download a ZIP file with all of the tutorial results, and you can copy the `04-ListView` edition of `LunchList` to use as a starting point. If you are using Eclipse, these instructions will help you load the project into a workspace.

Step #1: Create a Stub Custom Adapter

First, let us create a stub implementation of a `RestaurantAdapter` that will be where we put our logic for creating our own custom rows. That can look like this, implemented as an inner class of `LunchList`:

```
class RestaurantAdapter extends ArrayAdapter<Restaurant> {
  RestaurantAdapter() {
    super(LunchList.this,
        android.R.layout.simple_list_item_1,
        model);
  }
}
```

We hard-wire in the `android.R.layout.simple_list_item_1` layout for now, and we get our `Activity` and model from `LunchList` itself.

We also need to change our `adapter` data member to be a `RestaurantAdapter`, both where it is declared and where it is instantiated in `onCreate()`. Make these changes, then rebuild and reinstall the application and confirm it works as it did at the end of the previous tutorial.

Step #2: Design Our Row

Next, we want to design a row that incorporates all three of our model elements: name, address, and type. For the type, we will use three icons, one for each specific type (sit down, take-out, delivery). You can use whatever icons you wish, but they need to be named `ball_red.png`, `ball_yellow.png`, and `ball_green.png`, all located in `res/drawable/` in your project.

NOTE: If your project has no `res/drawable/` directory, but does have `res/drawable-ldpi/` and others with similar suffixes, rename `res/drawable-mdpi/` to `res/drawable/` directory for use in this project, and delete the other `res/drawable-*` directories.

NOTE #2: Links to download the three icons used in this tutorial are:

- ball_green.png[21]
- ball_red.png[22]
- ball_yellow.png[23]

The general layout is to have the icon on the left and the name stacked atop the address to the right:

Figure 40. A fancy row for our fancy list

To achieve this look, we use a nested pair of LinearLayout containers. And, once again, we have separate instructions for those of you using Eclipse and those of you who are not.

Eclipse

To add a new layout resource, simply right-click on the res/layout/ directory in the Package Explorer, and choose New > File from the options menu. That will bring up the new-file dialog:

---

21 https://github.com/commonsguy/cw-lunchlist/raw/master/05-FancyList/LunchList/res/drawable/ball_green.png

22 https://github.com/commonsguy/cw-lunchlist/raw/master/05-FancyList/LunchList/res/drawable/ball_red.png

23 https://github.com/commonsguy/cw-lunchlist/raw/master/05-FancyList/LunchList/res/drawable/ball_yellow.png

Figure 41. The Eclipse new-file dialog

Fill in row.xml as the name and click Finish. It will show up in your Package Explorer with a red X, indicating a problem:

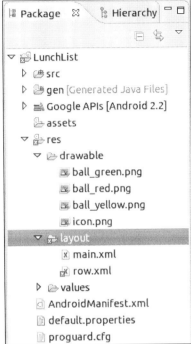

Figure 42. The Eclipse Package Explorer, showing our new and incomplete file

That is because there is no content in the file yet. To address this, from the Layouts section of the tool palette, drag a "LinearLayout (Horizontal)" into the open area of the graphical editor and drop it. That will set up the initial contents of the file, with our root container.

Then, right-click anywhere on the main area of the preview (basically, where our LinearLayout resides) and choose Properties > Padding from the context menu. Fill in a value of 4dip and click OK.

Next, in the "Images & Media" section of the tool palette, drag an ImageView into the LinearLayout. The ImageView is the widget in the upper-left corner of the "Images & Media" section of the tool palette – if you hover your mouse over it, the tool-tip will indicate the class. Immediately, you will be presented with a dialog to choose a "drawable resource" to apply to the image, via a Resource Chooser:

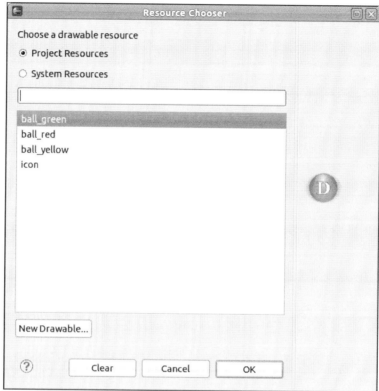

Figure 43. The Eclipse drawable Resource Chooser

We will get more into resources later in the book – for now, take it on faith that this is a list of all the images in your various resource directories. Click on ball_green and click OK. This will give you the following preview:

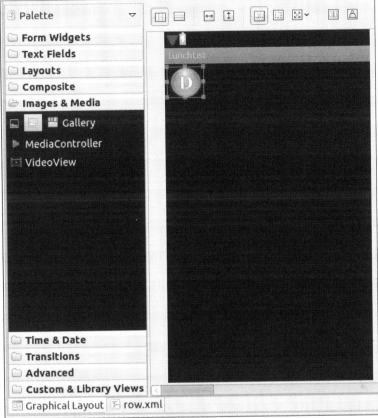

Figure 44. The current working edition of the row layout

Right-click over the ImageView, choose Edit ID... from the context menu, and fill in an ID of icon.

Our existing LinearLayout is set to fill the screen, which is not ideal for a row in the list. Click the toolbar button above the preview that looks like a pair of vertically-oriented arrowheads, to switch the height to be wrap_content. There will be no visual result, other than the toolbar button no longer being inset.

Now, we need to add a vertical LinearLayout for the two TextView widgets. From the Layouts section of the tool palette, drag a "LinearLayout (Vertical)" to the layout, dropping it to the right of the ImageView. Use the toolbar toggle button to change the width to match_parent (click the pair of horizontally-oriented arrowheads).

Next, from the "Form Widgets" section of the tool palette, drag a TextView into the newly-created vertical LinearLayout. Make the following adjustments to that widget:

- Give it an ID of title by choosing Edit ID... from the context menu

- Have it fill the width of the LinearLayout by toggling the width toolbar button (click the pair of horizontally-oriented arrowheads)

- Make it boldface by choosing Properties > Text Style > Bold from the context menu

- Set the maximum number of lines to be 1 by choosing Properties > Max Lines from the context menu

- Set the ellipsis rule to be end by choosing Properties > Ellipsize > End from the context menu

Now, drag another TextView into the vertical LinearLayout, below the TextView you just added. Make the following adjustments to that widget:

- Give it an ID of address by choosing Edit ID... from the context menu

- Have it fill the width of the LinearLayout by toggling the width toolbar button (click the pair of horizontally-oriented arrowheads)

- Set the maximum number of lines to be 1 by choosing Properties > Max Lines from the context menu

- Set the ellipsis rule to be end by choosing Properties > Ellipsize > End from the context menu

With the second TextView selected (has the blue outline and drag handles), shift-click on the top TextView (hold the Shift key while clicking) to select both widgets. Now, changes you make will affect both widgets. Click the "Change Gravity" toolbar button (sixth from left, looks like arrows pointing to the four corners) and choose "Center Vertical" from the popup menu. Then, click the "Distribute Weights Evenly" toolbar button (second from right, looks like a pair of rectangles separated by a vertical bar), dividing the total height of the row between them.

At this point, you can save your changes, using the standard Eclipse save-file options (e.g., Ctrl-S).

Outside of Eclipse

Use the following XML as the basis for `LunchList/res/layout/row.xml`:

```xml
<LinearLayout xmlns:android="http://schemas.android.com/apk/res/android"
  android:layout_width="match_parent"
  android:layout_height="wrap_content"
  android:orientation="horizontal"
  android:padding="4dip"
  >
  <ImageView android:id="@+id/icon"
    android:layout_width="wrap_content"
    android:layout_height="match_parent"
    android:layout_alignParentTop="true"
    android:layout_alignParentBottom="true"
    android:layout_marginRight="4dip"
  />
  <LinearLayout
    android:layout_width="match_parent"
    android:layout_height="wrap_content"
    android:orientation="vertical"
    >
    <TextView android:id="@+id/title"
      android:layout_width="match_parent"
      android:layout_height="wrap_content"
      android:layout_weight="1"
      android:gravity="center_vertical"
      android:textStyle="bold"
      android:maxLines="1"
      android:ellipsize="end"
    />
    <TextView android:id="@+id/address"
      android:layout_width="match_parent"
      android:layout_height="wrap_content"
      android:layout_weight="1"
      android:gravity="center_vertical"
      android:maxLines="1"
      android:ellipsize="end"
    />
  </LinearLayout>
</LinearLayout>
```

Some of the unusual attributes applied in this layout include:

- android:padding, which arranges for some whitespace to be put outside the actual widget contents but still be considered part of the widget (or container) itself when calculating its size

- android:textStyle, where we can indicate that some text is in bold or italics

- android:maxLines, which indicates how many lines the text should appear on, at most

- android:ellipsize, which indicates where text should be truncated and ellipsized if it is too long for the available space

Step #3: Override getView(): The Simple Way

Next, we need to use this layout ourselves in our RestaurantAdapter. To do this, we need to override getView() and inflate the layout as needed for rows.

Modify RestaurantAdapter to look like the following:

```
class RestaurantAdapter extends ArrayAdapter<Restaurant> {
  RestaurantAdapter() {
    super(LunchList.this,
          android.R.layout.simple_list_item_1,
          model);
  }

  public View getView(int position, View convertView,
                      ViewGroup parent) {
    View row=convertView;

    if (row==null) {
      LayoutInflater inflater=getLayoutInflater();

      row=inflater.inflate(R.layout.row, null);
    }

    Restaurant r=model.get(position);

    ((TextView)row.findViewById(R.id.title)).setText(r.getName());
    ((TextView)row.findViewById(R.id.address)).setText(r.getAddress());

    ImageView icon=(ImageView)row.findViewById(R.id.icon);
```

```
    if (r.getType().equals("sit_down")) {
      icon.setImageResource(R.drawable.ball_red);
    }
    else if (r.getType().equals("take_out")) {
      icon.setImageResource(R.drawable.ball_yellow);
    }
    else {
      icon.setImageResource(R.drawable.ball_green);
    }

    return(row);
  }
}
```

Notice how we create a row only if needed, recycling existing rows. But, we still pick out each `TextView` and `ImageView` from each row and populate it from the restaurant at the indicated position.

Step #4: Create a RestaurantHolder

To improve performance and encapsulation, we should move the logic that populates a row from a restaurant into a separate class, one that can cache the `TextView` and `ImageView` widgets.

To do this, add the following static inner class to `LunchList`:

```
static class RestaurantHolder {
  private TextView name=null;
  private TextView address=null;
  private ImageView icon=null;

  RestaurantHolder(View row) {
    name=(TextView)row.findViewById(R.id.title);
    address=(TextView)row.findViewById(R.id.address);
    icon=(ImageView)row.findViewById(R.id.icon);
  }

  void populateFrom(Restaurant r) {
    name.setText(r.getName());
    address.setText(r.getAddress());

    if (r.getType().equals("sit_down")) {
      icon.setImageResource(R.drawable.ball_red);
    }
    else if (r.getType().equals("take_out")) {
      icon.setImageResource(R.drawable.ball_yellow);
```

```
    }
    else {
       icon.setImageResource(R.drawable.ball_green);
    }
  }
}
```

Step #5: Recycle Rows via RestaurantHolder

To take advantage of the new RestaurantHolder, we need to modify
getView() in RestaurantAdapter. Following the holder pattern, we need to
create a RestaurantHolder when we inflate a new row, cache that wrapper in
the row via setTag(), then get it back later via getTag().

Change getView() to look like the following:

```
public View getView(int position, View convertView,
                    ViewGroup parent) {
  View row=convertView;
  RestaurantHolder holder=null;

  if (row==null) {
    LayoutInflater inflater=getLayoutInflater();

    row=inflater.inflate(R.layout.row, parent, false);
    holder=new RestaurantHolder(row);
    row.setTag(holder);
  }
  else {
    holder=(RestaurantHolder)row.getTag();
  }

  holder.populateFrom(model.get(position));

  return(row);
}
```

This means the whole LunchList class looks like:

```
package apt.tutorial;

import android.app.Activity;
import android.os.Bundle;
import android.view.View;
import android.view.ViewGroup;
import android.view.LayoutInflater;
import android.widget.ArrayAdapter;
```

```
import android.widget.Button;
import android.widget.EditText;
import android.widget.ImageView;
import android.widget.ListView;
import android.widget.RadioGroup;
import android.widget.TextView;
import java.util.ArrayList;
import java.util.List;

public class LunchList extends Activity {
  List<Restaurant> model=new ArrayList<Restaurant>();
  RestaurantAdapter adapter=null;

  @Override
  public void onCreate(Bundle savedInstanceState) {
    super.onCreate(savedInstanceState);
    setContentView(R.layout.main);

    Button save=(Button)findViewById(R.id.save);

    save.setOnClickListener(onSave);

    ListView list=(ListView)findViewById(R.id.restaurants);

    adapter=new RestaurantAdapter();
    list.setAdapter(adapter);
  }

  private View.OnClickListener onSave=new View.OnClickListener() {
    public void onClick(View v) {
      Restaurant r=new Restaurant();
      EditText name=(EditText)findViewById(R.id.name);
      EditText address=(EditText)findViewById(R.id.addr);

      r.setName(name.getText().toString());
      r.setAddress(address.getText().toString());

      RadioGroup types=(RadioGroup)findViewById(R.id.types);

      switch (types.getCheckedRadioButtonId()) {
        case R.id.sit_down:
          r.setType("sit_down");
          break;

        case R.id.take_out:
          r.setType("take_out");
          break;

        case R.id.delivery:
          r.setType("delivery");
          break;
      }

      adapter.add(r);
```

```
    }
};

class RestaurantAdapter extends ArrayAdapter<Restaurant> {
  RestaurantAdapter() {
    super(LunchList.this, R.layout.row, model);
  }

  public View getView(int position, View convertView,
                        ViewGroup parent) {
    View row=convertView;
    RestaurantHolder holder=null;

    if (row==null) {
      LayoutInflater inflater=getLayoutInflater();

      row=inflater.inflate(R.layout.row, parent, false);
      holder=new RestaurantHolder(row);
      row.setTag(holder);
    }
    else {
      holder=(RestaurantHolder)row.getTag();
    }

    holder.populateFrom(model.get(position));

    return(row);
  }
}

static class RestaurantHolder {
  private TextView name=null;
  private TextView address=null;
  private ImageView icon=null;

  RestaurantHolder(View row) {
    name=(TextView)row.findViewById(R.id.title);
    address=(TextView)row.findViewById(R.id.address);
    icon=(ImageView)row.findViewById(R.id.icon);
  }

  void populateFrom(Restaurant r) {
    name.setText(r.getName());
    address.setText(r.getAddress());

    if (r.getType().equals("sit_down")) {
      icon.setImageResource(R.drawable.ball_red);
    }
    else if (r.getType().equals("take_out")) {
      icon.setImageResource(R.drawable.ball_yellow);
    }
    else {
      icon.setImageResource(R.drawable.ball_green);
    }
```

```
    }
  }
}
```

Rebuild and reinstall the application, then try adding several restaurants and confirm that, when the list is scrolled, everything appears as it should – the name, address, and icon all change.

Note that you may experience a problem, where your EditText widgets shrink, failing to follow the android:stretchColumns rule. This is a bug in Android[24] that will hopefully be repaired one day.

Extra Credit

Here are some things you can try beyond those step-by-step instructions:

- Customize the rows beyond just the icon based on each restaurant, such as applying different colors to the name based upon certain criteria.

- Use three different layouts for the three different restaurant types. To do this, you will need to override getItemViewType() and getViewTypeCount() in the custom adapter to return the appropriate data.

Further Reading

Using custom Adapter classes and creating list rows that are more than mere strings is covered in the "Getting Fancy with Lists" chapter of The Busy Coder's Guide to Android Development[25].

---

24 http://code.google.com/p/android/issues/detail?id=6089
25 http://commonsware.com/Android

TUTORIAL 6

Splitting the Tab

In this tutorial, we will move our `ListView` onto one tab and our form onto a separate tab of a `TabView`. Along the way, we will also arrange to update our form based on a `ListView` selections or clicks, even though the Save button will still only add new restaurants to our list.

Step-By-Step Instructions

First, you need to have completed the previous tutorial. If you are beginning the tutorials here, or if you wish to not use your existing work, you can download a ZIP file with all of the tutorial results, and you can copy the `05-FancyList` edition of `LunchList` to use as a starting point. If you are using Eclipse, these instructions will help you load the project into a workspace.

Step #1: Rework the Layout

First, we need to change our layout around, to introduce the tabs and split our UI between a list tab and a details tab. This involves:

- Removing the `RelativeLayout` and the layout attributes leveraging it, as that was how we had the list and form on a single screen

- Add in a `TabHost`, `TabWidget`, and `FrameLayout`, the latter of which is parent to the list and details

Once again, this sort of refactoring is not readily possible in Eclipse using drag-and-drop. Hence, Eclipse users will need to edit the XML of the layout file using the `main.xml` sub-tab, just as non-Eclipse users would edit the XML.

Hence, to accomplish this, replace your current `LunchList/res/layout/main.xml` with the following:

```xml
<?xml version="1.0" encoding="utf-8"?>
<TabHost xmlns:android="http://schemas.android.com/apk/res/android"
  android:id="@android:id/tabhost"
  android:layout_width="match_parent"
  android:layout_height="match_parent">
  <LinearLayout
    android:orientation="vertical"
    android:layout_width="match_parent"
    android:layout_height="match_parent">
    <TabWidget android:id="@android:id/tabs"
      android:layout_width="match_parent"
      android:layout_height="wrap_content"
    />
    <FrameLayout android:id="@android:id/tabcontent"
      android:layout_width="match_parent"
      android:layout_height="match_parent"
    >
      <ListView android:id="@+id/restaurants"
        android:layout_width="match_parent"
        android:layout_height="match_parent"
      />
      <TableLayout android:id="@+id/details"
        android:layout_width="match_parent"
        android:layout_height="wrap_content"
        android:stretchColumns="1"
        android:shrinkColumns="1"
        android:paddingTop="4dip"
      >
      <TableRow>
        <TextView android:text="Name:" />
        <EditText android:id="@+id/name" />
      </TableRow>
      <TableRow>
        <TextView android:text="Address:" />
        <EditText android:id="@+id/addr" />
      </TableRow>
      <TableRow>
        <TextView android:text="Type:" />
        <RadioGroup android:id="@+id/types">
          <RadioButton android:id="@+id/take_out"
            android:text="Take-Out"
            android:checked="true"
          />
```

```
        <RadioButton android:id="@+id/sit_down"
           android:text="Sit-Down"
        />
        <RadioButton android:id="@+id/delivery"
           android:text="Delivery"
        />
      </RadioGroup>
    </TableRow>
    <Button android:id="@+id/save"
      android:layout_width="match_parent"
      android:layout_height="wrap_content"
      android:text="Save"
    />
   </TableLayout>
  </FrameLayout>
 </LinearLayout>
</TabHost>
```

Step #2: Wire In the Tabs

Next, we need to modify the LunchList itself, so it is a TabActivity (rather than a plain Activity) and teaches the TabHost how to use our FrameLayout contents for the individual tab panes. To do this:

1. Add imports to LunchList for android.app.TabActivity and android.widget.TabHost

2. Make LunchList extend TabActivity

3. Obtain 32px high icons from some source to use for the list and details tab icons, place them in LunchList/res/drawable as list.png and restaurant.png, respectively – if you wish to use the ones shown in the book, they are linked to here as list.png[26] and restaurant.png[27]

4. Add the following code to the end of your onCreate() method:

```
TabHost.TabSpec spec=getTabHost().newTabSpec("tag1");

spec.setContent(R.id.restaurants);
spec.setIndicator("List", getResources()
                          .getDrawable(R.drawable.list));
getTabHost().addTab(spec);

spec=getTabHost().newTabSpec("tag2");
```

26 https://github.com/commonsguy/cw-lunchlist/raw/master/06-Tabs/LunchList/res/drawable/list.png

27 https://github.com/commonsguy/cw-lunchlist/raw/master/06-Tabs/LunchList/res/drawable/restaurant.png

```
spec.setContent(R.id.details);
spec.setIndicator("Details", getResources()
                           .getDrawable(R.drawable.restaurant));
getTabHost().addTab(spec);

getTabHost().setCurrentTab(0);
```

At this point, you can recompile and reinstall the application and try it out.
You should see a two-tab UI like this:

Figure 45. The first tab of the two-tab LunchList

Figure 46. The second tab of the two-tab LunchList

Step #3: Get Control On List Events

Next, we need to detect when the user clicks on one of our restaurants in the list, so we can update our detail form with that information.

First, add an import for `android.widget.AdapterView` to `LunchList`. Then, create an `AdapterView.OnItemClickListener` named `onListClick`:

```
private AdapterView.OnItemClickListener onListClick=new
AdapterView.OnItemClickListener() {
  public void onItemClick(AdapterView<?> parent,
                          View view, int position,
                          long id) {

  }
};
```

Finally, call `setOnItemClickListener()` on the `ListView` in the activity's `onCreate()` to connect the `ListView` to the `onListClick` listener object (`list.setOnItemClickListener(onListClick);`)

Step #4: Update Our Restaurant Form On Clicks

Next, now that we have control in a list item click, we need to actually find the associated restaurant and update our details form.

To do this, you need to do two things. First, move the name, address, and types variables into data members and populate them in the activity's onCreate() – our current code has them as local variables in the onSave listener object's onClick() method. So, you should have some data members like:

```
EditText name=null;
EditText address=null;
RadioGroup types=null;
```

And some code after the call to setContentView() in onCreate() like:

```
name=(EditText)findViewById(R.id.name);
address=(EditText)findViewById(R.id.addr);
types=(RadioGroup)findViewById(R.id.types);
```

Then, add smarts to onListClick to update the details form:

```
private AdapterView.OnItemClickListener onListClick=new
AdapterView.OnItemClickListener() {
  public void onItemClick(AdapterView<?> parent,
                          View view, int position,
                          long id) {
    Restaurant r=model.get(position);

    name.setText(r.getName());
    address.setText(r.getAddress());

    if (r.getType().equals("sit_down")) {
      types.check(R.id.sit_down);
    }
    else if (r.getType().equals("take_out")) {
      types.check(R.id.take_out);
    }
    else {
      types.check(R.id.delivery);
    }
  }
};
```

Note how we find the clicked-upon restaurant via the position parameter, which is an index into our ArrayList of restaurants.

Step #5: Switch Tabs On Clicks

Finally, we want to switch to the detail form when the user clicks a restaurant in the list.

This is just one extra line of code, in the onItemClick() method of our onListClick listener object:

```
getTabHost().setCurrentTab(1);
```

This just changes the current tab to the one known as index 1, which is the second tab (tabs start counting at 0).

At this point, you should be able to recompile and reinstall the application and test out the new functionality.

Here is the complete source code to our LunchList activity, after all of the changes made in this tutorial:

```
package apt.tutorial;

import android.app.TabActivity;
import android.os.Bundle;
import android.view.View;
import android.view.ViewGroup;
import android.view.LayoutInflater;
import android.widget.AdapterView;
import android.widget.ArrayAdapter;
import android.widget.Button;
import android.widget.EditText;
import android.widget.ImageView;
import android.widget.ListView;
import android.widget.RadioGroup;
import android.widget.TabHost;
import android.widget.TextView;
import java.util.ArrayList;
import java.util.List;

public class LunchList extends TabActivity {
  List<Restaurant> model=new ArrayList<Restaurant>();
```

```
RestaurantAdapter adapter=null;
EditText name=null;
EditText address=null;
RadioGroup types=null;

@Override
public void onCreate(Bundle savedInstanceState) {
  super.onCreate(savedInstanceState);
  setContentView(R.layout.main);

  name=(EditText)findViewById(R.id.name);
  address=(EditText)findViewById(R.id.addr);
  types=(RadioGroup)findViewById(R.id.types);

  Button save=(Button)findViewById(R.id.save);

  save.setOnClickListener(onSave);

  ListView list=(ListView)findViewById(R.id.restaurants);

  adapter=new RestaurantAdapter();
  list.setAdapter(adapter);

  TabHost.TabSpec spec=getTabHost().newTabSpec("tag1");

  spec.setContent(R.id.restaurants);
  spec.setIndicator("List", getResources()
                            .getDrawable(R.drawable.list));
  getTabHost().addTab(spec);

  spec=getTabHost().newTabSpec("tag2");
  spec.setContent(R.id.details);
  spec.setIndicator("Details", getResources()
                            .getDrawable(R.drawable.restaurant));
  getTabHost().addTab(spec);

  getTabHost().setCurrentTab(0);

  list.setOnItemClickListener(onListClick);
}

private View.OnClickListener onSave=new View.OnClickListener() {
  public void onClick(View v) {
    Restaurant r=new Restaurant();
    r.setName(name.getText().toString());
    r.setAddress(address.getText().toString());

    switch (types.getCheckedRadioButtonId()) {
      case R.id.sit_down:
        r.setType("sit_down");
        break;

      case R.id.take_out:
        r.setType("take_out");
```

```
        break;

      case R.id.delivery:
        r.setType("delivery");
        break;
    }

    adapter.add(r);
  }
};

private AdapterView.OnItemClickListener onListClick=new
AdapterView.OnItemClickListener() {
  public void onItemClick(AdapterView<?> parent,
                          View view, int position,
                          long id) {
    Restaurant r=model.get(position);

    name.setText(r.getName());
    address.setText(r.getAddress());

    if (r.getType().equals("sit_down")) {
      types.check(R.id.sit_down);
    }
    else if (r.getType().equals("take_out")) {
      types.check(R.id.take_out);
    }
    else {
      types.check(R.id.delivery);
    }

    getTabHost().setCurrentTab(1);
  }
};

class RestaurantAdapter extends ArrayAdapter<Restaurant> {
  RestaurantAdapter() {
    super(LunchList.this, R.layout.row, model);
  }

  public View getView(int position, View convertView,
                      ViewGroup parent) {
    View row=convertView;
    RestaurantHolder holder=null;

    if (row==null) {
      LayoutInflater inflater=getLayoutInflater();

      row=inflater.inflate(R.layout.row, parent, false);
      holder=new RestaurantHolder(row);
      row.setTag(holder);
    }
    else {
      holder=(RestaurantHolder)row.getTag();
```

```
      }

    holder.populateFrom(model.get(position));

    return(row);
  }
}

static class RestaurantHolder {
  private TextView name=null;
  private TextView address=null;
  private ImageView icon=null;

  RestaurantHolder(View row) {
    name=(TextView)row.findViewById(R.id.title);
    address=(TextView)row.findViewById(R.id.address);
    icon=(ImageView)row.findViewById(R.id.icon);
  }

  void populateFrom(Restaurant r) {
    name.setText(r.getName());
    address.setText(r.getAddress());

    if (r.getType().equals("sit_down")) {
      icon.setImageResource(R.drawable.ball_red);
    }
    else if (r.getType().equals("take_out")) {
      icon.setImageResource(R.drawable.ball_yellow);
    }
    else {
      icon.setImageResource(R.drawable.ball_green);
    }
  }
}
}
```

Extra Credit

Here are some things you can try beyond those step-by-step instructions:

- Add a date in the restaurant model to note the last time you visited the restaurant, then use either DatePicker or DatePickerDialog to allow users to set the date when they create their restaurant objects.

- Try making a version of the activity that uses a ViewFlipper and a Button to flip from the list to the detail form, rather than using two tabs.

Further Reading

The use of tabs in an Android activity is covered in the "Still More Widgets and Containers" chapter of The Busy Coder's Guide to Android Development[28].

---

28 http://commonsware.com/Android

Menus and Messages

In this tutorial, we will add an EditText for a note to our detail form and restaurant model. Then, we will add an options menu that will display the note as a Toast.

Step-By-Step Instructions

First, you need to have completed the previous tutorial. If you are beginning the tutorials here, or if you wish to not use your existing work, you can download a ZIP file with all of the tutorial results, and you can copy the 06-Tabs edition of LunchList to use as a starting point. If you are using Eclipse, these instructions will help you load the project into a workspace.

Step #1: Add Notes to the Restaurant

First, our restaurant model does not have any spot for notes. Add a String notes data member plus an associated getter and setter. Your resulting class should look like:

```
package apt.tutorial;

public class Restaurant {
  private String name="";
  private String address="";
  private String type="";
  private String notes="";
```

```
  public String getName() {
    return(name);
  }

  public void setName(String name) {
    this.name=name;
  }

  public String getAddress() {
    return(address);
  }

  public void setAddress(String address) {
    this.address=address;
  }

  public String getType() {
    return(type);
  }

  public void setType(String type) {
    this.type=type;
  }

  public String getNotes() {
    return(notes);
  }

  public void setNotes(String notes) {
    this.notes=notes;
  }

  public String toString() {
    return(getName());
  }
}
```

Step #2: Add Notes to the Detail Form

Next, we need LunchList to make use of the notes.

Unfortunately for Eclipse users, it does not appear to be possible to do drag-and-drop editing of a tabbed UI in the r12 version of the Android Developer Tools plugin. In Tutorial 12, we will be replacing the tabs with two separate activities, at which point you will be able to edit the main layout file via drag-and-drop. For now, you will need to modify the XML directly.

To do this, first add the following `TableRow` above the Save button in our `TableLayout` in `LunchList/res/layout/main.xml`:

```
<TableRow>
  <TextView android:text="Notes:" />
  <EditText android:id="@+id/notes"
    android:singleLine="false"
    android:gravity="top"
    android:lines="2"
    android:scrollHorizontally="false"
    android:maxLines="2"
    android:maxWidth="200sp"
  />
</TableRow>
```

Then, we need to modify the `LunchList` activity itself, by:

1. Adding another data member for the `notes EditText` widget defined above

2. Find our `notes EditText` widget as part of `onCreate()`, like we do with other `EditText` widgets

3. Save our notes to our restaurant in `onSave`

4. Restore our notes to the `EditText` in `onListClick`

At this point, you can recompile and reinstall the application to see your notes field in action:

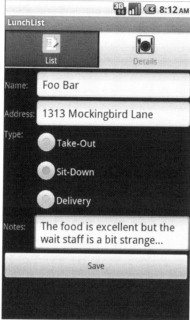

Figure 47. The notes field in the detail form

Step #3: Define the Options Menu

Now, we need to create an options menu and arrange for it to be displayed when the user clicks the [MENU] button.

Options menu items have icons, so you will need some image to work with. For the purposes of this tutorial, any 32px image or so should be fine, but the file should be named toast.png and put in your project's res/drawable/ directory. If you wish to use the image shown in these examples, you can find it here[29].

Eclipse users can use a graphical editor for defining menu resources, while non-Eclipse users will create XML directly.

---

29 https://github.com/commonsguy/cw-lunchlist/raw/master/07-
    MenusMessages/LunchList/res/drawable/toast.png

Eclipse

Add a menu/ folder to your project's res/ directory (e.g., right-click on res/ and choose New > Folder from the context menu).

Then, add a option.xml file to the res/menu/ directory (e.g., right-click on res/menu/ and choose New > File from the context menu). This will bring up the menu editor:

Figure 48. The Eclipse menu resource editor

If you wish, you can immediately save the file with the minimal default XML that the Android Developer Tools adds, to get rid of the error indicator in the Package Explorer.

In the menu resource editor, click the Add... button, and choose Item from the dialog of available entries to add to the menu resource. This adds an empty menu item and gives you a number of values you can specify for it on the right:

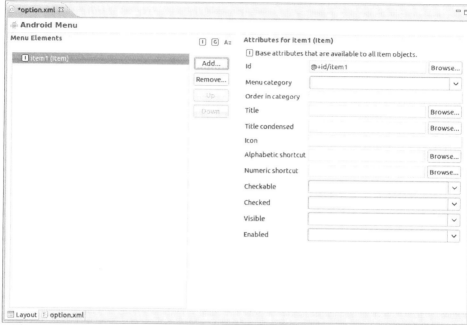

Figure 49. The Eclipse menu resource editor, showing an newly-added menu item

Make the following adjustments:

- Change the Id to be @+id/toast, most easily accomplished simply by typing into the field

- Change the Title to be Raise Toast, also most easily accomplished simply by typing into the field

- Change the Icon to be @drawable/toast, to refer to the toast.png file in our drawable resources

At this point, you can save the file using normal Eclipse procedures (e.g., Ctrl-S).

Outside of Eclipse

The menu itself can be defined as a small piece of XML. Enter the following as LunchList/res/menu/option.xml:

```
<?xml version="1.0" encoding="utf-8"?>
<menu xmlns:android="http://schemas.android.com/apk/res/android">
  <item android:id="@+id/toast"
    android:title="Raise Toast"
    android:icon="@drawable/toast"
  />
</menu>
```

This code relies upon an icon stored in LunchList/res/drawable/toast.png. Find something suitable to use, preferably around 32px high.

Step #4: Support the Options Menu

To arrange for the menu to be displayed, add the following method to LunchList:

```
@Override
public boolean onCreateOptionsMenu(Menu menu) {
  new MenuInflater(this).inflate(R.menu.option, menu);

  return(super.onCreateOptionsMenu(menu));
}
```

Note that you will also need to define imports for android.view.Menu and android.view.MenuInflater for this to compile cleanly.

At this point, you can rebuild and reinstall the application. Click the [MENU] button, from either tab, to see the options menu with its icon:

Figure 50. The LunchList options menu, displayed, with one menu choice

Step #5: Show the Notes as a Toast

Finally, we need to get control when the user selects the Raise Toast menu choice and display the notes in a `Toast`.

The problem is that, to do this, we need to know what restaurant to show. So far, we have not been holding onto a specific restaurant except when we needed it, such as when we populate the detail form. Now, we need to know our current restaurant, defined as the one visible in the detail form...which could be none, if we have not yet saved anything in the form.

To make all of this work, do the following:

1. Add another data member, `current`, to hold the current `Restaurant`. Be sure to initialize it to `null`.

2. In `onSave` and `onListClick`, rather than declaring local restaurant variables, use `current` to hold the restaurant we are saving (in

onSave) or have clicked on (in onListClick). You will need to change all references to the old r variable to be current in these two objects.

3. Add imports for android.view.MenuItem and android.widget.Toast.

4. Add the following implementation of onOptionsItemSelected() to your LunchList class:

```
@Override
public boolean onOptionsItemSelected(MenuItem item) {
  if (item.getItemId()==R.id.toast) {
    String message="No restaurant selected";

    if (current!=null) {
      message=current.getNotes();
    }

    Toast.makeText(this, message, Toast.LENGTH_LONG).show();

    return(true);
  }

  return(super.onOptionsItemSelected(item));
}
```

Note how we will either display "No restaurant selected" (if current is null) or the restaurant's notes, depending on our current state.

You can now rebuild and reinstall the application. Enter and save a restaurant, with notes, then choose the Raise Toast options menu item, and you will briefly see your notes in a Toast:

Figure 51. The Toast displayed, with some notes

The LunchList activity, as a whole, is shown below, incorporating all of the changes outlined in this tutorial:

```
package apt.tutorial;

import android.app.TabActivity;
import android.os.Bundle;
import android.view.Menu;
import android.view.MenuInflater;
import android.view.MenuItem;
import android.view.View;
import android.view.ViewGroup;
import android.view.LayoutInflater;
import android.widget.AdapterView;
import android.widget.ArrayAdapter;
import android.widget.Button;
import android.widget.EditText;
import android.widget.ImageView;
import android.widget.ListView;
import android.widget.RadioGroup;
import android.widget.TabHost;
import android.widget.TextView;
import android.widget.Toast;
import java.util.ArrayList;
import java.util.List;
```

```
public class LunchList extends TabActivity {
  List<Restaurant> model=new ArrayList<Restaurant>();
  RestaurantAdapter adapter=null;
  EditText name=null;
  EditText address=null;
  EditText notes=null;
  RadioGroup types=null;
  Restaurant current=null;

  @Override
  public void onCreate(Bundle savedInstanceState) {
    super.onCreate(savedInstanceState);
    setContentView(R.layout.main);

    name=(EditText)findViewById(R.id.name);
    address=(EditText)findViewById(R.id.addr);
    notes=(EditText)findViewById(R.id.notes);
    types=(RadioGroup)findViewById(R.id.types);

    Button save=(Button)findViewById(R.id.save);

    save.setOnClickListener(onSave);

    ListView list=(ListView)findViewById(R.id.restaurants);

    adapter=new RestaurantAdapter();
    list.setAdapter(adapter);

    TabHost.TabSpec spec=getTabHost().newTabSpec("tag1");

    spec.setContent(R.id.restaurants);
    spec.setIndicator("List", getResources()
                            .getDrawable(R.drawable.list));
    getTabHost().addTab(spec);

    spec=getTabHost().newTabSpec("tag2");
    spec.setContent(R.id.details);
    spec.setIndicator("Details", getResources()
                            .getDrawable(R.drawable.restaurant));
    getTabHost().addTab(spec);

    getTabHost().setCurrentTab(0);

    list.setOnItemClickListener(onListClick);
  }

  @Override
  public boolean onCreateOptionsMenu(Menu menu) {
    new MenuInflater(this).inflate(R.menu.option, menu);

    return(super.onCreateOptionsMenu(menu));
  }
```

```
  @Override
  public boolean onOptionsItemSelected(MenuItem item) {
    if (item.getItemId()==R.id.toast) {
      String message="No restaurant selected";

      if (current!=null) {
        message=current.getNotes();
      }

      Toast.makeText(this, message, Toast.LENGTH_LONG).show();

      return(true);
    }

    return(super.onOptionsItemSelected(item));
  }

  private View.OnClickListener onSave=new View.OnClickListener() {
    public void onClick(View v) {
      current=new Restaurant();
      current.setName(name.getText().toString());
      current.setAddress(address.getText().toString());
      current.setNotes(notes.getText().toString());

      switch (types.getCheckedRadioButtonId()) {
        case R.id.sit_down:
          current.setType("sit_down");
          break;

        case R.id.take_out:
          current.setType("take_out");
          break;

        case R.id.delivery:
          current.setType("delivery");
          break;
      }

      adapter.add(current);
    }
  };

  private AdapterView.OnItemClickListener onListClick=new
AdapterView.OnItemClickListener() {
    public void onItemClick(AdapterView<?> parent,
                            View view, int position,
                            long id) {
      current=model.get(position);

      name.setText(current.getName());
      address.setText(current.getAddress());
      notes.setText(current.getNotes());

      if (current.getType().equals("sit_down")) {
```

```
      types.check(R.id.sit_down);
    }
    else if (current.getType().equals("take_out")) {
      types.check(R.id.take_out);
    }
    else {
      types.check(R.id.delivery);
    }

    getTabHost().setCurrentTab(1);
  }
};

class RestaurantAdapter extends ArrayAdapter<Restaurant> {
  RestaurantAdapter() {
    super(LunchList.this, R.layout.row, model);
  }

  public View getView(int position, View convertView,
                      ViewGroup parent) {
    View row=convertView;
    RestaurantHolder holder=null;

    if (row==null) {
      LayoutInflater inflater=getLayoutInflater();

      row=inflater.inflate(R.layout.row, parent, false);
      holder=new RestaurantHolder(row);
      row.setTag(holder);
    }
    else {
      holder=(RestaurantHolder)row.getTag();
    }

    holder.populateFrom(model.get(position));

    return(row);
  }
}

static class RestaurantHolder {
  private TextView name=null;
  private TextView address=null;
  private ImageView icon=null;

  RestaurantHolder(View row) {
    name=(TextView)row.findViewById(R.id.title);
    address=(TextView)row.findViewById(R.id.address);
    icon=(ImageView)row.findViewById(R.id.icon);
  }

  void populateFrom(Restaurant r) {
    name.setText(r.getName());
    address.setText(r.getAddress());
```

```
    if (r.getType().equals("sit_down")) {
      icon.setImageResource(R.drawable.ball_red);
    }
    else if (r.getType().equals("take_out")) {
      icon.setImageResource(R.drawable.ball_yellow);
    }
    else {
      icon.setImageResource(R.drawable.ball_green);
    }
  }
 }
}
```

Step #6: Add a ScrollView

The soft keyboard (technically, the "input method editor") on Android will tend to cover up the lower part of the screen. This makes it difficult to type and see what you are typing in. A simple solution for this is to wrap part or all of your layout in a ScrollView widget, as Android will automatically scroll the ScrollView to try to keep the EditText visible when it is being typed into.

Alas, once again, Eclipse users cannot directly interact with the contents of the tabs from the graphical editor, and as such are forced to modify the XML directly, as developers using other tools must do.

With that in mind, adjust the res/layout/main.xml to look like this:

```xml
<?xml version="1.0" encoding="utf-8"?>
<TabHost xmlns:android="http://schemas.android.com/apk/res/android"
  android:id="@android:id/tabhost"
  android:layout_width="match_parent"
  android:layout_height="match_parent">
  <LinearLayout
    android:orientation="vertical"
    android:layout_width="match_parent"
    android:layout_height="match_parent">
    <TabWidget android:id="@android:id/tabs"
      android:layout_width="match_parent"
      android:layout_height="wrap_content"
    />
    <FrameLayout android:id="@android:id/tabcontent"
      android:layout_width="match_parent"
      android:layout_height="match_parent"
    >
      <ListView android:id="@+id/restaurants"
```

```
      android:layout_width="match_parent"
      android:layout_height="match_parent"
  />
  <ScrollView
      android:layout_width="match_parent"
      android:layout_height="wrap_content">
      <TableLayout android:id="@+id/details"
        android:layout_width="match_parent"
        android:layout_height="wrap_content"
        android:stretchColumns="1"
        android:shrinkColumns="1"
        android:paddingTop="4dip"
      >
      <TableRow>
        <TextView android:text="Name:" />
        <EditText android:id="@+id/name" />
      </TableRow>
      <TableRow>
        <TextView android:text="Address:" />
        <EditText android:id="@+id/addr" />
      </TableRow>
      <TableRow>
        <TextView android:text="Type:" />
        <RadioGroup android:id="@+id/types">
          <RadioButton android:id="@+id/take_out"
            android:text="Take-Out"
            android:checked="true"
          />
          <RadioButton android:id="@+id/sit_down"
            android:text="Sit-Down"
          />
          <RadioButton android:id="@+id/delivery"
            android:text="Delivery"
          />
        </RadioGroup>
      </TableRow>
      <TableRow>
        <TextView android:text="Notes:" />
        <EditText android:id="@+id/notes"
          android:inputType="textMultiLine"
          android:gravity="top"
          android:lines="2"
          android:scrollHorizontally="false"
          android:maxLines="2"
        />
      </TableRow>
      <Button android:id="@+id/save"
        android:layout_width="match_parent"
        android:layout_height="wrap_content"
        android:text="Save"
      />
    </TableLayout>
  </ScrollView>
</FrameLayout>
```

```
    </LinearLayout>
</TabHost>
```

The TableLayout is now wrapped in a ScrollView, which will give you better results when you go to type text into the form.

Extra Credit

Here are some things you can try beyond those step-by-step instructions:

- Try using an AlertDialog instead of a Toast to display the message.

- Try adding a menu option to switch you between tabs. In particular, change the text and icon on the menu option to reflect the other tab (i.e., on the List tab, the menu should show "Details" and the details tab icon; on the Details tab, the menu should show "List" and the List tab icon).

- Try creating an ErrorDialog designed to display exceptions in a "pleasant" format to the end user. The ErrorDialog should also log the exceptions via android.util.Log. Use some sort of runtime exception (e.g., division by zero) for generating exceptions to pass to the dialog.

Further Reading

You can learn more about menus – both options menus and context menus – in the "Applying Menus" chapter of The Busy Coder's Guide to Android Development[30]. The use of a Toast is covered in the "Showing Pop-Up Messages" chapter of the same book.

---

30 http://commonsware.com/Android

Sitting in the Background

In this tutorial, we will simulate having the LunchList do some background processing in a secondary thread, updating the user interface via a progress bar. While all of these tutorials are somewhat contrived, this one will be more contrived than most, as there is not much we are really able to do in a LunchList that would even require long processing in a background thread. So, please forgive us if this tutorial is a bit goofy.

Step-By-Step Instructions

First, you need to have completed the previous tutorial. If you are beginning the tutorials here, or if you wish to not use your existing work, you can download a ZIP file with all of the tutorial results, and you can copy the 07-MenusMessages edition of LunchList to use as a starting point. If you are using Eclipse, these instructions will help you load the project into a workspace.

Step #1: Initialize the Progress Bar

For this application, rather than use a ProgressBar widget, we will use the progress bar feature of the Activity window. This will put a progress bar in the title bar, rather than clutter up our layouts.

This requires a bit of initialization. Specifically, we need to add a line to onCreate() that will request this feature be activated. We have to do this before calling setContentView(), so we add it right after chaining to the superclass:

```
@Override
public void onCreate(Bundle savedInstanceState) {
  super.onCreate(savedInstanceState);
  requestWindowFeature(Window.FEATURE_PROGRESS);
  setContentView(R.layout.main);

  name=(EditText)findViewById(R.id.name);
  address=(EditText)findViewById(R.id.addr);
  notes=(EditText)findViewById(R.id.notes);
  types=(RadioGroup)findViewById(R.id.types);

  Button save=(Button)findViewById(R.id.save);

  save.setOnClickListener(onSave);

  ListView list=(ListView)findViewById(R.id.restaurants);

  adapter=new RestaurantAdapter();
  list.setAdapter(adapter);

  TabHost.TabSpec spec=getTabHost().newTabSpec("tag1");

  spec.setContent(R.id.restaurants);
  spec.setIndicator("List", getResources()
                            .getDrawable(R.drawable.list));
  getTabHost().addTab(spec);

  spec=getTabHost().newTabSpec("tag2");
  spec.setContent(R.id.details);
  spec.setIndicator("Details", getResources()
                            .getDrawable(R.drawable.restaurant));
  getTabHost().addTab(spec);

  getTabHost().setCurrentTab(0);

  list.setOnItemClickListener(onListClick);
}
```

Also, add another data member, an int named progress.

Step #2: Create the Work Method

The theory of this demo is that we have something that takes a long time, and we want to have that work done in a background thread and update the progress along the way. So, the first step is to build something that will run a long time.

To do that, first, implement a `doSomeLongWork()` method on `LunchList` as follows:

```
private void doSomeLongWork(final int incr) {
  SystemClock.sleep(250);  // should be something more useful!
}
```

Here, we sleep for 250 milliseconds, simulating doing some meaningful work.

Then, create a private `Runnable` in `LunchList` that will fire off `doSomeLongWork()` a number of times, as follows:

```
private Runnable longTask=new Runnable() {
  public void run() {
    for (int i=0;i<20;i++) {
      doSomeLongWork(500);
    }
  }
};
```

Here, we just loop 20 times, so the overall background thread will run for 5 seconds.

Step #3: Fork the Thread from the Menu

We need to arrange to do this (fake) long work at some point. The easiest way to do that is add another menu choice.

First, we should obtain our menu icon. Any image around 32px high should be fine, so long as it is in your res/drawable/ directory and is named run.png. If you wish to use the image shown in these examples, you can find it here[31].

---

31 https://github.com/commonsguy/cw-lunchlist/raw/master/08-
    Threads/LunchList/res/drawable/run.png

Next, update the `LunchList/res/menu/option.xml` file to look like the following:

```xml
<?xml version="1.0" encoding="utf-8"?>
<menu xmlns:android="http://schemas.android.com/apk/res/android">
  <item android:id="@+id/toast"
    android:title="Raise Toast"
    android:icon="@drawable/toast"
  />
  <item android:id="@+id/run"
    android:title="Run Long Task"
    android:icon="@drawable/run"
  />
</menu>
```

Eclipse users can accomplish this by:

- Double-clicking on the `res/menu/option.xml` resource to bring it up in the graphical editor

- Clicking the Add... button to add a new menu item – in the dialog that appears, you will need to toggle the radio button to add a child to the root element rather than a sub-item of whatever the selected menu item happens to be

- Changing the new menu item to have an ID of `@+id/run`, `Run Long Task` as the title, and `@drawable/run` as the icon

- Saving your changes via <Ctrl>-<S>

Since the menu item is in the menu XML, we do not need to do anything special to display the item – it will just be added to the menu automatically. We do, however, need to arrange to do something useful when the menu choice is chosen. So, update `onOptionsItemSelected()` in `LunchList` to look like the following:

```java
@Override
public boolean onOptionsItemSelected(MenuItem item) {
  if (item.getItemId()==R.id.toast) {
    String message="No restaurant selected";

    if (current!=null) {
      message=current.getNotes();
    }

    Toast.makeText(this, message, Toast.LENGTH_LONG).show();
```

```
    return(true);
  }
  else if (item.getItemId()==R.id.run) {
    new Thread(longTask).start();
  }

  return(super.onOptionsItemSelected(item));
}
```

You are welcome to recompile, reinstall, and run the application. However, since our background thread does not do anything visible at the moment, all you will see that is different is the new menu item:

Figure 52. The Run Long Task menu item

Step #4: Manage the Progress Bar

Finally, we need to actually make use of the progress indicator. This involves making it visible when we start our long-running task, updating it as the task proceeds, and hiding it again when the task is complete.

First, make it visible by updating onOptionsItemSelected() to show it:

```
@Override
public boolean onOptionsItemSelected(MenuItem item) {
  if (item.getItemId()==R.id.toast) {
    String message="No restaurant selected";

    if (current!=null) {
      message=current.getNotes();
    }

    Toast.makeText(this, message, Toast.LENGTH_LONG).show();

    return(true);
  }
  else if (item.getItemId()==R.id.run) {
    setProgressBarVisibility(true);
    progress=0;
    new Thread(longTask).start();

    return(true);
  }

  return(super.onOptionsItemSelected(item));
}
```

Notice the extra line that makes progress visible.

Then, we need to update the progress bar on each pass, so make this change to doSomeLongWork():

```
private void doSomeLongWork(final int incr) {
  runOnUiThread(new Runnable() {
    public void run() {
      progress+=incr;
      setProgress(progress);
    }
  });

  SystemClock.sleep(250); // should be something more useful!
}
```

Notice how we use runOnUiThread() to make sure our progress bar update occurs on the UI thread.

Finally, we need to hide the progress bar when we are done, so make this change to our longTask Runnable:

```
private Runnable longTask=new Runnable() {
  public void run() {
    for (int i=0;i<20;i++) {
      doSomeLongWork(500);
    }

    runOnUiThread(new Runnable() {
      public void run() {
        setProgressBarVisibility(false);
      }
    });
  }
};
```

At this point, you can rebuild, reinstall, and run the application. When you choose the Run Long Task menu item, you will see the progress bar appear for five seconds, progressively updated as the "work" gets done:

Figure 53. The progress bar in action

Extra Credit

Here are some things you can try beyond those step-by-step instructions:

- Have the background thread also update some UI element when the work is completed, beyond dismissing the progress bar. Make sure you arrange to update the UI on the UI thread!

- Instead of using `Activity#runOnUiThread()`, try using a `Handler` for communication between the background thread and the UI thread.

- Instead of starting a `Thread` from the menu choice, have the `Thread` be created in `onCreate()` and have it monitor a `LinkedBlockingQueue` (from `java.util.concurrent`) as a source of work to be done. Create a `FakeJob` that does what our current long-running method does, and a `KillJob` that causes the `Thread` to fall out of its queue-monitoring loop.

Further Reading

Coverage of the Android concept of "the UI thread" and tools like the Handler for managing communication between threads can be found in the "Dealing with Threads" chapter of The Busy Coder's Guide to Android Development[32]. You will also learn about `AsyncTask` in that chapter, which is another important means of coordinating background and UI thread operations.

If you are interested in Java threading in general, particularly the use of the `java.util.concurrent` set of thread-management classes, the book Java Concurrency in Practice[33] is a popular source of information.

---

32 http://commonsware.com/Android
33 http://www.amazon.com/Java-Concurrency-Practice-Brian-Goetz/dp/0321349601

Life and Times

In this tutorial, we will make our background task take a bit longer, then arrange to pause the background work when we start up another activity and restart the background work when our activity regains control. This pattern – stopping unnecessary background work when the activity is paused – is a good design pattern and is not merely something used for a tutorial.

Step-By-Step Instructions

First, you need to have completed the previous tutorial. If you are beginning the tutorials here, or if you wish to not use your existing work, you can download a ZIP file with all of the tutorial results, and you can copy the 08-Threads edition of LunchList to use as a starting point. If you are using Eclipse, these instructions will help you load the project into a workspace.

Step #1: Lengthen the Background Work

First, let us make the background work take a bit longer, so we have a bigger "window" in which to test whether our pause-and-resume logic works. It is also helpful, in our case, to synchronize our loop with our progress, so rather than counting 0 to 20 by 1, we should count from 0 to 10000 by 200, so the loop counter and progress are the same.

In the `longTask Runnable`, change the loop to look like this:

```
for (int i=progress;
    i<10000;
    i+=200) {
  doSomeLongWork(200);
}
```

Step #2: Pause in onPause()

Now, we need to arrange to have our thread stop running when the activity is paused (e.g., some other activity has taken over the screen). Since threads are relatively cheap to create and destroy, we can simply have our current running thread stop and start a fresh one, if needed, in `onResume()`.

While there are some deprecated methods on `Thread` to try to forcibly terminate them, it is generally better to let the `Thread` stop itself by falling out of whatever processing loop it is in. So, what we want to do is let the background thread know the activity is not active.

To do this, first import `java.util.concurrent.atomic.AtomicBoolean` in `LunchList` and add an `AtomicBoolean` data member named `isActive`, initially set to `true` (`new AtomicBoolean(true);`).

Then, in the `longTask Runnable`, change the loop to also watch for the state of `isActive`, falling out of the loop if the activity is no longer active:

```
for (int i=progress;
    i<10000 && isActive.get();
    i+=200) {
  doSomeLongWork(200);
}
```

Finally, implement `onPause()` to update the state of `isActive`:

```
@Override
public void onPause() {
  super.onPause();

  isActive.set(false);
}
```

Note how we chain to the superclass in `onPause()` – if we fail to do this, we will get a runtime error.

With this implementation, our background thread will run to completion or until `isActive` is `false`, whichever comes first.

Step #3: Resume in onResume()

Now, we need to restart our thread if it is needed. It will be needed if the progress is greater than 0, indicating we were in the middle of our background work when our activity was so rudely interrupted.

So, add the following implementation of `onResume()`:

```
@Override
public void onResume() {
  super.onResume();

  isActive.set(true);

  if (progress>0) {
    startWork();
  }
}
```

This assumes we have pulled out our thread-starting logic into a `startWork()` method, which you should implement as follows:

```
private void startWork() {
  setProgressBarVisibility(true);
  new Thread(longTask).start();
}
```

And you can change our menu handler to also use `startWork()`:

```
@Override
public boolean onOptionsItemSelected(MenuItem item) {
  if (item.getItemId()==R.id.toast) {
    String message="No restaurant selected";

    if (current!=null) {
      message=current.getNotes();
    }
```

```
    Toast.makeText(this, message, Toast.LENGTH_LONG).show();

    return(true);
  }
  else if (item.getItemId()==R.id.run) {
    startWork();

    return(true);
  }

  return(super.onOptionsItemSelected(item));
}
```

Finally, we need to not reset and hide the progress indicator when our background thread ends if it ends because our activity is not active. Otherwise, we will never restart it, since the progress will be reset to 0 every time. So, change longTask one more time, to look like this:

```
private Runnable longTask=new Runnable() {
  public void run() {
    for (int i=progress;
         i<10000 && isActive.get();
         i+=200) {
      doSomeLongWork(200);
    }

    if (isActive.get()) {
      runOnUiThread(new Runnable() {
        public void run() {
          setProgressBarVisibility(false);
          progress=0;
        }
      });
    }
  }
};
```

What this does is reset the progress only if we are active when the work is complete, so we are ready for the next round of work. If we are inactive, and fell out of our loop for that reason, we leave the progress as-is.

At this point, recompile and reinstall the application. To test this feature:

1. Use the [MENU] button to run the long task.

2. While it is running, click the green phone button on the emulator (lower-left corner of the "phone"). This will bring up the call log activity and, as a result, pause our LunchList activity.

3. After a while, click the BACK button – you should see the LunchList resuming the background work from the point where it left off.

Here is the full LunchList implementation, including the changes shown above:

```
package apt.tutorial;

import android.app.TabActivity;
import android.os.Bundle;
import android.os.SystemClock;
import android.view.Menu;
import android.view.MenuInflater;
import android.view.MenuItem;
import android.view.View;
import android.view.ViewGroup;
import android.view.LayoutInflater;
import android.view.Window;
import android.widget.AdapterView;
import android.widget.ArrayAdapter;
import android.widget.Button;
import android.widget.EditText;
import android.widget.ImageView;
import android.widget.ListView;
import android.widget.RadioGroup;
import android.widget.TabHost;
import android.widget.TextView;
import android.widget.Toast;
import java.util.ArrayList;
import java.util.List;
import java.util.concurrent.atomic.AtomicBoolean;

public class LunchList extends TabActivity {
  List<Restaurant> model=new ArrayList<Restaurant>();
  RestaurantAdapter adapter=null;
  EditText name=null;
  EditText address=null;
  EditText notes=null;
  RadioGroup types=null;
  Restaurant current=null;
  AtomicBoolean isActive=new AtomicBoolean(true);
  int progress=0;

  @Override
  public void onCreate(Bundle savedInstanceState) {
    super.onCreate(savedInstanceState);
    requestWindowFeature(Window.FEATURE_PROGRESS);
```

```
    setContentView(R.layout.main);

    name=(EditText)findViewById(R.id.name);
    address=(EditText)findViewById(R.id.addr);
    notes=(EditText)findViewById(R.id.notes);
    types=(RadioGroup)findViewById(R.id.types);

    Button save=(Button)findViewById(R.id.save);

    save.setOnClickListener(onSave);

    ListView list=(ListView)findViewById(R.id.restaurants);

    adapter=new RestaurantAdapter();
    list.setAdapter(adapter);

    TabHost.TabSpec spec=getTabHost().newTabSpec("tag1");

    spec.setContent(R.id.restaurants);
    spec.setIndicator("List", getResources()
                            .getDrawable(R.drawable.list));
    getTabHost().addTab(spec);

    spec=getTabHost().newTabSpec("tag2");
    spec.setContent(R.id.details);
    spec.setIndicator("Details", getResources()
                            .getDrawable(R.drawable.restaurant));
    getTabHost().addTab(spec);

    getTabHost().setCurrentTab(0);

    list.setOnItemClickListener(onListClick);
  }

@Override
public void onPause() {
  super.onPause();

  isActive.set(false);
}

@Override
public void onResume() {
  super.onResume();

  isActive.set(true);

  if (progress>0) {
    startWork();
  }
}

@Override
public boolean onCreateOptionsMenu(Menu menu) {
```

```
    new MenuInflater(this).inflate(R.menu.option, menu);

    return(super.onCreateOptionsMenu(menu));
}

@Override
public boolean onOptionsItemSelected(MenuItem item) {
  if (item.getItemId()==R.id.toast) {
    String message="No restaurant selected";

    if (current!=null) {
      message=current.getNotes();
    }

    Toast.makeText(this, message, Toast.LENGTH_LONG).show();

    return(true);
  }
  else if (item.getItemId()==R.id.run) {
    startWork();

    return(true);
  }

  return(super.onOptionsItemSelected(item));
}

private void startWork() {
  setProgressBarVisibility(true);
  new Thread(longTask).start();
}

private void doSomeLongWork(final int incr) {
  runOnUiThread(new Runnable() {
    public void run() {
      progress+=incr;
      setProgress(progress);
    }
  });

  SystemClock.sleep(250); // should be something more useful!
}

private View.OnClickListener onSave=new View.OnClickListener() {
  public void onClick(View v) {
    current=new Restaurant();
    current.setName(name.getText().toString());
    current.setAddress(address.getText().toString());
    current.setNotes(notes.getText().toString());

    switch (types.getCheckedRadioButtonId()) {
      case R.id.sit_down:
        current.setType("sit_down");
        break;
```

```
    case R.id.take_out:
      current.setType("take_out");
      break;

    case R.id.delivery:
      current.setType("delivery");
      break;
  }

  adapter.add(current);
  }
};

private AdapterView.OnItemClickListener onListClick=new
AdapterView.OnItemClickListener() {
  public void onItemClick(AdapterView<?> parent,
                          View view, int position,
                          long id) {
    current=model.get(position);

    name.setText(current.getName());
    address.setText(current.getAddress());
    notes.setText(current.getNotes());

    if (current.getType().equals("sit_down")) {
      types.check(R.id.sit_down);
    }
    else if (current.getType().equals("take_out")) {
      types.check(R.id.take_out);
    }
    else {
      types.check(R.id.delivery);
    }

    getTabHost().setCurrentTab(1);
  }
};

private Runnable longTask=new Runnable() {
  public void run() {
    for (int i=progress;
         i<10000 && isActive.get();
         i+=200) {
      doSomeLongWork(200);
    }

    if (isActive.get()) {
      runOnUiThread(new Runnable() {
        public void run() {
          setProgressBarVisibility(false);
          progress=0;
        }
      });
```

```
      }
    }
  };

  class RestaurantAdapter extends ArrayAdapter<Restaurant> {
    RestaurantAdapter() {
      super(LunchList.this, R.layout.row, model);
    }

    public View getView(int position, View convertView,
                        ViewGroup parent) {
      View row=convertView;
      RestaurantHolder holder=null;

      if (row==null) {
        LayoutInflater inflater=getLayoutInflater();

        row=inflater.inflate(R.layout.row, parent, false);
        holder=new RestaurantHolder(row);
        row.setTag(holder);
      }
      else {
        holder=(RestaurantHolder)row.getTag();
      }

      holder.populateFrom(model.get(position));

      return(row);
    }
  }

  static class RestaurantHolder {
    private TextView name=null;
    private TextView address=null;
    private ImageView icon=null;

    RestaurantHolder(View row) {
      name=(TextView)row.findViewById(R.id.title);
      address=(TextView)row.findViewById(R.id.address);
      icon=(ImageView)row.findViewById(R.id.icon);
    }

    void populateFrom(Restaurant r) {
      name.setText(r.getName());
      address.setText(r.getAddress());

      if (r.getType().equals("sit_down")) {
        icon.setImageResource(R.drawable.ball_red);
      }
      else if (r.getType().equals("take_out")) {
        icon.setImageResource(R.drawable.ball_yellow);
      }
      else {
        icon.setImageResource(R.drawable.ball_green);
```

```
        }
      }
    }
  }
}
```

Extra Credit

Here are some things you can try beyond those step-by-step instructions:

- Have the progress position be persisted via onSaveInstanceState(). When the activity is started in onCreate(), see if the background work was in progress when the activity was shut down (i.e., progress further than 0), and restart the background thread immediately if it was. To test this, you can press <Ctrl>-<F12> to simulate opening the keyboard and rotating the screen – by default, this causes your activity to be destroyed and recreated, with onSaveInstanceState() called along the way.

- Try moving the pause/resume logic to onStop() and onStart().

Further Reading

You can find material on the topics shown in this tutorial in the "Handling Activity Lifecycle Events" chapter of The Busy Coder's Guide to Android Development[34].

You are also strongly encouraged to read the class overview for Activity in the JavaDocs[35].

---

34 http://commonsware.com/Android
35 http://developer.android.com/reference/android/app/Activity.html

A Few Good Resources

We have already used many types of resources in the preceding tutorials. After reviewing what we have used so far, we set up an alternate layout for our LunchList activity to be used when the activity is in landscape orientation instead of portrait.

Step-By-Step Instructions

First, you need to have completed the previous tutorial. If you are beginning the tutorials here, or if you wish to not use your existing work, you can download a ZIP file with all of the tutorial results, and you can copy the 09-Lifecycle edition of LunchList to use as a starting point. If you are using Eclipse, these instructions will help you load the project into a workspace.

Step #1: Review our Current Resources

Now that we have completed ten tutorials, this is a good time to recap what resources we have been using along the way. Right now, LunchList has:

- Several icons in LunchList/res/drawable/, all PNGs

- Two XML files in LunchList/res/layout/, representing the main LunchList UI and the definition of each row

- One XML file in `LunchList/res/menu/`, containing our options menu definition

- The system-created `strings.xml` file in `LunchList/res/values/`

Step #2: Create a Landscape Layout

In the emulator, with `LunchList` running and showing the detail form, press `<Ctrl>-<F12>`. This simulates opening and closing the keyboard, causing the screen to rotate to landscape and portrait, respectively. Our current layout is not very good in landscape orientation:

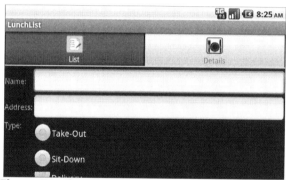

Figure 54. The LunchList in landscape orientation

So, let us come up with an alternative layout that will work better. Since Eclipse and tabs do not get along well, Eclipse users will have to perform this work by modifying the XML directly, as will developers not using Eclipse.

First, create a `LunchList/res/layout-land/` directory in your project. This will hold layout files that we wish to use when the device (or emulator) is in the landscape orientation.

Then, create a main.xml file in `LunchList/res/layout-land/` that looks like:

```
<?xml version="1.0" encoding="utf-8"?>
<TabHost xmlns:android="http://schemas.android.com/apk/res/android"
  android:id="@android:id/tabhost"
  android:layout_width="match_parent"
```

```
android:layout_height="match_parent">
<LinearLayout
   android:orientation="vertical"
   android:layout_width="match_parent"
   android:layout_height="match_parent">
<TabWidget android:id="@android:id/tabs"
   android:layout_width="match_parent"
   android:layout_height="wrap_content"
/>
<FrameLayout android:id="@android:id/tabcontent"
   android:layout_width="match_parent"
   android:layout_height="match_parent"
   >
<ListView android:id="@+id/restaurants"
   android:layout_width="match_parent"
   android:layout_height="wrap_content"
/>
<ScrollView
   android:layout_width="match_parent"
   android:layout_height="wrap_content">
<TableLayout android:id="@+id/details"
   android:layout_width="match_parent"
   android:layout_height="wrap_content"
   android:stretchColumns="1,3"
   android:shrinkColumns="3"
   android:paddingTop="4dip"
   >
<TableRow>
  <TextView
     android:text="Name:"
     android:paddingRight="2dip"
  />
  <EditText
     android:id="@+id/name"
     android:maxWidth="140sp"
  />
  <TextView
     android:text="Address:"
     android:paddingLeft="2dip"
     android:paddingRight="2dip"
  />
  <EditText
     android:id="@+id/addr"
     android:maxWidth="140sp"
  />
</TableRow>
<TableRow>
  <TextView android:text="Type:" />
  <RadioGroup android:id="@+id/types">
    <RadioButton android:id="@+id/take_out"
       android:text="Take-Out"
       android:checked="true"
    />
    <RadioButton android:id="@+id/sit_down"
```

```
                              android:text="Sit-Down"
                          />
                          <RadioButton android:id="@+id/delivery"
                             android:text="Delivery"
                          />
                      </RadioGroup>
                      <TextView
                          android:text="Notes:"
                          android:paddingLeft="2dip"
                      />
                      <LinearLayout
                          android:layout_width="match_parent"
                          android:layout_height="match_parent"
                          android:orientation="vertical"
                          >
                          <EditText android:id="@+id/notes"
                              android:inputType="textMultiLine"
                              android:gravity="top"
                              android:lines="3"
                              android:scrollHorizontally="false"
                              android:maxLines="3"
                              android:layout_width="match_parent"
                              android:layout_height="wrap_content"
                          />
                          <Button android:id="@+id/save"
                              android:layout_width="match_parent"
                              android:layout_height="wrap_content"
                              android:text="Save"
                          />
                      </LinearLayout>
                  </TableRow>
              </TableLayout>
          </ScrollView>
      </FrameLayout>
  </LinearLayout>
</TabHost>
```

In this revised layout, we:

- Switched to four columns in our table, with columns #1 and #3 as stretchable

- Put the name and address labels and fields on the same row

- Put the type, notes, and Save button on the same row, with the notes and Save button stacked via a LinearLayout

- Made the notes three lines instead of two, since we have the room

- Fixed the maximum width of the EditText widgets to 140 scaled pixels (sp), so they do not automatically grow outlandishly large if we type a lot

- Added a bit of padding in places to make the placement of the labels and fields look a bit better

If you rebuild and reinstall the application, then run it in landscape mode, you will see a form that looks like this:

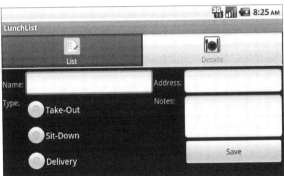

Figure 55. The LunchList in landscape orientation, revised

Note that we did not create a LunchList/res/layout-land/ edition of our row layout (row.xml). Android, upon not finding one in LunchList/res/layout-land/, will fall back to the one in LunchList/res/layout/. Since we do not really need our row to change, we can leave it as-is.

Note that when you change the screen orientation, your existing restaurants will vanish. That is because we are not persisting them anywhere, and rotating the screen by default destroys and recreates the activity. These issues will be addressed in later tutorials.

Extra Credit

Here are some things you can try beyond those step-by-step instructions:

- Find some other icons to use and create a LunchList/res/drawable-land directory with the replacement icons, using the same names as found in `LunchList/res/drawable`. See if exposing the keyboard swaps the icons as well as the layouts.

- Change the text of the labels in our main layout file to be string resources. You will need to add those values to `LunchList/res/values/strings.xml` and reference them in `LunchList/res/layout/main.xml`.

- Use `onSaveInstanceState()` to save the current contents of the detail form, and restore those contents in `onCreate()` if an instance state is available (e.g., after the screen was rotated). Note how this does not cover the list – you will still lose all existing restaurants on a rotation event. However, in a later tutorial, we will move that data to the database, which will solve that problem.

Further Reading

You can learn more about resource sets, particularly with respect to UI impacts, in the "Working with Resources" chapter of The Busy Coder's Guide to Android Development[36].

You will also find "Table 2" in the Alternate Resources section[37] of the Android developer guide to be of great use for determining the priority of different resource set suffixes.

---

36 http://commonsware.com/Android
37 http://developer.android.com/guide/topics/resources/resources-i18n.html#AlternateResources

The Restaurant Store

In this tutorial, we will create a database and table for holding our restaurant data and switch from our `ArrayAdapter` to a `CursorAdapter`, to make use of that database. This will allow our restaurants to persist from run to run of `LunchList`.

Step-By-Step Instructions

First, you need to have completed the previous tutorial. If you are beginning the tutorials here, or if you wish to not use your existing work, you can download a ZIP file with all of the tutorial results, and you can copy the `10-Resources` edition of `LunchList` to use as a starting point. If you are using Eclipse, these instructions will help you load the project into a workspace.

Step #1: Create a Stub SQLiteOpenHelper

First, we need to be able to define what our database name is, what the schema is for the table for our restaurants, etc. That is best wrapped up in a `SQLiteOpenHelper` implementation.

So, create `LunchList/src/apt/tutorial/RestaurantHelper.java`, and enter in the following code:

```
package apt.tutorial;

import android.content.Context;
import android.database.SQLException;
import android.database.sqlite.SQLiteOpenHelper;
import android.database.sqlite.SQLiteDatabase;
import android.database.sqlite.SQLiteQueryBuilder;

class RestaurantHelper extends SQLiteOpenHelper {
  private static final String DATABASE_NAME="lunchlist.db";
  private static final int SCHEMA_VERSION=1;

  public RestaurantHelper(Context context) {
    super(context, DATABASE_NAME, null, SCHEMA_VERSION);
  }

  @Override
  public void onCreate(SQLiteDatabase db) {
  }

  @Override
  public void onUpgrade(SQLiteDatabase db, int oldVersion, int newVersion) {
  }
}
```

Eclipse users can right-click over apt.tutorial in the Package Explorer and choose New > Class from the context menu to bring up the new class dialog. Set the class name to be RestaurantHelper and set the parent class to be android.content.database.SQLiteOpenHelper. Then, edit the resulting class to look like the above code listing.

This says that our database name is lunchlist.db, we are using the first version of the schema...and not much else. However, the project should still compile cleanly after adding this class.

Step #2: Manage our Schema

Next, we need to flesh out the onCreate() and onUpgrade() methods in RestaurantHelper, to actually create the schema we want.

To do this, add an import for android.database.Cursor and use the following implementation of onCreate():

```
@Override
public void onCreate(SQLiteDatabase db) {
  db.execSQL("CREATE TABLE restaurants (_id INTEGER PRIMARY KEY AUTOINCREMENT,
name TEXT, address TEXT, type TEXT, notes TEXT);");
}
```

Here, we are simply executing a SQL statement to create a restaurant table with a particular schema.

For onUpgrade(), there is nothing we really need to do now, since this method will not be executed until we have at least two schema versions. So far, we barely have our first schema version. So, just put a comment to that effect in onUpgrade(), perhaps something like this:

```
@Override
public void onUpgrade(SQLiteDatabase db, int oldVersion, int newVersion) {
  // no-op, since will not be called until 2nd schema
  // version exists
}
```

In a production system, of course, we would want to make a temporary table, copy our current data to it, fix up the real table's schema, then migrate the data back.

Step #3: Remove Extraneous Code from LunchList

With our menu and thread samples behind us, we can get rid of our options menu and simplify the code. Get rid of the following items from your implementation of LunchList:

- The isActive and progress data members

- The call to requestWindowFeature() in onCreate()

- The implementations of onPause(), onResume(), onCreateOptionsMenu(), and onOptionsItemSelected()

- The startWork() and doSomeLongWork() methods, along with the longTask Runnable

Step #4: Get Access to the Helper

We will be using RestaurantHelper as our bridge to the database. Hence, LunchList will need a RestaurantHelper, to retrieve existing restaurants and add new ones.

In order to really use the database, though, we need to open and close access to it from LunchList.

First, in LunchList, create a RestaurantHelper data member named helper.

Then, in onCreate() in LunchList, after the call to setContentView(), initialize RestaurantHelper like this:

```
helper=new RestaurantHelper(this);
```

Finally, implement onDestroy() on LunchList as follows:

```
@Override
public void onDestroy() {
  super.onDestroy();

  helper.close();
}
```

All we do in onDestroy(), besides chain to the superclass, is close the helper we opened in onCreate(). This will close the underlying SQLite database as well.

Step #5: Save a Restaurant to the Database

We are going to be replacing our restaurant object model (and its associated ArrayList) with the database and a Cursor representing the roster of restaurants. This will involve adding some more logic to RestaurantHelper to aid in this process, while also starting to use it from LunchList.

First, add an import statement for `android.content.ContentValues` to `RestaurantHelper`.

Then, implement `insert()` on `RestaurantHelper` as follows:

```
public void insert(String name, String address,
                   String type, String notes) {
  ContentValues cv=new ContentValues();

  cv.put("name", name);
  cv.put("address", address);
  cv.put("type", type);
  cv.put("notes", notes);

  getWritableDatabase().insert("restaurants", "name", cv);
}
```

With this code, we pour the individual pieces of a restaurant (e.g., its name) into a `ContentValues` and tell the `SQLiteDatabase` to insert it into the database. We call `getWritableDatabase()` to get at the `SQLiteDatabase`. Our helper will automatically open the database in write mode if it has not already been opened by the helper before.

Finally, we need to actually call `insert()` at the appropriate time. Right now, our Save button adds a restaurant to our `RestaurantAdapter` – now, we need it to persist the restaurant to the database. So, modify the `onSave` object in `LunchList` to look like this:

```
private View.OnClickListener onSave=new View.OnClickListener() {
    public void onClick(View v) {
      String type=null;

      switch (types.getCheckedRadioButtonId()) {
        case R.id.sit_down:
          type="sit_down";
          break;
        case R.id.take_out:
          type="take_out";
          break;
        case R.id.delivery:
          type="delivery";
          break;
      }

      helper.insert(name.getText().toString(),
                    address.getText().toString(), type,
```

```
                    notes.getText().toString());
    }
 };
```

We simply get the four pieces of data from their respective widgets and call
`insert()`.

Step #6: Get the List of Restaurants from the Database

This puts restaurants into the database. Presumably, it would be useful to
get them back out sometime. Hence, we need some logic that can query the
database and return a `Cursor` with columnar data from our `restaurant` table.
A `Cursor` in Android is much like a cursor in other database access libraries
– it is an encapsulation of the result set of the query, plus the query that
was used to create it.

To do this, add the following method to `RestaurantHelper`:

```
public Cursor getAll() {
  return(getReadableDatabase()
          .rawQuery("SELECT _id, name, address, type, notes FROM restaurants
ORDER BY name",
                  null));
}
```

Here, we get access to the underlying `SQLiteDatabase` (opening it in read
mode if it is not already open) and call `rawQuery()`, passing in a suitable
query string to retrieve all restaurants, sorted by name.

We will also need to have some way to get the individual pieces of data out
of the `Cursor` (e.g., name). To that end, add a few getter-style methods to
`RestaurantHelper` that will retrieve the proper columns from a `Cursor`
positioned on the desired row:

```
public String getName(Cursor c) {
  return(c.getString(1));
}

public String getAddress(Cursor c) {
```

```
  return(c.getString(2));
}

public String getType(Cursor c) {
  return(c.getString(3));
}

public String getNotes(Cursor c) {
  return(c.getString(4));
}
```

Step #7: Change our Adapter and Wrapper

Of course, our existing RestaurantAdapter extends ArrayAdapter and cannot use a Cursor very effectively. So, we need to change our RestaurantAdapter into something that can use a Cursor...such as a CursorAdapter. Just as an ArrayAdapter creates a View for every needed item in an array or List, CursorAdapter creates a View for every needed row in a Cursor.

A CursorAdapter does not use getView(), but rather bindView() and newView(). The newView() method handles the case where we need to inflate a new row; bindView() is when we are recycling an existing row. So, our current getView() logic needs to be split between bindView() and newView().

Replace our existing RestaurantAdapter implementation in LunchList with the following:

```
class RestaurantAdapter extends CursorAdapter {
  RestaurantAdapter(Cursor c) {
    super(LunchList.this, c);
  }

  @Override
  public void bindView(View row, Context ctxt,
                       Cursor c) {
    RestaurantHolder holder=(RestaurantHolder)row.getTag();

    holder.populateFrom(c, helper);
  }

  @Override
  public View newView(Context ctxt, Cursor c,
                      ViewGroup parent) {
    LayoutInflater inflater=getLayoutInflater();
    View row=inflater.inflate(R.layout.row, parent, false);
```

```
    RestaurantHolder holder=new RestaurantHolder(row);

    row.setTag(holder);

    return(row);
  }
}
```

Then, you need to make use of this refined adapter, by changing the model in LunchList from an ArrayList to a Cursor. After you have changed that data member, replace the current onCreate() code that populates our RestaurantAdapter with the following:

```
model=helper.getAll();
startManagingCursor(model);
adapter=new RestaurantAdapter(model);
list.setAdapter(adapter);
```

After getting the Cursor from getAll(), we call startManagingCursor(), so Android will deal with refreshing its contents if the activity is paused and resumed. Then, we hand the Cursor off to the RestaurantAdapter.

Also, you will need to import android.content.Context and android.widget.CursorAdapter in LunchList.

Then, we need to update RestaurantHolder to work with Cursor objects rather than a restaurant directly. Replace the existing implementation with the following:

```
static class RestaurantHolder {
  private TextView name=null;
  private TextView address=null;
  private ImageView icon=null;

  RestaurantHolder(View row) {
    name=(TextView)row.findViewById(R.id.title);
    address=(TextView)row.findViewById(R.id.address);
    icon=(ImageView)row.findViewById(R.id.icon);
  }

  void populateFrom(Cursor c, RestaurantHelper helper) {
    name.setText(helper.getName(c));
    address.setText(helper.getAddress(c));

    if (helper.getType(c).equals("sit_down")) {
```

```
    icon.setImageResource(R.drawable.ball_red);
  }
  else if (helper.getType(c).equals("take_out")) {
    icon.setImageResource(R.drawable.ball_yellow);
  }
  else {
    icon.setImageResource(R.drawable.ball_green);
  }
 }
}
```

Step #8: Clean Up Lingering ArrayList References

Since we changed our model in LunchList from an ArrayList to a Cursor, anything that still assumes an ArrayList will not work.

Notably, the onListClick listener object tries to obtain a restaurant from the ArrayList. Now, we need to move the Cursor to the appropriate position and get a restaurant from that. So, modify onListClick to use the Cursor and the property getter methods on RestaurantHelper instead:

```
private AdapterView.OnItemClickListener onListClick=new
AdapterView.OnItemClickListener() {
  public void onItemClick(AdapterView<?> parent,
                          View view, int position,
                          long id) {
    model.moveToPosition(position);
    name.setText(helper.getName(model));
    address.setText(helper.getAddress(model));
    notes.setText(helper.getNotes(model));

    if (helper.getType(model).equals("sit_down")) {
      types.check(R.id.sit_down);
    }
    else if (helper.getType(model).equals("take_out")) {
      types.check(R.id.take_out);
    }
    else {
      types.check(R.id.delivery);
    }

    getTabHost().setCurrentTab(1);
  }
};
```

At this point, you can recompile and reinstall your application. If you try using it, it will launch and you can save restaurants to the database.

However, you will find that the list of restaurants will not update unless you exit and restart the LunchList activity.

Step #9: Refresh Our List

The reason the list does not update is because neither the Cursor nor the CursorAdapter realize that the database contents have changed when we save our restaurant. To resolve this, add model.requery(); immediately after the call to insert() in the onSave object in LunchList. This causes the Cursor to reload its contents from the database, which in turn will cause the CursorAdapter to redisplay the list.

Rebuild and reinstall the application and try it out. You should have all the functionality you had before, with the added benefit of restaurants living from run to run of LunchList.

Here is an implementation of LunchList that incorporates all of the changes shown in this tutorial:

```
package apt.tutorial;

import android.app.TabActivity;
import android.content.Context;
import android.database.Cursor;
import android.os.Bundle;
import android.view.View;
import android.view.ViewGroup;
import android.view.LayoutInflater;
import android.widget.AdapterView;
import android.widget.CursorAdapter;
import android.widget.Button;
import android.widget.EditText;
import android.widget.ImageView;
import android.widget.ListView;
import android.widget.RadioGroup;
import android.widget.TabHost;
import android.widget.TextView;

public class LunchList extends TabActivity {
  Cursor model=null;
  RestaurantAdapter adapter=null;
  EditText name=null;
  EditText address=null;
  EditText notes=null;
```

```
RadioGroup types=null;
RestaurantHelper helper=null;

@Override
public void onCreate(Bundle savedInstanceState) {
  super.onCreate(savedInstanceState);
  setContentView(R.layout.main);

  helper=new RestaurantHelper(this);

  name=(EditText)findViewById(R.id.name);
  address=(EditText)findViewById(R.id.addr);
  notes=(EditText)findViewById(R.id.notes);
  types=(RadioGroup)findViewById(R.id.types);

  Button save=(Button)findViewById(R.id.save);

  save.setOnClickListener(onSave);

  ListView list=(ListView)findViewById(R.id.restaurants);

  model=helper.getAll();
  startManagingCursor(model);
  adapter=new RestaurantAdapter(model);
  list.setAdapter(adapter);

  TabHost.TabSpec spec=getTabHost().newTabSpec("tag1");

  spec.setContent(R.id.restaurants);
  spec.setIndicator("List", getResources()
                          .getDrawable(R.drawable.list));
  getTabHost().addTab(spec);

  spec=getTabHost().newTabSpec("tag2");
  spec.setContent(R.id.details);
  spec.setIndicator("Details", getResources()
                          .getDrawable(R.drawable.restaurant));
  getTabHost().addTab(spec);

  getTabHost().setCurrentTab(0);

  list.setOnItemClickListener(onListClick);
}

@Override
public void onDestroy() {
  super.onDestroy();

  helper.close();
}

private View.OnClickListener onSave=new View.OnClickListener() {
  public void onClick(View v) {
    String type=null;
```

```
    switch (types.getCheckedRadioButtonId()) {
      case R.id.sit_down:
        type="sit_down";
        break;
      case R.id.take_out:
        type="take_out";
        break;
      case R.id.delivery:
        type="delivery";
        break;
    }

    helper.insert(name.getText().toString(),
                  address.getText().toString(), type,
                  notes.getText().toString());
    model.requery();
  }
};

  private AdapterView.OnItemClickListener onListClick=new
AdapterView.OnItemClickListener() {
    public void onItemClick(AdapterView<?> parent,
                            View view, int position,
                            long id) {
    model.moveToPosition(position);
    name.setText(helper.getName(model));
    address.setText(helper.getAddress(model));
    notes.setText(helper.getNotes(model));

    if (helper.getType(model).equals("sit_down")) {
      types.check(R.id.sit_down);
    }
    else if (helper.getType(model).equals("take_out")) {
      types.check(R.id.take_out);
    }
    else {
      types.check(R.id.delivery);
    }

    getTabHost().setCurrentTab(1);
  }
};

  class RestaurantAdapter extends CursorAdapter {
    RestaurantAdapter(Cursor c) {
      super(LunchList.this, c);
    }

    @Override
    public void bindView(View row, Context ctxt,
                         Cursor c) {
      RestaurantHolder holder=(RestaurantHolder)row.getTag();
```

```
      holder.populateFrom(c, helper);
    }

  @Override
  public View newView(Context ctxt, Cursor c,
                      ViewGroup parent) {
    LayoutInflater inflater=getLayoutInflater();
    View row=inflater.inflate(R.layout.row, parent, false);
    RestaurantHolder holder=new RestaurantHolder(row);

    row.setTag(holder);

    return(row);
  }
}

static class RestaurantHolder {
  private TextView name=null;
  private TextView address=null;
  private ImageView icon=null;

  RestaurantHolder(View row) {
    name=(TextView)row.findViewById(R.id.title);
    address=(TextView)row.findViewById(R.id.address);
    icon=(ImageView)row.findViewById(R.id.icon);
  }

  void populateFrom(Cursor c, RestaurantHelper helper) {
    name.setText(helper.getName(c));
    address.setText(helper.getAddress(c));

    if (helper.getType(c).equals("sit_down")) {
      icon.setImageResource(R.drawable.ball_red);
    }
    else if (helper.getType(c).equals("take_out")) {
      icon.setImageResource(R.drawable.ball_yellow);
    }
    else {
      icon.setImageResource(R.drawable.ball_green);
    }
  }
}
}
```

Similarly, here is a full implementation of `RestaurantHelper` that contains the modifications from this tutorial:

```
package apt.tutorial;

import android.content.Context;
import android.content.ContentValues;
import android.database.Cursor;
```

```
import android.database.SQLException;
import android.database.sqlite.SQLiteOpenHelper;
import android.database.sqlite.SQLiteDatabase;
import android.database.sqlite.SQLiteQueryBuilder;

class RestaurantHelper extends SQLiteOpenHelper {
  private static final String DATABASE_NAME="lunchlist.db";
  private static final int SCHEMA_VERSION=1;

  public RestaurantHelper(Context context) {
    super(context, DATABASE_NAME, null, SCHEMA_VERSION);
  }

  @Override
  public void onCreate(SQLiteDatabase db) {
    db.execSQL("CREATE TABLE restaurants (_id INTEGER PRIMARY KEY AUTOINCREMENT,
name TEXT, address TEXT, type TEXT, notes TEXT);");
  }

  @Override
  public void onUpgrade(SQLiteDatabase db, int oldVersion, int newVersion) {
    // no-op, since will not be called until 2nd schema
    // version exists
  }

  public Cursor getAll() {
    return(getReadableDatabase()
            .rawQuery("SELECT _id, name, address, type, notes FROM restaurants
ORDER BY name",
                     null));
  }

  public void insert(String name, String address,
                     String type, String notes) {
    ContentValues cv=new ContentValues();

    cv.put("name", name);
    cv.put("address", address);
    cv.put("type", type);
    cv.put("notes", notes);

    getWritableDatabase().insert("restaurants", "name", cv);
  }

  public String getName(Cursor c) {
    return(c.getString(1));
  }

  public String getAddress(Cursor c) {
    return(c.getString(2));
  }

  public String getType(Cursor c) {
    return(c.getString(3));
```

```
  }

  public String getNotes(Cursor c) {
    return(c.getString(4));
  }
}
```

Extra Credit

Here are some things you can try beyond those step-by-step instructions:

- Download the database off the emulator (or device) and examine it using a SQLite client program. You can use `adb pull` to download `/data/data/apt.tutorial/databases/lunchlist.db`, or use Eclipse or DDMS to browse the emulator graphically to retrieve the same file.

- Use `adb shell` and the `sqlite3` program built into the emulator to examine the database in the emulator itself, without downloading it.

Further Reading

You can learn more about how Android and SQLite work together in the "Managing and Accessing Local Databases" chapter of The Busy Coder's Guide to Android Development[38].

However, if you are looking for more general documentation on SQLite itself, such as it's particular flavor of SQL, you will want to use the SQLite site[39], or perhaps The Definitive Guide to SQLite[40].

---

38 http://commonsware.com/Android
39 http://sqlite.org
40 http://www.amazon.com/Definitive-Guide-SQLite-Mike-Owens/dp/1590596730

Getting More Active

In this tutorial, we will add support for both creating new restaurants and editing ones that were previously entered. Along the way, we will get rid of our tabs, splitting the application into two activities: one for the list, and one for the detail form.

Step-By-Step Instructions

First, you need to have completed the previous tutorial. If you are beginning the tutorials here, or if you wish to not use your existing work, you can download a ZIP file with all of the tutorial results, and you can copy the 11-Database edition of LunchList to use as a starting point. If you are using Eclipse, these instructions will help you load the project into a workspace.

Also, for this specific tutorial, since there is a lot of cutting and pasting, you may wish to save off a copy of your current work before starting in on the modifications, so you can clip code from the original and paste it where it is needed.

Step #1: Create a Stub Activity

The first thing we need to do is create an activity to serve as our detail form. In a flash of inspiration, let's call it DetailForm. So, create a LunchList/src/apt/tutorial/DetailForm.java file with the following content:

```
package apt.tutorial;

import android.app.Activity;
import android.os.Bundle;

public class DetailForm extends Activity {
  @Override
  public void onCreate(Bundle savedInstanceState) {
    super.onCreate(savedInstanceState);
//    setContentView(R.layout.main);
  }
}
```

Eclipse users can do this by right-clicking over the `apt.tutorial` package in the Package Explorer and choosing New > Class from the context menu. Indicate that the class name is `DetailForm` and the superclass is `android.app.Activity`. Then, fill in the `onCreate()` method shown in the listing above.

This is just a stub activity, except it has the `setContentView()` line commented out. That is because we do not want to use `main.xml`, as that is the layout for `LunchList`. Since we do not have another layout ready yet, we can just comment out the line. As we will see, this is perfectly legal, but it means the activity will have no UI.

Step #2: Launch the Stub Activity on List Click

Now, we need to arrange to display this activity when the user clicks on a `LunchList` list item, instead of flipping to the original detail form tab in `LunchList`.

First, we need to add `DetailForm` to the `AndroidManifest.xml` file, so it is recognized by the system as being an available activity. Change the manifest to look like the following:

```xml
<?xml version="1.0" encoding="utf-8"?>
<manifest android:versionCode="1"
          android:versionName="1.0"
          package="apt.tutorial"
          xmlns:android="http://schemas.android.com/apk/res/android">

  <supports-screens android:largeScreens="true"
```

```
                  android:normalScreens="true"
                  android:smallScreens="false" />
  <application android:label="@string/app_name">
    <activity android:label="@string/app_name"
              android:name=".LunchList">
      <intent-filter>
        <action android:name="android.intent.action.MAIN" />
        <category android:name="android.intent.category.LAUNCHER" />
      </intent-filter>
    </activity>
    <activity android:name=".DetailForm"></activity>
  </application>
</manifest>
```

Notice the second <activity> element, referencing the DetailForm class. Also note that it does not need an <intent-filter>, since we will be launching it ourselves rather than expecting the system to launch it for us.

Eclipse users can accomplish the preceding step by:

- Double-clicking on the AndroidManifest.xml file in the PackageExplorer to launch the graphical manifest editor

- Switching to the Application sub-tab of the editor

- Clicking the Add... button next to the Application Nodes list

- Choosing Activity from the list of possible elements to add

- Clicking the Browse... button next to the Name field and choosing DetailForm from the list of activities

Then, we need to start this activity when the list item is clicked. That is handled by our onListClick listener object in LunchList. So, replace our current implementation with the following:

```
private AdapterView.OnItemClickListener onListClick=new
AdapterView.OnItemClickListener() {
  public void onItemClick(AdapterView<?> parent,
                          View view, int position,
                          long id) {
    Intent i=new Intent(LunchList.this, DetailForm.class);

    startActivity(i);
  }
};
```

Here we create an `Intent` that points to our `DetailForm` and call `startActivity()` on that `Intent`. You will need to add an import for `android.content.Intent` to `LunchList`.

At this point, you should be able to recompile and reinstall the application. If you run it and click on an item in the list, it will open up the empty `DetailForm`. From there, you can click the BACK button to return to the main `LunchList` activity.

Step #3: Move the Detail Form Layout

Now, the shredding begins – we need to start moving our detail form smarts out of `LunchList` and its layout to `DetailForm`.

Create a `LunchList/res/layout/detail_form.xml`, using the detail form from `LunchList/res/layout/main.xml` as a basis:

```
<ScrollView xmlns:android="http://schemas.android.com/apk/res/android"
  android:layout_width="match_parent"
  android:layout_height="wrap_content">
  <TableLayout
    android:layout_width="match_parent"
    android:layout_height="wrap_content"
    android:stretchColumns="1"
    android:shrinkColumns="1"
  >
  <TableRow>
    <TextView android:text="Name:" />
    <EditText android:id="@+id/name" />
  </TableRow>
  <TableRow>
    <TextView android:text="Address:" />
    <EditText android:id="@+id/addr" />
  </TableRow>
  <TableRow>
    <TextView android:text="Type:" />
    <RadioGroup android:id="@+id/types">
      <RadioButton android:id="@+id/take_out"
        android:text="Take-Out"
        android:checked="true"
      />
      <RadioButton android:id="@+id/sit_down"
        android:text="Sit-Down"
      />
      <RadioButton android:id="@+id/delivery"
```

```
        android:text="Delivery"
      />
    </RadioGroup>
  </TableRow>
  <TableRow>
    <TextView android:text="Notes:" />
    <EditText android:id="@+id/notes"
      android:inputType="textMultiLine"
      android:gravity="top"
      android:lines="2"
      android:scrollHorizontally="false"
      android:maxLines="2"
    />
  </TableRow>
  <Button android:id="@+id/save"
    android:layout_width="match_parent"
    android:layout_height="wrap_content"
    android:text="Save"
  />
</TableLayout>
</ScrollView>
```

Eclipse users can accomplish the above by copying res/layout/main.xml
(right-click on the file and choose Copy), pasting it back into res/layout/ as
detail_form.xml (right-click on the res/layout/ folder and choose Paste),
and then editing the XML.

This is just the detail form turned into its own standalone layout file. You
are getting rid of everything before the <ScrollView> and after the
</ScrollView> tags, after moving the android:xmlns attribute on the root
element to the ScrollView element.

Step #4: Move the Detail Form Code

Un-comment the setContentView() call in onCreate() in DetailForm and have
it load this layout:

```
setContentView(R.layout.detail_form);
```

Then, we need to add all our logic for accessing the various form widgets,
plus an onSave listener for our Save button, plus all necessary imports.

Set the import list for DetailForm to be:

```
import android.app.Activity;
import android.database.Cursor;
import android.os.Bundle;
import android.view.View;
import android.widget.Button;
import android.widget.EditText;
import android.widget.RadioGroup;
import android.widget.TextView;
```

Then, add the following data members to the DetailForm class:

```
EditText name=null;
EditText address=null;
EditText notes=null;
RadioGroup types=null;
RestaurantHelper helper=null;
```

Then, copy the widget finders and stuff from onCreate() in LunchList into the same spot in DetailForm:

```
helper=new RestaurantHelper(this);

name=(EditText)findViewById(R.id.name);
address=(EditText)findViewById(R.id.addr);
notes=(EditText)findViewById(R.id.notes);
types=(RadioGroup)findViewById(R.id.types);

Button save=(Button)findViewById(R.id.save);

save.setOnClickListener(onSave);
```

Finally, add the onSave listener object with a subset of the implementation from LunchList:

```
private View.OnClickListener onSave=new View.OnClickListener() {
  public void onClick(View v) {
    String type=null;

    switch (types.getCheckedRadioButtonId()) {
      case R.id.sit_down:
        type="sit_down";
        break;
      case R.id.take_out:
        type="take_out";
        break;
      case R.id.delivery:
        type="delivery";
        break;
```

```
    }
  }
};
```

You will notice that we are not using the type variable – we will put that to use in a later step of the tutorial.

Step #5: Clean Up the Original Layout

Now we need to clean up LunchList and its layout to reflect the fact that we moved much of the logic over to DetailForm.

First, we need to get rid of the tabs and the detail form from LunchList/res/layout/main.xml and alter the ListView's android:id to the @android:id/list value required for use with ListActivity. Also, it would be nice, now that we are using ListActivity, to support the "empty view" – a View in our layout that will be displayed when the list of restaurants is empty.

In what is sure to be a shock to you, there are separate instructions for those of you using Eclipse and those of you not using Eclipse.

Eclipse

It will be simplest to start this layout from scratch. Delete the existing main.xml layout resource by right-clicking over it, choosing Delete from the context menu, and confirming this move. Then, right-click over res/layout/, choose New > File from the context menu, and name it main.xml. Once again, you will get complaints in Eclipse about not having any content in this file, but we will fix that next.

From the Layouts section of the tool palette, drag a FrameLayout into the editing area. Your preview image will appear, though, as with most layouts, there is nothing visible at this point.

From the Composite section of the tool palette, drag a ListView into the editing area, dropping it on your (invisible) FrameLayout. It will appear as a transparent widget with a selection outline and grab handles:

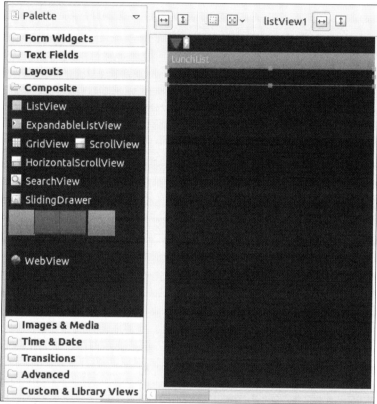

Figure 56. The new LunchList main layout, with a FrameLayout and ListView

Then, toggle over to the XML, and assign @android:id/list to the android:id attribute on the ListView element – due to a bug in the tools, you cannot define this one via the context menu.

Back in the "Graphical Layout" sub-tab, from the "Form Widgets" section of the tool palette, drag a TextView onto the FrameLayout (do not drag it onto the ListView!). This will add it to the FrameLayout, visually placing it in the top-left corner. Then, toggle over to the XML, and assign @android:id/empty to the android:id attribute on the TextView element – again, due to a bug in the tools, you cannot define this one via the context menu.

Back in the "Graphical Layout" sub-tab, with the TextView selected, click both the horizontal and vertical stretch toggle toolbar buttons (first two on the left in the toolbar above the preview), to say that the TextView should fill the entire screen. Then, right-click on the TextView, choose Properties > Text from the context menu, and fill in Click the MENU button to add a restaurant! as the text.

Now, right-click over the TextView and choose Select > Select Siblings from the context menu. This will cause both the TextView and the ListView to be selected in the graphical editor:

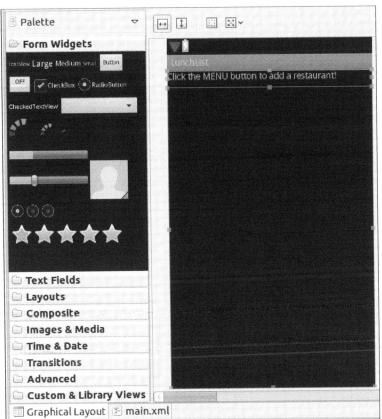

Figure 57. The new LunchList main layout, with both the TextView and the ListView selected

Click the second toolbar button from the left above the editing area (looks like vertical arrowheads) to indicate that both the `ListView` and the `TextView` should fill all available vertical space. `ListActivity` will arrange for only one of these widgets to be visible at a time.

At this point, you can save your layout via Ctrl-S or the main Eclipse menu. Also, you can delete the `res/layout-land/main.xml` file (right-click over it, choose Delete, and confirm your decision), as we will create an updated version of the landscape layout in a later tutorial.

Outside of Eclipse

To make those changes, replace your existing `LunchList/res/layout/main.xml` with the following:

```xml
<?xml version="1.0" encoding="utf-8"?>
<FrameLayout xmlns:android="http://schemas.android.com/apk/res/android"
  android:layout_width="match_parent"
  android:layout_height="match_parent">
  <ListView
    android:id="@android:id/list"
    android:layout_width="match_parent"
    android:layout_height="match_parent"
  />
  <TextView
    android:id="@android:id/empty"
    android:layout_width="match_parent"
    android:layout_height="match_parent"
    android:text="Click the MENU button to add a restaurant!"/>
</FrameLayout>
```

You will notice that our `ListView` is wrapped inside of a `FrameLayout`, with a `TextView` as a peer. The `TextView`, courtesy of the magic `@android:id/empty` ID, will be displayed when the list is empty. Flipping between the `TextView` and `ListView` is handled for us automatically by `ListActivity`.

Next, delete `LunchList/res/layout_land/main.xml`, as we will revisit landscape layouts in a later tutorial.

Step #6: Clean Up the Original Code

At present, LunchList extends TabActivity, which is no longer what we need. Change it to extend ListActivity instead, adding an import for android.app.ListActivity.

Finally, get rid of the code from onCreate() that sets up the tabs and the Save button, since they are no longer needed. Also, you no longer need to find the ListView widget, since you can call setListAdapter() on the ListActivity to associate your RestaurantAdapter with the ListActivity's ListView. You also no longer need to access the form widgets, since they are no longer in this activity. The resulting onCreate() implementation should look like:

```
@Override
public void onCreate(Bundle savedInstanceState) {
  super.onCreate(savedInstanceState);
  setContentView(R.layout.main);

  helper=new RestaurantHelper(this);
  model=helper.getAll();
  startManagingCursor(model);
  adapter=new RestaurantAdapter(model);
  setListAdapter(adapter);
}
```

You can also get rid of the onSave object, as we will be using the onSave that exists in the DetailForm class.

Step #7: Pass the Restaurant _ID

Now, let's step back a bit and think about what we are trying to achieve.

We want to be able to use DetailForm for both adding new restaurants and editing an existing restaurant. DetailForm needs to be able to tell those two scenarios apart. Also, DetailForm needs to know which item is to be edited.

To achieve this, we will pass an "extra" in our Intent that launches DetailForm, containing the ID (_id column) of the restaurant to edit. We will use this if the DetailForm was launched by clicking on an existing restaurant. If DetailForm receives an Intent lacking our "extra", it will know to add a new restaurant.

First, we need to define a name for this "extra", so add the following data member to LunchList:

```
public final static String ID_EXTRA="apt.tutorial._ID";
```

We use the apt.tutorial namespace to ensure our "extra" name will not collide with any names perhaps used by the Android system.

Next, convert the onListClick object to an onListItemClick() method (available to us on ListActivity) and have it add this "extra" to the Intent it uses to start the DetailForm:

```
@Override
public void onListItemClick(ListView list, View view,
                            int position, long id) {
  Intent i=new Intent(LunchList.this, DetailForm.class);

  i.putExtra(ID_EXTRA, String.valueOf(id));
  startActivity(i);
}
```

The _id of the restaurant happens to be provided to us as the fourth parameter to onListItemClick(). We turn it into a String because DetailForm will want it in String format, as we will see shortly.

Next, add the following data member to DetailForm:

```
String restaurantId=null;
```

This will be null if we are adding a new restaurant or the string form of the ID if we are editing an existing restaurant.

Finally, add the following line to the end of onCreate() in DetailForm:

```
restaurantId=getIntent().getStringExtra(LunchList.ID_EXTRA);
```

This will pull out our "extra", or leave `restaurantId` as `null` if there is no such "extra".

Step #8: Load the Restaurant Into the Form

In the case where we are editing an existing restaurant, we need to load that restaurant from the database, then load it into the `DetailForm`.

Since we created a `RestaurantHelper` in `onCreate()`, we need to close it again, so add an `onDestroy()` implementation to `DetailForm` as follows:

```
@Override
public void onDestroy() {
  super.onDestroy();

  helper.close();
}
```

Now that we have a handle to the database, we need to load a restaurant given its ID. So, add the following method to `RestaurantHelper`:

```
public Cursor getById(String id) {
  String[] args={id};

  return(getReadableDatabase()
          .rawQuery("SELECT _id, name, address, type, notes FROM restaurants
WHERE _ID=?",
                    args));
}
```

Then, add the following lines to the bottom of `onCreate()` in `DetailForm`, to load in the specified restaurant into the form if its ID was specified in the `Intent`:

```
if (restaurantId!=null) {
  load();
}
```

The code snippet above references a `load()` method, which we need to add to `DetailForm`, based off of code originally in `LunchList`:

```
private void load() {
  Cursor c=helper.getById(restaurantId);

  c.moveToFirst();
  name.setText(helper.getName(c));
  address.setText(helper.getAddress(c));
  notes.setText(helper.getNotes(c));

  if (helper.getType(c).equals("sit_down")) {
    types.check(R.id.sit_down);
  }
  else if (helper.getType(c).equals("take_out")) {
    types.check(R.id.take_out);
  }
  else {
    types.check(R.id.delivery);
  }

  c.close();
}
```

Step #9: Add an "Add" Menu Option

We have most of the logic in place to edit existing restaurants. However, we still need to add a menu item for adding a new restaurant.

First, we need an icon for that menu option. In our case, we will use one from the Android SDK. Go to the directory where you installed the SDK, and go into the platforms/ directory inside of it. Then, go into the directory for some version of Android (e.g., android-8/), and into data/res/drawable-mdpi/. You will find ic_menu_add.png in there – copy it into your project. Eclipse users may have to press <F5> to get Eclipse to recognize the new image, if you copied it using your development machine's operating system (e.g., copied it using Windows Explorer).

Now we need to change LunchList/res/menu/option.xml to replace the existing options with one for add:

```
<?xml version="1.0" encoding="utf-8"?>
<menu xmlns:android="http://schemas.android.com/apk/res/android">
  <item android:id="@+id/add"
    android:title="Add"
    android:icon="@drawable/ic_menu_add"
  />
</menu>
```

Eclipse users can accomplish this by:

- Double-clicking on the res/menu/option.xml resource to bring it up in the graphical editor

- Selecting one of the existing menu options and clicking the Remove... button to get rid of it

- Selecting the other menu option and changing it to have an ID of @+id/add, Add as the title, and @drawable/ic_menu_add as the icon

- Saving your changes via <Ctrl>-<S>

Now that we have the menu option, we need to adjust our menu handling to match. Restore our older implementation of onCreateOptionMenu() to LunchList:

```
@Override
public boolean onCreateOptionsMenu(Menu menu) {
  new MenuInflater(this).inflate(R.menu.option, menu);

  return(super.onCreateOptionsMenu(menu));
}
```

Then, add an onOptionsItemSelected() implementation in LunchList with the following:

```
@Override
public boolean onOptionsItemSelected(MenuItem item) {
  if (item.getItemId()==R.id.add) {
    startActivity(new Intent(LunchList.this, DetailForm.class));

    return(true);
  }

  return(super.onOptionsItemSelected(item));
}
```

Here, we launch the DetailForm activity without our "extra", signalling to DetailForm that it is to add a new restaurant. You will need imports again for android.view.Menu, android.view.MenuInflater, and android.view.MenuItem.

Step #10: Detail Form Supports Add and Edit

Last, but certainly not least, we need to have `DetailForm` properly do useful work when the Save button is clicked. Specifically, we need to either insert or update the database. It would also be nice if we dismissed the `DetailForm` at that point and returned to the main `LunchList` activity.

To accomplish this, we first need to add an `update()` method to `RestaurantHelper` that can perform a database update:

```
public void update(String id, String name, String address,
                   String type, String notes) {
  ContentValues cv=new ContentValues();
  String[] args={id};

  cv.put("name", name);
  cv.put("address", address);
  cv.put("type", type);
  cv.put("notes", notes);

  getWritableDatabase().update("restaurants", cv, "_ID=?",
                       args);
}
```

Then, we need to adjust our `onSave` listener object in `DetailForm` to call the right method (`save()` or `update()`) and `finish()` our activity:

```
private View.OnClickListener onSave=new View.OnClickListener() {
  public void onClick(View v) {
    String type=null;

    switch (types.getCheckedRadioButtonId()) {
      case R.id.sit_down:
        type="sit_down";
        break;
      case R.id.take_out:
        type="take_out";
        break;
      case R.id.delivery:
        type="delivery";
        break;
    }

    if (restaurantId==null) {
      helper.insert(name.getText().toString(),
                    address.getText().toString(), type,
                    notes.getText().toString());
```

```
    }
    else {
      helper.update(restaurantId, name.getText().toString(),
                    address.getText().toString(), type,
                    notes.getText().toString());
    }

    finish();
  }
};
```

At this point, you should be able to recompile and reinstall the application. When you first bring up the application, it will no longer show the tabs:

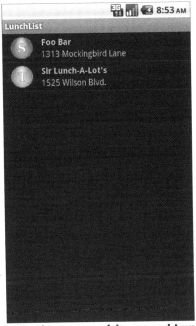

Figure 58. The new-and-improved LunchList

However, it will have an "add" menu option:

Figure 59. The LunchList options menu, with Add

If you choose the "add" menu option, it will bring up a blank DetailForm:

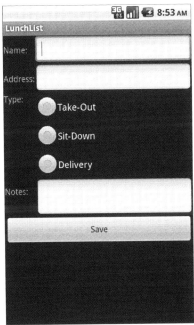

Figure 60. The DetailForm activity

If you fill out the form and click Save, it will return you to the LunchList and immediately shows the new restaurant (courtesy of our using a managed Cursor in LunchList):

Figure 61. The LunchList with an added Restaurant

If you click an existing restaurant, it will bring up the DetailForm for that object:

Figure 62. The DetailForm on an existing Restaurant

Making changes and clicking Save will update the database and list:

Figure 63. The LunchList with an edited Restaurant

Here is one implementation of LunchList that incorporates all of this tutorial's changes:

```
package apt.tutorial;

import android.app.ListActivity;
import android.content.Context;
import android.content.Intent;
import android.database.Cursor;
import android.os.Bundle;
import android.view.Menu;
import android.view.MenuInflater;
import android.view.MenuItem;
import android.view.View;
import android.view.ViewGroup;
import android.view.LayoutInflater;
import android.widget.AdapterView;
import android.widget.CursorAdapter;
import android.widget.ImageView;
import android.widget.ListView;
import android.widget.TextView;

public class LunchList extends ListActivity {
  public final static String ID_EXTRA="apt.tutorial._ID";
  Cursor model=null;
```

```
RestaurantAdapter adapter=null;
RestaurantHelper helper=null;

@Override
public void onCreate(Bundle savedInstanceState) {
  super.onCreate(savedInstanceState);
  setContentView(R.layout.main);

  helper=new RestaurantHelper(this);
  model=helper.getAll();
  startManagingCursor(model);
  adapter=new RestaurantAdapter(model);
  setListAdapter(adapter);
}

@Override
public void onDestroy() {
  super.onDestroy();

  helper.close();
}

@Override
public void onListItemClick(ListView list, View view,
                            int position, long id) {
  Intent i=new Intent(LunchList.this, DetailForm.class);

  i.putExtra(ID_EXTRA, String.valueOf(id));
  startActivity(i);
}

@Override
public boolean onCreateOptionsMenu(Menu menu) {
  new MenuInflater(this).inflate(R.menu.option, menu);

  return(super.onCreateOptionsMenu(menu));
}

@Override
public boolean onOptionsItemSelected(MenuItem item) {
  if (item.getItemId()==R.id.add) {
    startActivity(new Intent(LunchList.this, DetailForm.class));

    return(true);
  }

  return(super.onOptionsItemSelected(item));
}

class RestaurantAdapter extends CursorAdapter {
  RestaurantAdapter(Cursor c) {
    super(LunchList.this, c);
  }
```

```
    @Override
    public void bindView(View row, Context ctxt,
                         Cursor c) {
      RestaurantHolder holder=(RestaurantHolder)row.getTag();

      holder.populateFrom(c, helper);
    }

    @Override
    public View newView(Context ctxt, Cursor c,
                        ViewGroup parent) {
      LayoutInflater inflater=getLayoutInflater();
      View row=inflater.inflate(R.layout.row, parent, false);
      RestaurantHolder holder=new RestaurantHolder(row);

      row.setTag(holder);

      return(row);
    }
  }

  static class RestaurantHolder {
    private TextView name=null;
    private TextView address=null;
    private ImageView icon=null;

    RestaurantHolder(View row) {
      name=(TextView)row.findViewById(R.id.title);
      address=(TextView)row.findViewById(R.id.address);
      icon=(ImageView)row.findViewById(R.id.icon);
    }

    void populateFrom(Cursor c, RestaurantHelper helper) {
      name.setText(helper.getName(c));
      address.setText(helper.getAddress(c));

      if (helper.getType(c).equals("sit_down")) {
        icon.setImageResource(R.drawable.ball_red);
      }
      else if (helper.getType(c).equals("take_out")) {
        icon.setImageResource(R.drawable.ball_yellow);
      }
      else {
        icon.setImageResource(R.drawable.ball_green);
      }
    }
  }
}
```

Here is one implementation of DetailForm that works with the revised
LunchList:

```
package apt.tutorial;

import android.app.Activity;
import android.database.Cursor;
import android.os.Bundle;
import android.view.View;
import android.widget.Button;
import android.widget.EditText;
import android.widget.RadioGroup;
import android.widget.TextView;

public class DetailForm extends Activity {
  EditText name=null;
  EditText address=null;
  EditText notes=null;
  RadioGroup types=null;
  RestaurantHelper helper=null;
  String restaurantId=null;

  @Override
  public void onCreate(Bundle savedInstanceState) {
    super.onCreate(savedInstanceState);
    setContentView(R.layout.detail_form);

    helper=new RestaurantHelper(this);

    name=(EditText)findViewById(R.id.name);
    address=(EditText)findViewById(R.id.addr);
    notes=(EditText)findViewById(R.id.notes);
    types=(RadioGroup)findViewById(R.id.types);

    Button save=(Button)findViewById(R.id.save);

    save.setOnClickListener(onSave);

    restaurantId=getIntent().getStringExtra(LunchList.ID_EXTRA);

    if (restaurantId!=null) {
      load();
    }
  }

  @Override
  public void onDestroy() {
    super.onDestroy();

    helper.close();
  }

  private void load() {
    Cursor c=helper.getById(restaurantId);

    c.moveToFirst();
    name.setText(helper.getName(c));
```

```
    address.setText(helper.getAddress(c));
    notes.setText(helper.getNotes(c));

    if (helper.getType(c).equals("sit_down")) {
      types.check(R.id.sit_down);
    }
    else if (helper.getType(c).equals("take_out")) {
      types.check(R.id.take_out);
    }
    else {
      types.check(R.id.delivery);
    }

    c.close();
  }

  private View.OnClickListener onSave=new View.OnClickListener() {
    public void onClick(View v) {
      String type=null;

      switch (types.getCheckedRadioButtonId()) {
        case R.id.sit_down:
          type="sit_down";
          break;
        case R.id.take_out:
          type="take_out";
          break;
        case R.id.delivery:
          type="delivery";
          break;
      }

      if (restaurantId==null) {
        helper.insert(name.getText().toString(),
                     address.getText().toString(), type,
                     notes.getText().toString());
      }
      else {
        helper.update(restaurantId, name.getText().toString(),
                     address.getText().toString(), type,
                     notes.getText().toString());
      }

      finish();
    }
  };
}
```

And, here is an implementation of `RestaurantHelper` with the changes needed by `DetailForm`:

```
package apt.tutorial;

import android.content.Context;
import android.content.ContentValues;
import android.database.Cursor;
import android.database.SQLException;
import android.database.sqlite.SQLiteOpenHelper;
import android.database.sqlite.SQLiteDatabase;
import android.database.sqlite.SQLiteQueryBuilder;

class RestaurantHelper extends SQLiteOpenHelper {
  private static final String DATABASE_NAME="lunchlist.db";
  private static final int SCHEMA_VERSION=1;

  public RestaurantHelper(Context context) {
    super(context, DATABASE_NAME, null, SCHEMA_VERSION);
  }

  @Override
  public void onCreate(SQLiteDatabase db) {
    db.execSQL("CREATE TABLE restaurants (_id INTEGER PRIMARY KEY AUTOINCREMENT,
name TEXT, address TEXT, type TEXT, notes TEXT);");
  }

  @Override
  public void onUpgrade(SQLiteDatabase db, int oldVersion, int newVersion) {
    // no-op, since will not be called until 2nd schema
    // version exists
  }

  public Cursor getAll() {
    return(getReadableDatabase()
            .rawQuery("SELECT _id, name, address, type, notes FROM restaurants
ORDER BY name",
                      null));
  }

  public Cursor getById(String id) {
    String[] args={id};

    return(getReadableDatabase()
            .rawQuery("SELECT _id, name, address, type, notes FROM restaurants
WHERE _ID=?",
                      args));
  }

  public void insert(String name, String address,
                     String type, String notes) {
    ContentValues cv=new ContentValues();

    cv.put("name", name);
    cv.put("address", address);
    cv.put("type", type);
    cv.put("notes", notes);
```

```
      getWritableDatabase().insert("restaurants", "name", cv);
  }

  public void update(String id, String name, String address,
                     String type, String notes) {
    ContentValues cv=new ContentValues();
    String[] args={id};

    cv.put("name", name);
    cv.put("address", address);
    cv.put("type", type);
    cv.put("notes", notes);

    getWritableDatabase().update("restaurants", cv, "_ID=?",
                                 args);
  }

  public String getName(Cursor c) {
    return(c.getString(1));
  }

  public String getAddress(Cursor c) {
    return(c.getString(2));
  }

  public String getType(Cursor c) {
    return(c.getString(3));
  }

  public String getNotes(Cursor c) {
    return(c.getString(4));
  }
}
```

Extra Credit

Here are some things you can try beyond those step-by-step instructions:

- Have the database hold a URL for the restaurant's Web site. Update the UI to collect this address in the detail form. Launch that URL via startActivity() via an options menu choice from the restaurant list, so you can view the restaurant's Web site.

- Add an options menu to delete a restaurant. Raise an AlertDialog to confirm that the user wants the restaurant deleted. Delete it from the database and refresh the list if the user confirms the deletion.

Further Reading

You can read up on having multiple activities in your application, or linking to activities supplied by others, in the "Launching Activities and Sub-Activities" chapter of The Busy Coder's Guide to Android Development[41].

---

41 http://commonsware.com/Android

What's Your Preference?

In this tutorial, we will add a preference setting for the sort order of the restaurant list. To do this, we will create a `PreferenceScreen` definition in XML, load that into a `PreferenceActivity`, connect that activity to the application, and finally actually use the preference to control the sort order.

Step-By-Step Instructions

First, you need to have completed the previous tutorial. If you are beginning the tutorials here, or if you wish to not use your existing work, you can download a ZIP file with all of the tutorial results, and you can copy the `12-Activities` edition of `LunchList` to use as a starting point. If you are using Eclipse, these instructions will help you load the project into a workspace.

Step #1: Define the Preference XML

Preferences are described in the form of a preference XML resource, located in a `res/xml/` resource directory. Not surprisingly, there are separate instructions for setting up the XML, depending upon whether or not you are using Eclipse.

Eclipse

The preference that we are going to use is a ListPreference. A ListPreference, as the name suggests, gives the user a list of things to choose from. That list of things to choose from comes in the form of a string-array resource, as does a corresponding list of actual values to be stored – think of this as being the difference between the text in an HTML <option> tag compared to the tag's value attribute.

So, first, we need to set up these arrays. To do that, right-click over the res/values/ directory in your project and choose New > File from the context menu. Give the file the name of arrays.xml and click OK. This will create an empty file, and give you an error message to that effect:

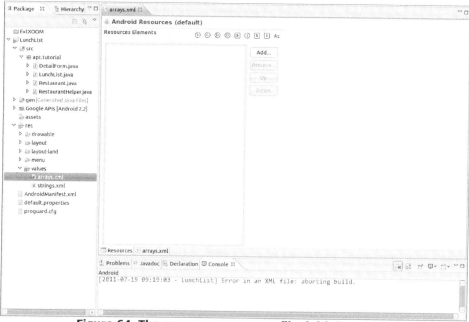

Figure 64. The new array resource file, initially empty

Click the Add... button, choose "String Array" in the dialog, and click OK to create a new string-array resource:

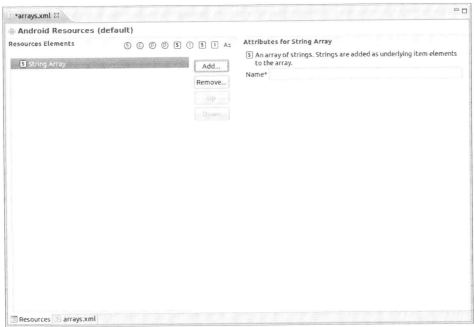

Figure 65. The new, empty string-array resource

Fill in sort_names for the name in the field on the right. Then, with the string-array resource highlighted, click the Add... button, choose "Item" in the dialog, and click OK to put a new item in this string-array resource:

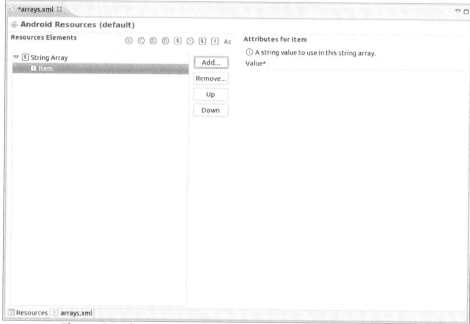

Figure 66. The new, empty item in the string-array resource

Fill in By Name, Ascending as the value in the field on the right. Continue clicking the Add... button and adding new items to the array, with the following values:

- By Name, Descending
- By Type
- By Address, Ascending
- By Address, Descending

Click the Add... button once again, but this time, choose the top radio button ("Create a new element at the top level, in Resources"), then choose "String Array" and click OK. This will add another string-array resource as a peer to the first:

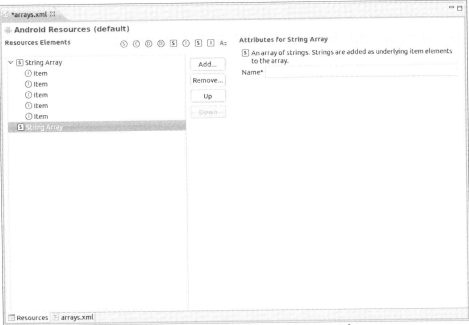

Figure 67. The arrays.xml resource file, now with two string-array resources

Give this string-array resource a name of `sort_clauses`. Then, add five items to it using the Add… button, with the following five values:

- name ASC

- name DESC

- type, name ASC

- address ASC

- address DESC

Note that you need to add these in the orders specified, or at least keep the two arrays synchronized.

When done, you can save this file using <Ctrl>-<S> or the File menu.

With that behind us, we can define the preference XML itself. Right-click over the `res/` directory and choose New > Folder from the context menu. Give the folder the name of `xml` and click OK. Then, right-click over the newly-created `res/xml/` folder and choose New > File from the context menu. Give the file the name of `preferences.xml` and click OK. And, since at this point there is no means of defining preference XML resources graphically in a useful fashion, switch to the Source sub-tab and paste in the following XML:

```
<PreferenceScreen
  xmlns:android="http://schemas.android.com/apk/res/android">
  <ListPreference
    android:key="sort_order"
    android:title="Sort Order"
    android:summary="Choose the order the list uses"
    android:entries="@array/sort_names"
    android:entryValues="@array/sort_clauses"
    android:dialogTitle="Choose a sort order" />
</PreferenceScreen>
```

This sets up a single-item `PreferenceScreen`. Note that it references the two string-array resources that we defined above.

Outside of Eclipse

First, add a `LunchList/res/xml/preferences.xml` file as follows:

```
<PreferenceScreen
  xmlns:android="http://schemas.android.com/apk/res/android">
  <ListPreference
    android:key="sort_order"
    android:title="Sort Order"
    android:summary="Choose the order the list uses"
    android:entries="@array/sort_names"
    android:entryValues="@array/sort_clauses"
    android:dialogTitle="Choose a sort order" />
</PreferenceScreen>
```

This sets up a single-item `PreferenceScreen`. Note that it references two string arrays, one for the display labels of the sort-order selection list, and one for the values actually stored in the `SharedPreferences`.

So, to define those string arrays, add a `LunchList/res/values/arrays.xml` file with the following content:

```
<?xml version="1.0" encoding="utf-8"?>
<resources>
  <string-array name="sort_names">
    <item>By Name, Ascending</item>
    <item>By Name, Descending</item>
    <item>By Type</item>
    <item>By Address, Ascending</item>
    <item>By Address, Descending</item>
  </string-array>
  <string-array name="sort_clauses">
    <item>name ASC</item>
    <item>name DESC</item>
    <item>type, name ASC</item>
    <item>address ASC</item>
    <item>address DESC</item>
  </string-array>
</resources>
```

Note we are saying that the value stored in the `SharedPreferences` will actually be an ORDER BY clause for use in our SQL query. This is a convenient trick, though it does tend to make the system a bit more fragile – if we change our column names, we might have to change our preferences to match and deal with older invalid preference values.

Step #2: Create the Preference Activity

Next, we need to create a `PreferenceActivity` that will actually use these preferences. Eclipse users can use the Eclipse new-class wizard (right-click over the `apt.tutorial` package in Package Explorer and choose New > Class) to create a subclass of `android.preference.PreferenceActivity` named `EditPreferences`. Non-Eclipse users can simply create a `LunchList/src/apt/tutorial/EditPreferences.java` file.

Regardless of how you create the class, its implementation should look like this:

```java
package apt.tutorial;

import android.app.Activity;
import android.os.Bundle;
import android.preference.PreferenceActivity;

public class EditPreferences extends PreferenceActivity {
  @Override
```

```
  public void onCreate(Bundle savedInstanceState) {
    super.onCreate(savedInstanceState);

    addPreferencesFromResource(R.xml.preferences);
  }
}
```

Here, we simply tell Android to allow the user to edit the preferences defined in that preference XML resource from the previous section.

We also need to update `AndroidManifest.xml` to reference this activity, so we can launch it later. Eclipse users should:

1. Double-click on the `AndroidManifest.xml` file in the project to open it up in the editor

2. Click on the Application sub-tab

3. Click the Add... button next to the "Application Nodes" list

4. Choose Activity in the dialog box and click OK

5. Click the Browse... button next to the Name field and choose `EditPreferences` from the resulting dialog (then press OK to close that dialog)

6. Save the changes to the manifest (e.g., <Ctrl>-<S>)

Non-Eclipse users can simply add the `<activity>` element for `EditPreferences` shown in the manifest file below:

```
<?xml version="1.0" encoding="utf-8"?>
<manifest android:versionCode="1"
          android:versionName="1.0"
          package="apt.tutorial"
          xmlns:android="http://schemas.android.com/apk/res/android">

  <supports-screens android:largeScreens="true"
                     android:normalScreens="true"
                     android:smallScreens="false" />
  <application android:label="@string/app_name">
    <activity android:label="@string/app_name"
              android:name=".LunchList">
      <intent-filter>
        <action android:name="android.intent.action.MAIN" />
        <category android:name="android.intent.category.LAUNCHER" />
      </intent-filter>
```

```
    </activity>
    <activity android:name=".DetailForm"></activity>
    <activity android:name=".EditPreferences"></activity>
  </application>
</manifest>
```

Step #3: Connect the Preference Activity to the Option Menu

Now, we can add a menu option to launch the `EditPreferences` activity.

First, we need another menu icon. Grab the `ic_menu_preferences.png` image from the Android SDK, from the same directory where you got `ic_menu_add.png`, and put it in your res/drawable/ directory in your project.

Then, we need to add another `<item>` to our `LunchList/res/menu/option.xml` file:

```xml
<?xml version="1.0" encoding="utf-8"?>
<menu xmlns:android="http://schemas.android.com/apk/res/android">
  <item android:id="@+id/add"
    android:title="Add"
    android:icon="@drawable/ic_menu_add"
  />
  <item android:id="@+id/prefs"
    android:title="Settings"
    android:icon="@drawable/ic_menu_preferences"
  />
</menu>
```

Eclipse users, instead of manually editing the XML, can do the following:

1. Double-click on the `res/menu/option.xml` file in the Package Explorer to open it up in the editor

2. Click the Add... button next to the list of menu items, choose Item in the dialog, and click OK to add a blank menu item

3. Assign `@+id/prefs` as the Id value for the menu item

4. Fill in `Settings` as the title for the menu item

5. Use `@drawable/ic_menu_preferences` for the icon for the menu item

6.   Save the resulting changes (e.g., <Ctrl>-<S>)

Of course, if we modify the menu XML, we also need to modify the
LunchList implementation of onOptionsItemSelected() to match, so replace
the current implementation with the following:

```
@Override
public boolean onOptionsItemSelected(MenuItem item) {
  if (item.getItemId()==R.id.add) {
    startActivity(new Intent(LunchList.this, DetailForm.class));

    return(true);
  }
  else if (item.getItemId()==R.id.prefs) {
    startActivity(new Intent(this, EditPreferences.class));

    return(true);
  }

  return(super.onOptionsItemSelected(item));
}
```

All we are doing is starting up our EditPreferences activity.

If you recompile and reinstall the application, you will see our new menu
option:

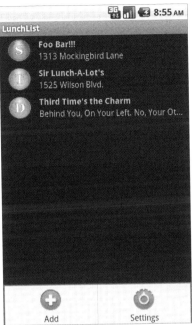

Figure 68. The LunchList with the new menu option

And if you choose that menu option, you will get the `EditPreferences` activity:

Figure 69. The preferences activity

Clicking the Sort Order item will bring up a selection list of available sort orders:

Figure 70. The available sort orders

Of course, none of this is actually having any effect on the sort order itself, which we will address in the next section.

Step #4: Apply the Sort Order on Startup

Now, given that the user has chosen a sort order, we need to actually use it. First, we can apply it when the application starts up – the next section will handle changing the sort order after the user changes the preference value.

First, the getAll() method on RestaurantHelper needs to take a sort order as a parameter, rather than apply one of its own. So, change that method as follows:

```
public Cursor getAll(String orderBy) {
  return(getReadableDatabase()
        .rawQuery("SELECT _id, name, address, type, notes FROM restaurants
ORDER BY "+orderBy,
                  null));
}
```

Then, we need to get our hands on our SharedPreferences instance. Add imports to LunchList for android.content.SharedPreferences and android.preference.PreferenceManager, along with a SharedPreferences data member named prefs.

Next, add this line near the top of onCreate() in LunchList, to initialize prefs to be the SharedPreferences our preference activity uses:

```
prefs=PreferenceManager.getDefaultSharedPreferences(this);
```

Finally, change the call to getAll() to use the SharedPreferences:

```
model=helper.getAll(prefs.getString("sort_order", "name"));
```

Here, we use name as the default value, so if the user has not specified a sort order yet, the sort order will be by name.

Now, if you recompile and reinstall the application, then set a sort order preference, you can see that preference take effect if you exit and reopen the application.

Step #5: Listen for Preference Changes

That works, but users will get annoyed if they have to exit the application just to get their preference choice to take effect. To change the sort order on the fly, we first need to know when they change the sort order.

SharedPreferences has the notion of a preference listener object, to be notified on such changes. To take advantage of this, add the following line at the end of onCreate() in LunchList:

```
prefs.registerOnSharedPreferenceChangeListener(prefListener);
```

This snippet refers to a prefListener object, so add the following code to LunchList to create a stub implementation of that object:

```
private SharedPreferences.OnSharedPreferenceChangeListener prefListener=
  new SharedPreferences.OnSharedPreferenceChangeListener() {
  public void onSharedPreferenceChanged(SharedPreferences sharedPrefs, String
key) {
    if (key.equals("sort_order")) {
    }
  }
};
```

All we are doing right now is watching for our specific preference of interest (sort_order), though we are not actually taking advantage of the changed value.

Step #6: Re-Apply the Sort Order on Changes

Finally, we actually need to change the sort order. For simple lists like this, the easiest way to accomplish this is to get a fresh Cursor representing our list (from getAll() on RestaurantHelper) with the proper sort order, and use the new Cursor instead of the old one.

First, pull some of the list-population logic out of onCreate(), by implementing an initList() method as follows:

```
private void initList() {
  if (model!=null) {
    stopManagingCursor(model);
    model.close();
  }

  model=helper.getAll(prefs.getString("sort_order", "name"));
  startManagingCursor(model);
  adapter=new RestaurantAdapter(model);
  setListAdapter(adapter);
}
```

Note that we call stopManagingCursor() so Android will ignore the old Cursor, then we close it, before we get and apply the new Cursor. Of course, we only do those things if there is an old Cursor.

The onCreate() method needs to change to take advantage of initList():

```
@Override
public void onCreate(Bundle savedInstanceState) {
  super.onCreate(savedInstanceState);
  setContentView(R.layout.main);

  helper=new RestaurantHelper(this);
  prefs=PreferenceManager.getDefaultSharedPreferences(this);
  initList();
  prefs.registerOnSharedPreferenceChangeListener(prefListener);
}
```

Also, we can call initList() from prefListener:

```
private SharedPreferences.OnSharedPreferenceChangeListener prefListener=
 new SharedPreferences.OnSharedPreferenceChangeListener() {
  public void onSharedPreferenceChanged(SharedPreferences sharedPrefs,
                                         String key) {
    if (key.equals("sort_order")) {
      initList();
    }
  }
};
```

At this point, if you recompile and reinstall the application, you should see the sort order change immediately as you change the order via the preferences.

Extra Credit

Here are some things you can try beyond those step-by-step instructions:

- Add a preference for the default type of restaurant (e.g., take-out). Use that preference in detail forms when creating a new restaurant.

- Add an options menu to the detail form activity and have it be able to start the preference activity the way we did from the option menu for the list.

- Rather than use preferences, store the preference values in a JSON file that you read in at startup and re-read in onResume() (to find out about changes). This means you will need to create your own preference UI, rather than rely upon the one created by the preference XML.

Further Reading

Learn more about setting up preference XML files and reading shared preferences in the "Using Preferences" chapter of The Busy Coder's Guide to Android Development[42].

---

42 http://commonsware.com/Android

Turn, Turn, Turn

In this tutorial, we will make our application somewhat more intelligent about screen rotations, ensuring that partially-entered restaurant information remains intact even after the screen rotates.

Step-By-Step Instructions

First, you need to have completed the previous tutorial. If you are beginning the tutorials here, or if you wish to not use your existing work, you can download a ZIP file with all of the tutorial results, and you can copy the 13-Prefs edition of LunchList to use as a starting point. If you are using Eclipse, these instructions will help you load the project into a workspace.

Step #1: Add a Stub onSaveInstanceState()

Since we are not holding onto network connections or other things that cannot be stored in a Bundle, we can use onSaveInstanceState() to track our state as the screen is rotated.

To that end, add a stub implementation of onSaveInstanceState() to DetailForm as follows:

```
@Override
public void onSaveInstanceState(Bundle state) {
```

```
    super.onSaveInstanceState(state);
}
```

Step #2: Pour the Form Into the Bundle

Now, fill in the details of onSaveInstanceState(), putting our widget contents into the supplied Bundle:

```
@Override
public void onSaveInstanceState(Bundle state) {
  super.onSaveInstanceState(state);

  state.putString("name", name.getText().toString());
  state.putString("address", address.getText().toString());
  state.putString("notes", notes.getText().toString());
  state.putInt("type", types.getCheckedRadioButtonId());
}
```

Step #3: Repopulate the Form

Next, we need to make use of that saved state. We could do this in onCreate(), if the passed-in Bundle is non-null. However, it is usually easier just to override onRestoreInstanceState(). This is called only when there is state to restore, supplying the Bundle with your state. So, add an implementation of onRestoreInstanceState() to DetailForm:

```
@Override
public void onRestoreInstanceState(Bundle state) {
  super.onRestoreInstanceState(state);

  name.setText(state.getString("name"));
  address.setText(state.getString("address"));
  notes.setText(state.getString("notes"));
  types.check(state.getInt("type"));
}
```

At this point, you can recompile and reinstall the application. Use <Ctrl>-<F12> to simulate rotating the screen of your emulator. If you do this after making changes (but not saving) on the DetailForm, you will see those changes survive the rotation.

Step #4: Fix Up the Landscape Detail Form

As you tested the work from the previous section, you no doubt noticed that the DetailForm layout is not well-suited for landscape – the notes text area is chopped off and the Save button is missing. To fix this, we need to create a LunchList/res/layout-land/detail_form.xml file, derived from our original, but set up to take advantage of the whitespace to the right of the radio buttons:

```xml
<ScrollView xmlns:android="http://schemas.android.com/apk/res/android"
  android:layout_width="match_parent"
  android:layout_height="wrap_content">
  <TableLayout
    android:layout_width="match_parent"
    android:layout_height="wrap_content"
    android:stretchColumns="3"
    android:shrinkColumns="3"
  >
    <TableRow>
      <TextView android:text="Name:" />
      <EditText android:id="@+id/name"
        android:layout_span="3"
      />
    </TableRow>
    <TableRow>
      <TextView android:text="Address:" />
      <EditText android:id="@+id/addr"
        android:layout_span="3"
      />
    </TableRow>
    <TableRow>
      <TextView android:text="Type:" />
      <RadioGroup android:id="@+id/types">
        <RadioButton android:id="@+id/take_out"
          android:text="Take-Out"
          android:checked="true"
        />
        <RadioButton android:id="@+id/sit_down"
          android:text="Sit-Down"
        />
        <RadioButton android:id="@+id/delivery"
          android:text="Delivery"
        />
      </RadioGroup>
      <TextView android:text="Notes:" />
      <LinearLayout android:orientation="vertical">
        <EditText android:id="@+id/notes"
          android:inputType="textMultiLine"
          android:gravity="top"
          android:lines="2"
```

```
                android:scrollHorizontally="false"
                android:maxLines="2"
                android:layout_width="match_parent"
                android:layout_height="wrap_content"
            />
            <Button android:id="@+id/save"
                android:layout_width="match_parent"
                android:layout_height="wrap_content"
                android:text="Save"
            />
        </LinearLayout>
      </TableRow>
    </TableLayout>
</ScrollView>
```

Eclipse users can right-click over the res/layout-land/ directory and choose New > File from the context menu. Name the new file detail_form.xml to match the one we have in res/layout/. Then, paste in the above XML in the source sub-tab.

Now, if you recompile and reinstall the application, you should see a better landscape rendition of the detail form.

Extra Credit

Here are some things you can try beyond those step-by-step instructions:

- Try switching to onRetainNonConfigurationInstance() instead of onSaveInstanceState().

- Try commenting out onSaveInstanceState() and onRestoreInstanceState(). Does the activity still retain its instance state? Why or why not?

Further Reading

Additional coverage of screen rotations and how to control what happens during them can be found in the "Handling Rotation" chapter of The Busy Coder's Guide to Android Development[43].

---

43 http://commonsware.com/Android

Feeding at Lunch

Right now, our LunchList application simply displays data that the user entered. It would be nice to collect more information about a restaurant, culled from other places online. In this tutorial, we allow users to attach an RSS feed URL to a restaurant. Then, we allow them to view the latest titles in the feed via a new ListActivity. To do this, we will need to download the feed from the Internet, then parse it – to do this, we will take advantage of a third-party JAR file.

Step-By-Step Instructions

First, you need to have completed the previous tutorial. If you are beginning the tutorials here, or if you wish to not use your existing work, you can download a ZIP file with all of the tutorial results, and you can copy the 14-Rotation edition of LunchList to use as a starting point. If you are using Eclipse, these instructions will help you load the project into a workspace.

Step #1: Add a Feed URL to the Data Model

First, we need to track the feed URL in our data model. This means we need to adjust our database and our RestaurantHelper (so we can retrieve and set the URL).

First, modify onCreate() of RestaurantHelper to add a new TEXT column named feed:

```
@Override
public void onCreate(SQLiteDatabase db) {
  db.execSQL("CREATE TABLE restaurants (_id INTEGER PRIMARY KEY AUTOINCREMENT,
name TEXT, address TEXT, type TEXT, notes TEXT, feed TEXT);");
}
```

This also means that we have changed our schema, so we need to change our SCHEMA_VERSION in RestaurantHelper to match:

```
private static final int SCHEMA_VERSION=2;
```

Also, now we need to contend with upgrading our existing database, for those users who already have LunchList installed and do not wish to lose all their precious restaurant data. This means we need to replace our original "no-op" RestaurantHelper onUpgrade() with one that will execute an ALTER TABLE statement to add this column:

```
@Override
public void onUpgrade(SQLiteDatabase db, int oldVersion, int newVersion) {
  db.execSQL("ALTER TABLE restaurants ADD COLUMN feed TEXT");
}
```

Plus, we need to adjust our RestaurantHelper methods that operate on the database, including getAll(), getById(), insert(), and update(), adding in support for the feed column:

```
public Cursor getAll(String orderBy) {
  return(getReadableDatabase()
          .rawQuery("SELECT _id, name, address, type, notes, feed FROM
restaurants ORDER BY "+orderBy,
                    null));
}

public Cursor getById(String id) {
  String[] args={id};

  return(getReadableDatabase()
          .rawQuery("SELECT _id, name, address, type, notes, feed FROM
restaurants WHERE _ID=?",
                    args));
}
```

```
public void insert(String name, String address,
                   String type, String notes,
                   String feed) {
  ContentValues cv=new ContentValues();

  cv.put("name", name);
  cv.put("address", address);
  cv.put("type", type);
  cv.put("notes", notes);
  cv.put("feed", feed);

  getWritableDatabase().insert("restaurants", "name", cv);
}

public void update(String id, String name, String address,
                   String type, String notes, String feed) {
  ContentValues cv=new ContentValues();
  String[] args={id};

  cv.put("name", name);
  cv.put("address", address);
  cv.put("type", type);
  cv.put("notes", notes);
  cv.put("feed", feed);

  getWritableDatabase().update("restaurants", cv, "_ID=?",
                               args);
}
```

And, we should add a new getFeed() method on RestaurantHelper to retrieve our feed URL from a Cursor returned by getAll() or getById():

```
public String getFeed(Cursor c) {
  return(c.getString(5));
}
```

The complete revised RestaurantHelper class now looks something like this:

```
package apt.tutorial;

import android.content.Context;
import android.content.ContentValues;
import android.database.Cursor;
import android.database.SQLException;
import android.database.sqlite.SQLiteOpenHelper;
import android.database.sqlite.SQLiteDatabase;
import android.database.sqlite.SQLiteQueryBuilder;

class RestaurantHelper extends SQLiteOpenHelper {
  private static final String DATABASE_NAME="lunchlist.db";
  private static final int SCHEMA_VERSION=2;
```

```
  public RestaurantHelper(Context context) {
    super(context, DATABASE_NAME, null, SCHEMA_VERSION);
  }

  @Override
  public void onCreate(SQLiteDatabase db) {
    db.execSQL("CREATE TABLE restaurants (_id INTEGER PRIMARY KEY AUTOINCREMENT,
name TEXT, address TEXT, type TEXT, notes TEXT, feed TEXT);");
  }

  @Override
  public void onUpgrade(SQLiteDatabase db, int oldVersion, int newVersion) {
    db.execSQL("ALTER TABLE restaurants ADD COLUMN feed TEXT");
  }

  public Cursor getAll(String orderBy) {
    return(getReadableDatabase()
            .rawQuery("SELECT _id, name, address, type, notes, feed FROM
restaurants ORDER BY "+orderBy,
                      null));
  }

  public Cursor getById(String id) {
    String[] args={id};

    return(getReadableDatabase()
            .rawQuery("SELECT _id, name, address, type, notes, feed FROM
restaurants WHERE _ID=?",
                      args));
  }

  public void insert(String name, String address,
                     String type, String notes,
                     String feed) {
  ContentValues cv=new ContentValues();

    cv.put("name", name);
    cv.put("address", address);
    cv.put("type", type);
    cv.put("notes", notes);
    cv.put("feed", feed);

    getWritableDatabase().insert("restaurants", "name", cv);
  }

  public void update(String id, String name, String address,
                     String type, String notes, String feed) {
  ContentValues cv=new ContentValues();
    String[] args={id};

    cv.put("name", name);
    cv.put("address", address);
    cv.put("type", type);
```

```
    cv.put("notes", notes);
    cv.put("feed", feed);

    getWritableDatabase().update("restaurants", cv, "_ID=?",
                                 args);
  }

  public String getName(Cursor c) {
    return(c.getString(1));
  }

  public String getAddress(Cursor c) {
    return(c.getString(2));
  }

  public String getType(Cursor c) {
    return(c.getString(3));
  }

  public String getNotes(Cursor c) {
    return(c.getString(4));
  }

  public String getFeed(Cursor c) {
    return(c.getString(5));
  }
}
```

Step #2: Update the Detail Form

The next problem is that our detail form is getting a wee bit crowded. We do not really have much room for adding another field, so we will need to use a bit of creativity to allow our form to still work on HVGA displays, in addition to larger ones.

Change the res/layout/detail_form.xml resource to look like this:

```xml
<ScrollView xmlns:android="http://schemas.android.com/apk/res/android"
  android:layout_width="match_parent"
  android:layout_height="wrap_content">
  <TableLayout
    android:layout_width="match_parent"
    android:layout_height="wrap_content"
    android:stretchColumns="1"
    android:shrinkColumns="1"
    >
    <TableRow>
      <TextView android:text="Name:" />
      <EditText android:id="@+id/name" />
```

```
    </TableRow>
    <TableRow>
      <TextView android:text="Address:" />
      <EditText android:id="@+id/addr" />
    </TableRow>
    <TableRow>
      <TextView android:text="Type:" />
      <RadioGroup android:id="@+id/types">
        <RadioButton android:id="@+id/take_out"
          android:text="Take-Out"
          android:checked="true"
        />
        <RadioButton android:id="@+id/sit_down"
          android:text="Sit-Down"
        />
        <RadioButton android:id="@+id/delivery"
          android:text="Delivery"
        />
      </RadioGroup>
    </TableRow>
    <EditText android:id="@+id/notes"
      android:inputType="textMultiLine"
      android:gravity="top"
      android:lines="2"
      android:scrollHorizontally="false"
      android:maxLines="2"
      android:hint="Notes"
    />
    <EditText android:id="@+id/feed"
      android:hint="Feed URL"
    />
    <Button android:id="@+id/save"
      android:layout_width="match_parent"
      android:layout_height="wrap_content"
      android:text="Save"
    />
  </TableLayout>
</ScrollView>
```

We have dropped the label for the notes field, replacing it with a hint. The hint will be displayed if the EditText is empty; otherwise, it will show what the user has typed in. Our new feed EditText also uses a hint instead of a label, and both are direct children of the TableLayout, like the Button, so they fill the entire row.

Because Eclipse does not support drag-and-drop of widgets in a TableLayout that are not in a TableRow, Eclipse users will need to edit the XML by hand.

Similarly, change the `res/layout-land/detail_form.xml` resource to look like this:

```xml
<ScrollView xmlns:android="http://schemas.android.com/apk/res/android"
  android:layout_width="match_parent"
  android:layout_height="wrap_content">
<TableLayout
    android:layout_width="match_parent"
    android:layout_height="wrap_content"
    android:stretchColumns="2"
    android:shrinkColumns="2"
  >
  <TableRow>
    <TextView android:text="Name:" />
    <EditText android:id="@+id/name"
      android:layout_span="2"
    />
  </TableRow>
  <TableRow>
    <TextView android:text="Address:" />
    <EditText android:id="@+id/addr"
      android:layout_span="2"
    />
  </TableRow>
  <TableRow>
    <TextView android:text="Type:" />
    <RadioGroup android:id="@+id/types">
      <RadioButton android:id="@+id/take_out"
        android:text="Take-Out"
        android:checked="true"
      />
      <RadioButton android:id="@+id/sit_down"
        android:text="Sit-Down"
      />
      <RadioButton android:id="@+id/delivery"
        android:text="Delivery"
      />
    </RadioGroup>
    <LinearLayout android:orientation="vertical">
      <EditText android:id="@+id/notes"
        android:inputType="textMultiLine"
        android:gravity="top"
        android:lines="2"
        android:scrollHorizontally="false"
        android:maxLines="2"
        android:layout_width="match_parent"
        android:layout_height="wrap_content"
        android:hint="Notes"
      />
      <EditText android:id="@+id/feed"
        android:layout_width="match_parent"
        android:layout_height="wrap_content"
        android:hint="Feed URL"
```

```
          />
          <Button android:id="@+id/save"
            android:layout_width="match_parent"
            android:layout_height="wrap_content"
            android:text="Save"
          />
        </LinearLayout>
      </TableRow>
    </TableLayout>
  </ScrollView>
```

Again, we have switched to hints instead of labels, plus added the `feed` EditText. Also, we have changed `android:stretchColumns` in the `TableLayout` element to 2, and similarly changed the `android:layout_span` attributes to 2, since we have removed one column.

Since Eclipse does not support changing the `android:layout_span` attribute graphically, Eclipse users will need to edit the XML by hand.

This also requires some changes to the `DetailForm` class. Add a new `EditText` data member named `feed`:

```
EditText feed=null;
```

Then, add a statement to the `onCreate()` method of `DetailForm` that uses `findViewById()` to retrieve that `EditText` widget from the inflated layout, after the similar statements for the other widgets:

```
feed=(EditText)findViewById(R.id.feed);
```

The `load()` method will need to populate the `feed` widget from the data model, so add a statement that performs that after all the other similar statements:

```
feed.setText(helper.getFeed(c));
```

Finally, the `onSave` object's `onClick()` method will need to change its calls to `insert()` and `update()` on the `RestaurantHelper` to add in the feed URL:

```
private View.OnClickListener onSave=new View.OnClickListener() {
  public void onClick(View v) {
```

```
  String type=null;

  switch (types.getCheckedRadioButtonId()) {
    case R.id.sit_down:
      type="sit_down";
      break;
    case R.id.take_out:
      type="take_out";
      break;
    case R.id.delivery:
      type="delivery";
      break;
  }

  if (restaurantId==null) {
    helper.insert(name.getText().toString(),
                  address.getText().toString(), type,
                  notes.getText().toString(),
                  feed.getText().toString());
  }
  else {
    helper.update(restaurantId, name.getText().toString(),
                  address.getText().toString(), type,
                  notes.getText().toString(),
                  feed.getText().toString());
  }

  finish();
  }
};
```

Step #3: Add a Feed Options Menu Item

Next, we need to give the user the ability to launch another activity to view the latest items from a restaurant's RSS feed. A likely way to do that would be via an options menu. Right now, though, the detail form does not have an options menu, so we will need to add one.

First, you will need to add a suitable icon to your project's `res/drawable/` directory as well, such as copying the `ic_menu_friendslist.png` file from your SDK installation – the same place where we have obtained most of the other menu drawables used in this project.

Then, we need to actually create the menu. Non-Eclipse users can create a new file, `res/menu/details_option.xml`, with the following content:

```
<?xml version="1.0" encoding="utf-8"?>
<menu xmlns:android="http://schemas.android.com/apk/res/android">
  <item android:id="@+id/feed"
    android:title="RSS Feed"
    android:icon="@drawable/ic_menu_friendslist"
  />
</menu>
```

It has a single menu item, to be used to view the feed.

Eclipse users should:

1. Right-click over the `res/menu/` folder and choose New > File from the context menu

2. Fill in `details_option.xml` in the dialog and click OK to create an empty menu XML resource

3. Click the Add... button next to the list of menu items, choose Item in the dialog, and click OK to add an empty menu item

4. Assign it `@+id/feed` as the Id value for the menu item

5. Use `RSS Feed` as the title for the menu item

6. Supply `@drawable/ic_menu_friendslist` as the icon for the menu item

7. Save the changes (e.g., <Ctrl>-<S>)

Then, add an `onCreateOptionsMenu()` method to `DetailForm`, using a `MenuInflater` object to load the menu resource and display it when the user chooses the menu:

```
@Override
public boolean onCreateOptionsMenu(Menu menu) {
  new MenuInflater(this).inflate(R.menu.details_option, menu);

  return(super.onCreateOptionsMenu(menu));
}
```

We will add the corresponding `onOptionsItemSelected()` method in the next section. Note that you will need to add imports to `android.view.Menu` and `android.view.MenuInflater`.

Step #4: Add Permissions and Check Connectivity

It would be nice if we would check to see if there is an Internet connection before going ahead and trying to fetch the feed given its URL. After all, if there is no connectivity, there is no point in trying and failing with some ugly error.

With that in mind, add an `onOptionsItemSelected()` method, and an accompanying `isNetworkAvailable()` method, to `DetailForm` that look like this:

```
@Override
public boolean onOptionsItemSelected(MenuItem item) {
  if (item.getItemId()==R.id.feed) {
    if (isNetworkAvailable()) {
      Intent i=new Intent(this, FeedActivity.class);

      i.putExtra(FeedActivity.FEED_URL, feed.getText().toString());
      startActivity(i);
    }
    else {
      Toast
        .makeText(this, "Sorry, the Internet is not available",
                Toast.LENGTH_LONG)
        .show();
    }

    return(true);
  }

  return(super.onOptionsItemSelected(item));
}

private boolean isNetworkAvailable() {
  ConnectivityManager
cm=(ConnectivityManager)getSystemService(CONNECTIVITY_SERVICE);
  NetworkInfo info=cm.getActiveNetworkInfo();

  return(info!=null);
}
```

Here, we call `getSystemService()` to obtain a `ConnectivityManager`. `ConnectivityManager` knows the state of data access overall, not via some particular technology (e.g., WiFi). Specifically, we see if `getActiveNetworkInfo()` returns a non-null object – if so, the device thinks it has a network connection. Of course, there could be problems with that connection (e.g., connected to a WiFi router, but unable to access certain URLs), but at least we can detect obvious problems.

If there is an Internet connection, `onOptionsItemSelected()` goes ahead and starts up a yet-to-be-defined activity named `FeedActivity`, tucking the feed URL in an Intent extra. If there is no Internet connection, we display a `Toast` instead.

You will need to add imports for:

- `android.content.Intent`

- `android.net.ConnectivityManager`

- `android.net.NetworkInfo`

- `android.view.MenuItem`

- `android.widget.Toast`

The complete modified `DetailForm` class should look something like this:

```
package apt.tutorial;

import android.app.Activity;
import android.content.Intent;
import android.database.Cursor;
import android.net.ConnectivityManager;
import android.net.NetworkInfo;
import android.os.Bundle;
import android.view.Menu;
import android.view.MenuInflater;
import android.view.MenuItem;
import android.view.View;
import android.widget.Button;
import android.widget.EditText;
import android.widget.RadioGroup;
import android.widget.TextView;
import android.widget.Toast;

public class DetailForm extends Activity {
  EditText name=null;
  EditText address=null;
  EditText notes=null;
  EditText feed=null;
  RadioGroup types=null;
  RestaurantHelper helper=null;
  String restaurantId=null;
```

```
@Override
public void onCreate(Bundle savedInstanceState) {
  super.onCreate(savedInstanceState);
  setContentView(R.layout.detail_form);

  helper=new RestaurantHelper(this);

  name=(EditText)findViewById(R.id.name);
  address=(EditText)findViewById(R.id.addr);
  notes=(EditText)findViewById(R.id.notes);
  types=(RadioGroup)findViewById(R.id.types);
  feed=(EditText)findViewById(R.id.feed);

  Button save=(Button)findViewById(R.id.save);

  save.setOnClickListener(onSave);

  restaurantId=getIntent().getStringExtra(LunchList.ID_EXTRA);

  if (restaurantId!=null) {
    load();
  }
}

@Override
public void onDestroy() {
  super.onDestroy();

  helper.close();
}

@Override
public boolean onCreateOptionsMenu(Menu menu) {
  new MenuInflater(this).inflate(R.menu.details_option, menu);

  return(super.onCreateOptionsMenu(menu));
}

@Override
public boolean onOptionsItemSelected(MenuItem item) {
  if (item.getItemId()==R.id.feed) {
    if (isNetworkAvailable()) {
      Intent i=new Intent(this, FeedActivity.class);

      i.putExtra(FeedActivity.FEED_URL, feed.getText().toString());
      startActivity(i);
    }
    else {
      Toast
        .makeText(this, "Sorry, the Internet is not available",
                  Toast.LENGTH_LONG)
        .show();
    }
```

```
      return(true);
    }

    return(super.onOptionsItemSelected(item));
  }

  private boolean isNetworkAvailable() {
    ConnectivityManager
cm=(ConnectivityManager)getSystemService(CONNECTIVITY_SERVICE);
    NetworkInfo info=cm.getActiveNetworkInfo();

    return(info!=null);
  }

  private void load() {
    Cursor c=helper.getById(restaurantId);

    c.moveToFirst();
    name.setText(helper.getName(c));
    address.setText(helper.getAddress(c));
    notes.setText(helper.getNotes(c));
    feed.setText(helper.getFeed(c));

    if (helper.getType(c).equals("sit_down")) {
      types.check(R.id.sit_down);
    }
    else if (helper.getType(c).equals("take_out")) {
      types.check(R.id.take_out);
    }
    else {
      types.check(R.id.delivery);
    }

    c.close();
  }

  private View.OnClickListener onSave=new View.OnClickListener() {
    public void onClick(View v) {
      String type=null;

      switch (types.getCheckedRadioButtonId()) {
        case R.id.sit_down:
          type="sit_down";
          break;
        case R.id.take_out:
          type="take_out";
          break;
        case R.id.delivery:
          type="delivery";
          break;
      }

      if (restaurantId==null) {
        helper.insert(name.getText().toString(),
```

```
                        address.getText().toString(), type,
                        notes.getText().toString(),
                        feed.getText().toString());
      }
    else {
      helper.update(restaurantId, name.getText().toString(),
                        address.getText().toString(), type,
                        notes.getText().toString(),
                        feed.getText().toString());
      }

    finish();
    }
  };
}
```

Also, we need to add our first permissions to our manifest, as we are starting to access device capabilities that require user agreement. Add the INTERNET and ACCESS_NETWORK_STATE permissions to your AndroidManifest.xml file, as children of the root <manifest> element:

```
<uses-permission android:name="android.permission.INTERNET" />
<uses-permission android:name="android.permission.ACCESS_NETWORK_STATE" />
```

Eclipse users can add these permissions by:

1. Double-clicking on AndroidManifest.xml in the Package Explorer to bring it up in the editor

2. Clicking on the Permissions sub-tab

3. Clicking the Add... button next to the permissions list, choosing "Uses Permission" in the dialog, and clicking OK

4. Choosing android.permission.INTERNET from the Name drop-down list

5. Repeating steps 2-3, then choosing android.permission.ACCESS_NETWORK_STATE for the second permission

6. Saving the results (e.g., <Ctrl>-<S>)

Step #5: Fetch the Feed

Now we are in position to start work on the `FeedActivity` – the class that will arrange to retrieve and display the RSS feed.

Start a new `FeedActivity` class, inheriting from `ListActivity`, in the project package. Do not worry about any methods on the class right now – we will add some of those in a bit. Eclipse users can do this by right-clicking over the `apt.tutorial` package in Package Explorer, choosing New > Class from the context menu, then specifying `FeedActivity` as the class name and `android.app.Activity` as the superclass.

Add `FeedActivity` to your manifest, by adding another `<activity>` element. The resulting `AndroidManifest.xml` file should look something like this:

```xml
<?xml version="1.0" encoding="utf-8"?>
<manifest android:versionCode="1"
          android:versionName="1.0"
          package="apt.tutorial"
          xmlns:android="http://schemas.android.com/apk/res/android">

  <uses-permission android:name="android.permission.INTERNET" />
  <uses-permission android:name="android.permission.ACCESS_NETWORK_STATE" />
  <supports-screens android:largeScreens="true"
                    android:normalScreens="true"
                    android:smallScreens="false" />
  <application android:label="@string/app_name">
    <activity android:label="@string/app_name"
              android:name=".LunchList">
      <intent-filter>
        <action android:name="android.intent.action.MAIN" />
        <category android:name="android.intent.category.LAUNCHER" />
      </intent-filter>
    </activity>
    <activity android:name=".DetailForm"></activity>
    <activity android:name=".EditPreferences"></activity>
    <activity android:name=".FeedActivity"></activity>
  </application>
</manifest>
```

Eclipse users can do this by:

1. Double-clicking on the `AndroidManifest.xml` file in Package Explorer to bring it up in the editor

2. Clicking on the Application sub-tab

3. Clicking on the Add... button next to the Application Nodes list

4. Choosing Activity in the node type dialog and clicking OK

5. Clicking the Browse... button next to the Name field and choosing FeedActivity

6. Saving changes (e.g., <Ctrl>-<S>)

Then, add a static inner class named FeedTask to FeedActivity that looks like this:

```
private static class FeedTask extends AsyncTask<String, Void, Void> {
  private Exception e=null;
  private FeedActivity activity=null;

  FeedTask(FeedActivity activity) {
    attach(activity);
  }

  @Override
  public Void doInBackground(String... urls) {
    try {
      DefaultHttpClient client=new DefaultHttpClient();
      HttpGet getMethod=new HttpGet(urls[0]);
      ResponseHandler<String> responseHandler=new BasicResponseHandler();
      String responseBody=client.execute(getMethod,
                                          responseHandler);

      Log.d("FeedActivity", responseBody);
    }
    catch (Exception e) {
      this.e=e;
    }

    return(null);
  }

  @Override
  public void onPostExecute(Void unused) {
    if (e==null) {
      // TODO
    }
    else {
      Log.e("LunchList", "Exception parsing feed", e);
      activity.goBlooey(e);
    }
  }
}
```

FeedTask is an AsyncTask, designed to wrap a thread and Handler and deal with background operations on our behalf. The doInBackground() method uses HttpClient[44] to fetch our feed, given its URL. Specifically:

- We create a DefaultHttpClient object, representing our executor of HTTP requests

- We create an HttpGet object to represent the request we wish to perform

- We create a BasicResponseHandler, whose job it is to get our data out of the server's response – specifically, we are looking for our feed

- We tell the client to execute the GET request by way of the response handler, giving us our feed, which we dump to LogCat

- If there is an exception – for example, we have a bad URL – we hold onto the Exception object and pass it to our activity

The FeedTask constructor takes the FeedActivity as a parameter. This is needed because FeedTask is a static inner class, and therefore does not automatically get access to the outer class instance. As we will see later in this tutorial, we need to attach and detach the activity from the task as part of handling configuration changes, such as screen rotations.

Also, go ahead and implement goBlooey() on FeedActivity, raising an AlertDialog if an Exception is encountered:

```
private void goBlooey(Throwable t) {
  AlertDialog.Builder builder=new AlertDialog.Builder(this);

  builder
    .setTitle("Exception!")
    .setMessage(t.toString())
    .setPositiveButton("OK", null)
    .show();
}
```

You will need the following imports:

- android.app.AlertDialog

- android.app.ListActivity

---

44 http://hc.apache.org/httpcomponents-client-ga/index.html

- `android.os.AsyncTask`

- `android.util.Log`

- `org.apache.http.client.ResponseHandler`

- `org.apache.http.client.HttpClient`

- `org.apache.http.client.methods.HttpGet`

- `org.apache.http.impl.client.BasicResponseHandler`

- `org.apache.http.impl.client.DefaultHttpClient`

If you are trying to use the emulator from some facility that requires a proxy server for external HTTP access, add the following lines of code to `doInBackground()` before creating the `DefaultHttpClient` object:

```
Properties systemSettings=System.getProperties();

systemSettings.put("http.proxyHost", "your.proxy.host.here");
systemSettings.put("http.proxyPort", "8080"); // use actual proxy port
```

Step #6: Install the RSS Library

To download and parse the feed, we could continue to use `HttpClient` to retrieve the content at the URL, then roll a DOM- or SAX-based parser to get at the data.

We could.

But we won't. Because we're *lazy*.

Instead, we will reuse an existing library for this purpose, android-rss[45], released under the Apache 2.0 license.

At the time of this writing, the author of that component only publishes source code, not a JAR, but you can download a JAR from http://misc.commonsware.com/android-rss.jar[46]. Readers of the digital

---

45 https://github.com/ahorn/android-rss
46 http://misc.commonsware.com/android-rss.jar

edition of this book can simply click on the link to begin downloading the file.

Copy that JAR into the libs/ directory of your project.

Eclipse users will also need to add the library to the build path – this is automatic if you are building via Ant. Eclipse users should right-click over the project name in the project explorer, then choose Build Path > Configure Build Path from the context menu. Click on the Libraries tab, then click the "Add JARs" button. Find the android-rss.jar file in your project's libs/ directory and select it. Then, you can close up this project properties window.

Step #7: Fetch and Parse the Feed (For Real This Time)

Get rid of the existing implementation of FeedTask in FeedActivity and replace it with one that looks like this:

```
private static class FeedTask extends AsyncTask<String, Void, RSSFeed> {
  private RSSReader reader=new RSSReader();
  private Exception e=null;
  private FeedActivity activity=null;

  FeedTask(FeedActivity activity) {
    attach(activity);
  }

  void attach(FeedActivity activity) {
    this.activity=activity;
  }

  void detach() {
    this.activity=null;
  }

  @Override
  public RSSFeed doInBackground(String... urls) {
    RSSFeed result=null;

    try {
      result=reader.load(urls[0]);
    }
    catch (Exception e) {
```

```
      this.e=e;
    }

    return(result);
  }

  @Override
  public void onPostExecute(RSSFeed feed) {
    if (e==null) {
      activity.setFeed(feed);
    }
    else {
      Log.e("LunchList", "Exception parsing feed", e);
      activity.goBlooey(e);
    }
  }
}
```

This time, the doInBackground() method uses an RSSReader object to load an RSSFeed, given the URL. This one statement takes care of downloading and parsing it, courtesy of our helper JAR. doInBackground() passes the RSSFeed object to onPostExecute(), which calls a setFeed() method that we will eventually implement on FeedActivity. If an exception occurs while retrieving or parsing the feed (e.g., the URL is not an RSS resource), doInBackground() catches the Exception and onPostExecute() logs it to LogCat and hands it to FeedActivity.

The FeedTask constructor takes the FeedActivity as a parameter. This is needed because FeedTask is a static inner class, and therefore does not automatically get access to the outer class instance. As we will see in the next two sections, we need to attach and detach the activity from the task as part of handling configuration changes, such as screen rotations.

You can remove all of the org.apache.http.* imports, as you will no longer need them. However, you will need to add the following imports:

- org.mcsoxford.rss.RSSReader
- org.mcsoxford.rss.RSSFeed

Step #8: Display the Feed Items

Finally, we need to actually use the ListView in FeedActivity to display the results of the feed.

Immediately, we run into yet another challenge. RSSFeed is our data model. It has a getItems() method that returns a List<RSSItem>. We could wrap that List in an ArrayAdapter. However, to demonstrate another solution, let's create a totally different adapter, a FeedAdapter, extended from BaseAdapter. BaseAdapter handles the basic adapter operations – we just need to override a handful of methods.

So, add an inner class named FeedAdapter to FeedActivity, that looks like this:

```java
private class FeedAdapter extends BaseAdapter {
  RSSFeed feed=null;

  FeedAdapter(RSSFeed feed) {
    super();

    this.feed=feed;
  }

  public int getCount() {
    return(feed.getItems().size());
  }

  public Object getItem(int position) {
    return(feed.getItems().get(position));
  }

  public long getItemId(int position) {
    return(position);
  }

  public View getView(int position, View convertView,
                      ViewGroup parent) {
    View row=convertView;

    if (row==null) {
      LayoutInflater inflater=getLayoutInflater();

      row=inflater.inflate(android.R.layout.simple_list_item_1,
                      parent, false);
    }
```

```
    RSSItem item=(RSSItem)getItem(position);

    ((TextView)row).setText(item.getTitle());

    return(row);
  }
 }
}
```

A `BaseAdapter` subclass, at minimum, needs to implement:

- `getCount()`, to return how many items are in the adapter

- `getItem()`, to return a model object (e.g., an `RSSItem`) given a position

- `getItemId()`, to return a unique long ID for a position – in this case, we just use the position itself

- `getView()`, as we would with an `ArrayAdapter`, except that we have to inflate rows ourself, rather than perhaps relying upon the superclass to do that for us

In the case of `getView()`, we simply pour each item's title into an `android.R.layout.simple_list_item_1` row.

The next problem is thinking about handling configuration changes. Any time you fork a background thread from an `Activity` – whether directly or via an `AsyncTask` – you really need to think about how you are going to deal with a screen rotation or other configuration change. We want to ensure that when our `FeedTask` gets to `onPostExecute()` that it is updating the `FeedActivity` instance that is on the screen, not a `FeedActivity` instance that happened to kick off the task but then was destroyed as part of the user changing device orientation. This is the reason we added the `attach()` and `detach()` methods to `FeedTask`, which we now need to make use of.

The recipe for configuration changes is:

- Use `onSaveInstanceState()` and `onRestoreInstanceState()` for simple stuff that can fit in the supplied `Bundle`

- In onRetainNonConfigurationInstance(), return some state object for things that cannot go in a Bundle, and update those objects as needed to indicate that the original Activity is going away

- In onCreate(), call getLastNonConfigurationInstance() – if that is not null, it is the object returned by the previous call to onRetainNonConfigurationInstance(), and so we can hook that state back up to the newly-created Activity

With all of that in mind, add another static inner class, this time named InstanceState:

```
private static class InstanceState {
  RSSFeed feed=null;
  FeedTask task=null;
}
```

This is a simple data structure holding onto our FeedTask and the RSSFeed. These objects are part of our state, but neither can go inside a Bundle. You should also add an InstanceState data member named state:

```
private InstanceState state=null;
```

Then, implement the following three methods on FeedActivity:

```
@Override
public void onCreate(Bundle savedInstanceState) {
  super.onCreate(savedInstanceState);

  state=(InstanceState)getLastNonConfigurationInstance();

  if (state==null) {
    state=new InstanceState();
    state.task=new FeedTask(this);
    state.task.execute(getIntent().getStringExtra(FEED_URL));
  }
  else {
    if (state.task!=null) {
      state.task.attach(this);
    }

    if (state.feed!=null) {
      setFeed(state.feed);
    }
  }
}
```

```
@Override
public Object onRetainNonConfigurationInstance() {
  if (state.task!=null) {
    state.task.detach();
  }

  return(state);
}

private void setFeed(RSSFeed feed) {
  state.feed=feed;
  setListAdapter(new FeedAdapter(feed));
}
```

In onCreate(), if getLastNonConfigurationInstance() is null, we must be starting up a brand-new copy of the FeedActivity. In that case, we set up a fresh InstanceState, a fresh FeedTask, and have the FeedTask set about downloading and parsing our feed, using the URL we were passed in the Intent extra. If, however, getLastNonConfigurationInstance() returns something other than null, it is the InstanceState we are returning from onRetainNonConfigurationInstance(). In that case, we can attach the new FeedActivity to our FeedTask, so onPostExecute() will update our new FeedActivity when results are in. And, if we already have our RSSFeed object, we call a setFeed() method, just like FeedTask does in onPostExecute().

setFeed() simply puts the RSSFeed into our InstanceState, plus wraps it in a FeedAdapter and puts the adapter into the ListView.

onRetainNonConfigurationInstance() merely detaches the old activity from the FeedTask before returning it.

Hence, the flow of events on an orientation change is:

- The user flicks their wrist, slides out the keyboard, or otherwise triggers the rotation

- onRetainNonConfigurationInstance() is called, where we detach the activity from the FeedTask and returns it

- A new FeedActivity is instantiated

- onCreate() of the new activity is called, where we attach to the FeedTask and, if available, use the already-parsed RSSFeed

FeedActivity also needs a static String data member named FEED_URL, to serve as our Intent extra key:

```
public static final String FEED_URL="apt.tutorial.FEED_URL";
```

And, we need a handful of new imports, including:

- android.os.Bundle
- android.view.LayoutInflater
- android.view.View
- android.view.ViewGroup
- android.widget.BaseAdapter
- android.widget.TextView
- org.mcsoxford.rss.RSSItem

The resulting FeedActivity class, including all inner classes, should look a bit like this:

```
package apt.tutorial;

import android.app.AlertDialog;
import android.app.ListActivity;
import android.os.AsyncTask;
import android.os.Bundle;
import android.util.Log;
import android.view.LayoutInflater;
import android.view.View;
import android.view.ViewGroup;
import android.widget.BaseAdapter;
import android.widget.TextView;
import org.mcsoxford.rss.RSSItem;
import org.mcsoxford.rss.RSSFeed;
import org.mcsoxford.rss.RSSReader;

public class FeedActivity extends ListActivity {
  public static final String FEED_URL="apt.tutorial.FEED_URL";
  private InstanceState state=null;

  @Override
  public void onCreate(Bundle savedInstanceState) {
    super.onCreate(savedInstanceState);
```

```
    state=(InstanceState)getLastNonConfigurationInstance();

  if (state==null) {
    state=new InstanceState();
    state.task=new FeedTask(this);
    state.task.execute(getIntent().getStringExtra(FEED_URL));
  }
  else {
    if (state.task!=null) {
      state.task.attach(this);
    }

    if (state.feed!=null) {
      setFeed(state.feed);
    }
  }
}

@Override
public Object onRetainNonConfigurationInstance() {
  if (state.task!=null) {
    state.task.detach();
  }

  return(state);
}

private void setFeed(RSSFeed feed) {
  state.feed=feed;
  setListAdapter(new FeedAdapter(feed));
}

private void goBlooey(Throwable t) {
  AlertDialog.Builder builder=new AlertDialog.Builder(this);

  builder
    .setTitle("Exception!")
    .setMessage(t.toString())
    .setPositiveButton("OK", null)
    .show();
}

private static class InstanceState {
  RSSFeed feed=null;
  FeedTask task=null;
}

private static class FeedTask extends AsyncTask<String, Void, RSSFeed> {
  private RSSReader reader=new RSSReader();
  private Exception e=null;
  private FeedActivity activity=null;

  FeedTask(FeedActivity activity) {
```

```
      attach(activity);
    }

  void attach(FeedActivity activity) {
    this.activity=activity;
  }

  void detach() {
    this.activity=null;
  }

  @Override
  public RSSFeed doInBackground(String... urls) {
    RSSFeed result=null;

    try {
      result=reader.load(urls[0]);
    }
    catch (Exception e) {
      this.e=e;
    }

    return(result);
  }

  @Override
  public void onPostExecute(RSSFeed feed) {
    if (e==null) {
      activity.setFeed(feed);
    }
    else {
      Log.e("LunchList", "Exception parsing feed", e);
      activity.goBlooey(e);
    }
  }
}

private class FeedAdapter extends BaseAdapter {
  RSSFeed feed=null;

  FeedAdapter(RSSFeed feed) {
    super();

    this.feed=feed;
  }

  public int getCount() {
    return(feed.getItems().size());
  }

  public Object getItem(int position) {
    return(feed.getItems().get(position));
  }
```

```
   public long getItemId(int position) {
     return(position);
   }

   public View getView(int position, View convertView,
                       ViewGroup parent) {
     View row=convertView;

     if (row==null) {
       LayoutInflater inflater=getLayoutInflater();

       row=inflater.inflate(android.R.layout.simple_list_item_1,
                           parent, false);
     }

     RSSItem item=(RSSItem)getItem(position);

     ((TextView)row).setText(item.getTitle());

     return(row);
   }
 }
}
```

Now you can compile and run your application. Fill in some likely RSS feed URL into the detail form (e.g., `http://rss.slashdot.org/Slashdot/slashdot`, also available as `http://goo.gl/UZBdM`), and click the RSS Feed options menu item:

Figure 71. The detail form, with an RSS feed and the options menu

If you click on the "RSS Feed" options menu item, it will bring up the
FeedActivity, which will momentarily show you the items in the feed:

Figure 72. FeedActivity, showing feed items

Extra Credit

Here are some things you can try beyond those step-by-step instructions:

- When the user clicks on an item in the FeedActivity's ListView, open up the Web browser on that particular feed item.

- The options menu item is always enabled, even if there is no feed URL available. Use onPrepareOptionsMenu() to check to see if there is a feed URL, then disable the FeedActivity menu item if there is no URL. Similarly, you can elect to disable the menu item if there is no connectivity, rather than displaying the "sorry!" Toast as is shown above.

- More gracefully handle various errors, such as supplying an Atom feed URL instead of one for an RSS feed.

- Support multiple feed URLs (or possibly other data sources), instead of just one.

Further Reading

Additional examples of interacting with the Internet from Android can be found in the "Communicating via the Internet" chapter of The Busy Coder's Guide to Android Development[47]. More information about dealing with third-party libraries, such as our RSS JAR, can be found in the "Leveraging Java Libraries" chapter of The Busy Coder's Guide to Android Development[48].

---

47 http://commonsware.com/Android
48 http://commonsware.com/Android

Serving Up Lunch

In the previous tutorial, we used an AsyncTask to retrieve the contents of the RSS feed. That was so we could get the network I/O off the main application thread, and therefore prevent our UI from becoming sluggish or "janky".

Another way we could solve that same problem is to use an IntentService. An IntentService is a separate component that accepts commands from activities, performs those commands on background threads, and optionally responds to the activities or the user. In this tutorial, we will set up such an IntentService as a replacement for the AsyncTask.

Step-By-Step Instructions

First, you need to have completed the previous tutorial. If you are beginning the tutorials here, or if you wish to not use your existing work, you can download a ZIP file with all of the tutorial results, and you can copy the 15-Internet edition of LunchList to use as a starting point. If you are using Eclipse, these instructions will help you load the project into a workspace.

Step #1: Create and Register a Stub IntentService

Add a new Java class file to the project, named FeedService.java, where you create a stub implementation of an IntentService:

```
package apt.tutorial;

import android.app.IntentService;
import android.content.Intent;

public class FeedService extends IntentService {
  public FeedService() {
    super("FeedService");
  }

  @Override
  public void onHandleIntent(Intent i) {
    // do something
  }
}
```

Eclipse users can add this class by right-clicking over the `apt.tutorial` package in the Package Explorer, choosing New > Class from the context menu, and specifying `FeedService` as the class name and `android.app.IntentService` as the superclass.

`IntentService`, unlike `Service`, requires you to implement a no-argument constructor and chain to the superclass, supplying a name for your `IntentService`. We will put some actual business logic in the implementation of `onHandleIntent()` in the next step.

We also need to add a `<service>` element to the manifest, identifying this service to Android. Your resulting `AndroidManifest.xml` file should look something like this:

```
<?xml version="1.0" encoding="utf-8"?>
<manifest android:versionCode="1"
          android:versionName="1.0"
          package="apt.tutorial"
          xmlns:android="http://schemas.android.com/apk/res/android">

  <uses-permission android:name="android.permission.INTERNET" />
  <uses-permission android:name="android.permission.ACCESS_NETWORK_STATE" />
  <supports-screens android:largeScreens="true"
                     android:normalScreens="true"
                     android:smallScreens="false" />
  <application android:label="@string/app_name">
    <activity android:label="@string/app_name"
              android:name=".LunchList">
      <intent-filter>
        <action android:name="android.intent.action.MAIN" />
        <category android:name="android.intent.category.LAUNCHER" />
```

```
      </intent-filter>
    </activity>
    <activity android:name=".DetailForm"></activity>
    <activity android:name=".EditPreferences"></activity>
    <activity android:name=".FeedActivity"></activity>
    <service android:name=".FeedService"></service>
  </application>
</manifest>
```

Eclipse users can do this by:

1. Double-clicking on the `AndroidManifest.xml` file in Package Explorer to bring it up in the editor

2. Clicking on the Application sub-tab

3. Clicking on the Add... button next to the Application Nodes list

4. Choosing Service in the node type dialog and clicking OK

5. Clicking the Browse... button next to the Name field and choosing `FeedService`

6. Saving changes (e.g., <Ctrl>-<S>)

Step #2: Move Feed Fetching and Parsing to the Service

The `onHandleIntent()` method of `IntentService` will be called on a background thread – one of the key reasons to use an `IntentService`. So, set up a preliminary version of `onHandleIntent()` that mirrors some of the logic from `doInBackground()` from the `FeedTask` set up in the previous tutorial:

```
@Override
public void onHandleIntent(Intent i) {
  RSSReader reader=new RSSReader();

  try {
    RSSFeed result=reader.load(i.getStringExtra(EXTRA_URL));
  }
  catch (Exception e) {
    Log.e("LunchList", "Exception parsing feed", e);
  }
}
```

All we do is load the RSS via an `RSSReader` and get an `RSSFeed` as a result. If there is an exception, we log it.

For this to work, we need to define `EXTRA_URL`, the key to our `Intent` extra that will identify the feed URL, so add this static data member to `FeedService`:

```
public static final String EXTRA_URL="apt.tutorial.EXTRA_URL";
```

Also, you will need to add imports for `android.util.Log`, `org.mcsoxford.rss.RSSFeed`, and `org.mcsoxford.rss.RSSReader`.

Step #3: Send the Feed to the Activity

Fetching and parsing the feed in the `FeedService` is all fine and well, but we need the feed items to get to the `FeedActivity`. That requires a bit more work, plus a new object: a `Messenger`.

A `Messenger` is tied to a `Handler` from an `Activity` (or, technically, any other component that has a `Handler`). Just as somebody with a `Handler` can send messages to the main application thread via the `Handler`, anyone with a `Handler`'s `Messenger` can send messages to the `Handler`. These are "handled" the same as any other `Handler` messages, via `handleMessage()`. And, the beauty of a `Messenger` is that it implements the `Parcelable` interface, and so can be packaged in an `Intent` extra as easily as can a `String`.

So, we will require that `FeedActivity` supply us with a `Messenger` that we can use to send results back to the `FeedActivity` itself.

With that in mind, update `onHandleIntent()` in `FeedService` to look like this:

```
@Override
public void onHandleIntent(Intent i) {
  RSSReader reader=new RSSReader();
  Messenger messenger=(Messenger)i.getExtras().get(EXTRA_MESSENGER);
  Message msg=Message.obtain();

  try {
```

```
    RSSFeed result=reader.load(i.getStringExtra(EXTRA_URL));

    msg.arg1=Activity.RESULT_OK;
    msg.obj=result;
  }
  catch (Exception e) {
    Log.e("LunchList", "Exception parsing feed", e);
    msg.arg1=Activity.RESULT_CANCELED;
    msg.obj=e;
  }

  try {
    messenger.send(msg);
  }
  catch (Exception e) {
    Log.w("LunchList", "Exception sending results to activity", e);
  }
}
```

Here, we get a Messenger object out of our Intent extras, keyed by an EXTRA_MESSENGER key. We then get an empty Message object for the Messenger. If the fetch-and-parse of the RSS feed succeeds, we put RESULT_OK in the arg1 public data member of the Message and put the RSSFeed in the obj public field of the Message. If an Exception is raised, we set arg1 to RESULT_CANCELED and obj to be the Exception.

Then, we tell the Messenger to send() the Message. If the activity is still on the screen – or if we handle configuration changes properly – this will succeed without incident. If, however, the activity has been permanently destroyed, such as by the user pressing BACK, we will get an exception, which we simply log as a warning.

For this to compile, we need to add a definition for EXTRA_MESSENGER:

```
public static final String EXTRA_MESSENGER="apt.tutorial.EXTRA_MESSENGER";
```

We also need to add four more imports:

- android.app.Activity
- android.os.Message
- android.os.Messenger
- org.mcsoxford.rss.RSSItem

The complete implementation of `FeedService`, therefore, should look a bit like this:

```
package apt.tutorial;

import android.app.Activity;
import android.app.IntentService;
import android.content.Intent;
import android.os.Message;
import android.os.Messenger;
import android.util.Log;
import org.mcsoxford.rss.RSSItem;
import org.mcsoxford.rss.RSSFeed;
import org.mcsoxford.rss.RSSReader;

public class FeedService extends IntentService {
  public static final String EXTRA_URL="apt.tutorial.EXTRA_URL";
  public static final String EXTRA_MESSENGER="apt.tutorial.EXTRA_MESSENGER";

  public FeedService() {
    super("FeedService");
  }

  @Override
  public void onHandleIntent(Intent i) {
    RSSReader reader=new RSSReader();
    Messenger messenger=(Messenger)i.getExtras().get(EXTRA_MESSENGER);
    Message msg=Message.obtain();

    try {
      RSSFeed result=reader.load(i.getStringExtra(EXTRA_URL));

      msg.arg1=Activity.RESULT_OK;
      msg.obj=result;
    }
    catch (Exception e) {
      Log.e("LunchList", "Exception parsing feed", e);
      msg.arg1=Activity.RESULT_CANCELED;
      msg.obj=e;
    }

    try {
      messenger.send(msg);
    }
    catch (Exception e) {
      Log.w("LunchList", "Exception sending results to activity", e);
    }
  }
}
```

Step #4: Display the Feed Items, Redux

Now we need to make the requisite changes to FeedActivity to work with FeedService instead of FeedTask.

We can start by converting FeedTask to FeedHandler, having it extend Handler instead of AsyncTask. We can retain the attach() and detach() methods, as we will need those for handling configuration changes. The doInBackground() method can be removed, as that logic is now handled by FeedService. The onPostExecute() method turns into a handleMessage() method, to take the Message object from FeedService and either call setFeed() or goBlooey() on FeedActivity, depending on whether we received RESULT_OK or RESULT_CANCELED in the Message.

The resulting FeedHandler would look like this:

```
private static class FeedHandler extends Handler {
  FeedActivity activity=null;

  FeedHandler(FeedActivity activity) {
    attach(activity);
  }

  void attach(FeedActivity activity) {
    this.activity=activity;
  }

  void detach() {
    this.activity=null;
  }

  @Override
  public void handleMessage(Message msg) {
    if (msg.arg1--RESULT_OK) {
      activity.setFeed((RSSFeed)msg.obj);
    }
    else {
      activity.goBlooey((Exception)msg.obj);
    }
  }
}
```

Since we no longer have FeedTask, we no longer need it in InstanceState. However, we do need to hold onto our Handler as part of our state, so when the user rotates the screen, our Messenger object can still communicate with the right `FeedActivity`. Hence, replace the `FeedTask` with `FeedHandler` in `InstanceState`:

```
private static class InstanceState {
  RSSFeed feed=null;
  FeedHandler handler=null;
}
```

This means that `onRetainNonConfigurationInstance()` needs to change, to accommodate the switch between `task` and `handler`:

```
@Override
public Object onRetainNonConfigurationInstance() {
  if (state.handler!=null) {
    state.handler.detach();
  }

  return(state);
}
```

Also, our `onCreate()` method needs to have a few changes:

- If `getLastNonConfigurationInstance()` is `null`, when we create the fresh `InstanceState`, we also call `startService()` on our `FeedService`, to request that it fetch and parse the RSS feed

- If `getLastNonConfigurationInstance()` is not `null`, we need to attach the new `FeedActivity` to the `handler`, not the `task` as before

The resulting `onCreate()` method would look like:

```
@Override
public void onCreate(Bundle savedInstanceState) {
  super.onCreate(savedInstanceState);

  state=(InstanceState)getLastNonConfigurationInstance();

  if (state==null) {
    state=new InstanceState();
    state.handler=new FeedHandler(this);

    Intent i=new Intent(this, FeedService.class);

    i.putExtra(FeedService.EXTRA_URL,
            getIntent().getStringExtra(FEED_URL));
    i.putExtra(FeedService.EXTRA_MESSENGER,
            new Messenger(state.handler));
```

```
    startService(i);
  }
  else {
    if (state.handler!=null) {
      state.handler.attach(this);
    }

    if (state.feed!=null) {
      setFeed(state.feed);
    }
  }
}
```

Everything else can remain the same, other than replacing some imports
(e.g., `AsyncTask` with `android.os.Handler`), removing the import for
`RSSReader`, and adding some other imports:

- `android.content.Intent`

- `android.os.Handler`

- `android.os.Message`

- `android.os.Messenger`

The entire `FeedActivity` implementation should resemble:

```
package apt.tutorial;

import android.app.AlertDialog;
import android.app.ListActivity;
import android.content.Intent;
import android.os.Bundle;
import android.os.Handler;
import android.os.Message;
import android.os.Messenger;
import android.view.LayoutInflater;
import android.view.View;
import android.view.ViewGroup;
import android.widget.BaseAdapter;
import android.widget.TextView;
import org.mcsoxford.rss.RSSItem;
import org.mcsoxford.rss.RSSFeed;

public class FeedActivity extends ListActivity {
  public static final String FEED_URL="apt.tutorial.FEED_URL";
  private InstanceState state=null;

  @Override
  public void onCreate(Bundle savedInstanceState) {
    super.onCreate(savedInstanceState);
```

```
    state=(InstanceState)getLastNonConfigurationInstance();

  if (state==null) {
    state=new InstanceState();
    state.handler=new FeedHandler(this);

    Intent i=new Intent(this, FeedService.class);

    i.putExtra(FeedService.EXTRA_URL,
            getIntent().getStringExtra(FEED_URL));
    i.putExtra(FeedService.EXTRA_MESSENGER,
            new Messenger(state.handler));

    startService(i);
  }
  else {
    if (state.handler!=null) {
      state.handler.attach(this);
    }

    if (state.feed!=null) {
      setFeed(state.feed);
    }
  }
}

@Override
public Object onRetainNonConfigurationInstance() {
  if (state.handler!=null) {
    state.handler.detach();
  }

  return(state);
}

private void setFeed(RSSFeed feed) {
  state.feed=feed;
  setListAdapter(new FeedAdapter(feed));
}

private void goBlooey(Throwable t) {
  AlertDialog.Builder builder=new AlertDialog.Builder(this);

  builder
    .setTitle("Exception!")
    .setMessage(t.toString())
    .setPositiveButton("OK", null)
    .show();
}

private static class InstanceState {
  RSSFeed feed=null;
  FeedHandler handler=null;
```

```
}

private class FeedAdapter extends BaseAdapter {
  RSSFeed feed=null;

  FeedAdapter(RSSFeed feed) {
    super();

    this.feed=feed;
  }

  public int getCount() {
    return(feed.getItems().size());
  }

  public Object getItem(int position) {
    return(feed.getItems().get(position));
  }

  public long getItemId(int position) {
    return(position);
  }

  public View getView(int position, View convertView,
                      ViewGroup parent) {
    View row=convertView;

    if (row==null) {
      LayoutInflater inflater=getLayoutInflater();

      row=inflater.inflate(android.R.layout.simple_list_item_1,
                           parent, false);
    }

    RSSItem item=(RSSItem)getItem(position);

    ((TextView)row).setText(item.getTitle());

    return(row);
  }
}

private static class FeedHandler extends Handler {
  FeedActivity activity=null;

  FeedHandler(FeedActivity activity) {
    attach(activity);
  }

  void attach(FeedActivity activity) {
    this.activity=activity;
  }

  void detach() {
```

```
    this.activity=null;
  }

  @Override
  public void handleMessage(Message msg) {
    if (msg.arg1==RESULT_OK) {
      activity.setFeed((RSSFeed)msg.obj);
    }
    else {
      activity.goBlooey((Exception)msg.obj);
    }
  }
 }
}
```

If you compile and run the new LunchList, nothing changes visibly. The user experience is identical.

So why bother with an IntentService?

In this case, perhaps it is not necessary. The big advantage of an IntentService, though, is that it can live beyond the scope of any activity. Suppose instead of downloading an RSS feed, we were downloading a PDF of a book that the user bought. We should not force the user to have to wait in our activity for the download to complete, yet if the activity is destroyed, any threads it forked may be killed off as well. The IntentService, on the other hand, can continue downloading, and it will automatically destroy itself when onHandleIntent() ends.

Extra Credit

Here are some things you can try beyond those step-by-step instructions:

- To confirm that our configuration handling works properly, add a call to sleep() on android.os.SystemClock in the FeedService, somewhere in onHandleIntent() before calling send() on the Messenger. While the service is asleep, you can rotate the screen of your device or emulator, and confirm that the message still makes it to the new FeedActivity instance.

- Experiment with other ways of having the FeedService send results to the FeedActivity, such as via a broadcast Intent, the PendingIntent created by calling createPendingResult() on an Activity, or a ResultReceiver.

- Experiment with having the FeedService go ahead and download/parse the RSS feed when the DetailsForm comes up, rather than waiting for the user to start the FeedActivity. This will require having some way of caching the results, such that you can make them available to the FeedActivity upon demand. You may find that it is simpler to do the download and the parsing in separate steps, caching the downloaded feed (pre-fetched when DetailsForm comes up) and parsing the cached feed only when FeedActivity requests it.

Further Reading

You can learn more about the roles of services and how to create them in a pair of chapters of The Busy Coder's Guide to Android Development[49].

---

[49] http://commonsware.com/Android

Locating Lunch

While we keep track of the address of our restaurants, it might also be useful to keep track of the GPS coordinates as well. In this tutorial, we will hook up to the LocationManager system service and find a restaurant's location via GPS, saving it in the database for later use.

WARNING: The Android 2.3 emulator has bugs related to simulating locations using DDMS. For this tutorial, you will need to use another emulator or a piece of hardware. The Android 2.3 problem is limited to the emulator – using a device's actual GPS should pose no problems, assuming you are someplace where you can get a GPS signal.

Step-By-Step Instructions

First, you need to have completed the previous tutorial. If you are beginning the tutorials here, or if you wish to not use your existing work, you can download a ZIP file with all of the tutorial results, and you can copy the 16-Services edition of LunchList to use as a starting point. If you are using Eclipse, these instructions will help you load the project into a workspace.

Step #1: Add Latitude and Longitude to the Data Model

Two tutorials ago, we modified our database and RestaurantHelper to add support for a feed URL. Now, we get to make more changes, to store the latitude and longitude of a restaurant.

So, add in a pair of REAL columns named lat and lon to the schema used in onCreate() of RestaurantHelper:

```
@Override
public void onCreate(SQLiteDatabase db) {
  db.execSQL("CREATE TABLE restaurants (_id INTEGER PRIMARY KEY AUTOINCREMENT,
name TEXT, address TEXT, type TEXT, notes TEXT, feed TEXT, lat REAL, lon
REAL);");
}
```

This will also require incrementing our SCHEMA_VERSION to 3:

```
private static final int SCHEMA_VERSION=3;
```

Modifying onUpgrade() in RestaurantHelper, though, becomes a bit trickier. Many users of our app will be on SCHEMA_REVISION 2 when they install our new copy of the application. However, it is possible that some users skipped upgrading LunchList along the way and are still back on SCHEMA_REVISION 1. As such, we need to handle upgrading 1->3 and 2->3, not just the latter. A typical solution for this is to do the upgrades in series, 1->2 where needed, then 2->3.

With that in mind, modify onUpgrade() to do our original ALTER TABLE for the feed column if the SCHEMA_REVISION is less than 2, plus add a new stanza to add our lat and lon columns if we are less than SCHEMA_REVISION 3:

```
@Override
public void onUpgrade(SQLiteDatabase db, int oldVersion, int newVersion) {
  if (oldVersion<2) {
    db.execSQL("ALTER TABLE restaurants ADD COLUMN feed TEXT");
  }

  if (oldVersion<3) {
    db.execSQL("ALTER TABLE restaurants ADD COLUMN lat REAL");
```

```
    db.execSQL("ALTER TABLE restaurants ADD COLUMN lon REAL");
  }
}
```

Our two RestaurantHelper query methods, getAll() and getById(), will also need to start returning the lat and lon columns:

```
public Cursor getAll(String orderBy) {
  return(getReadableDatabase()
          .rawQuery("SELECT _id, name, address, type, notes, lat, lon FROM
restaurants ORDER BY "+orderBy,
                    null));
}

public Cursor getById(String id) {
  String[] args={id};

  return(getReadableDatabase()
          .rawQuery("SELECT _id, name, address, type, notes, feed, lat, lon FROM
restaurants WHERE _ID=?",
                    args));
}
```

However, the user will not be modifying the location directly – expecting somebody to manually type in a latitude and longitude is probably asking too much. Later on, we will use an options menu item to allow the user to request a location via GPS. Hence, we do not need to worry about modifying insert() and update() in RestaurantHelper, as we will never be setting or changing the latitude and longitude when we call them. Rather, we need a new method in RestaurantHelper – call it updateLocation() – that will do a SQL UPDATE statement to put the latitude and longitude in a restaurant's row:

```
public void updateLocation(String id, double lat, double lon) {
  ContentValues cv=new ContentValues();
  String[] args={id};

  cv.put("lat", lat);
  cv.put("lon", lon);

  getWritableDatabase().update("restaurants", cv, "_ID=?",
                               args);
}
```

This, of course, assumes that our restaurant already exists in the database, a restriction we will need to enforce in the UI.

Finally, we need a couple of getter methods in `RestaurantHelper` to return the latitude and longitude from a `Cursor` returned by `getAll()` or `getById()`:

```
public double getLatitude(Cursor c) {
   return(c.getDouble(6));
}

public double getLongitude(Cursor c) {
   return(c.getDouble(7));
}
```

The revised `RestaurantHelper` should resemble:

```
package apt.tutorial;

import android.content.Context;
import android.content.ContentValues;
import android.database.Cursor;
import android.database.SQLException;
import android.database.sqlite.SQLiteOpenHelper;
import android.database.sqlite.SQLiteDatabase;
import android.database.sqlite.SQLiteQueryBuilder;

class RestaurantHelper extends SQLiteOpenHelper {
  private static final String DATABASE_NAME="lunchlist.db";
  private static final int SCHEMA_VERSION=3;

  public RestaurantHelper(Context context) {
    super(context, DATABASE_NAME, null, SCHEMA_VERSION);
  }

  @Override
  public void onCreate(SQLiteDatabase db) {
    db.execSQL("CREATE TABLE restaurants (_id INTEGER PRIMARY KEY AUTOINCREMENT,
name TEXT, address TEXT, type TEXT, notes TEXT, feed TEXT, lat REAL, lon
REAL);");
  }

  @Override
  public void onUpgrade(SQLiteDatabase db, int oldVersion, int newVersion) {
    if (oldVersion<2) {
      db.execSQL("ALTER TABLE restaurants ADD COLUMN feed TEXT");
    }

    if (oldVersion<3) {
      db.execSQL("ALTER TABLE restaurants ADD COLUMN lat REAL");
      db.execSQL("ALTER TABLE restaurants ADD COLUMN lon REAL");
    }
  }

  public Cursor getAll(String orderBy) {
```

```
      return(getReadableDatabase()
              .rawQuery("SELECT _id, name, address, type, notes, lat, lon FROM
restaurants ORDER BY "+orderBy,
                        null));
  }

  public Cursor getById(String id) {
    String[] args={id};

      return(getReadableDatabase()
              .rawQuery("SELECT _id, name, address, type, notes, feed, lat, lon
FROM restaurants WHERE _ID=?",
                        args));
  }

  public void insert(String name, String address,
                     String type, String notes,
                     String feed) {
    ContentValues cv=new ContentValues();

    cv.put("name", name);
    cv.put("address", address);
    cv.put("type", type);
    cv.put("notes", notes);
    cv.put("feed", feed);

    getWritableDatabase().insert("restaurants", "name", cv);
  }

  public void update(String id, String name, String address,
                     String type, String notes, String feed) {
    ContentValues cv=new ContentValues();
    String[] args={id};

    cv.put("name", name);
    cv.put("address", address);
    cv.put("type", type);
    cv.put("notes", notes);
    cv.put("feed", feed);

    getWritableDatabase().update("restaurants", cv, "_ID=?",
                                 args);
  }

  public void updateLocation(String id, double lat, double lon) {
    ContentValues cv=new ContentValues();
    String[] args={id};

    cv.put("lat", lat);
    cv.put("lon", lon);

    getWritableDatabase().update("restaurants", cv, "_ID=?",
                                 args);
  }
```

```
  public String getName(Cursor c) {
    return(c.getString(1));
  }

  public String getAddress(Cursor c) {
    return(c.getString(2));
  }

  public String getType(Cursor c) {
    return(c.getString(3));
  }

  public String getNotes(Cursor c) {
    return(c.getString(4));
  }

  public String getFeed(Cursor c) {
    return(c.getString(5));
  }

  public double getLatitude(Cursor c) {
    return(c.getDouble(6));
  }

  public double getLongitude(Cursor c) {
    return(c.getDouble(7));
  }
}
```

Step #2: Save the Restaurant in onPause()

We need to add a spot for displaying the GPS coordinates on the screen. Once again, we are running out of room.

One big chunk of screen space is taken up with our Save button. Most Android activities do not have such a button. Instead, they take one of two approaches:

- There is an options menu item to save

- The data is saved automatically when the activity is paused

Here, let's try the second approach – save the restaurant to the database when the activity is paused, such as the user pressing BACK or HOME.

To do this, first get rid of all references to the "save" `Button` from the `DetailForm` class. You can also get rid of the `android.widget.Button` import, which may help you determine what you need to get rid of.

Then, in the `DetailForm` class, convert the `onSave` `OnItemClickListener` object to a `save()` method, where that method just does what `onClick()` used to to in the `onSave` object, except that it skips the `finish()` call and only saves if the restaurant has a name.:

```
private void save() {
  if (name.getText().toString().length()>0) {
    String type=null;

    switch (types.getCheckedRadioButtonId()) {
      case R.id.sit_down:
        type="sit_down";
        break;
      case R.id.take_out:
        type="take_out";
        break;
      default:
        type="delivery";
        break;
    }

    if (restaurantId==null) {
      helper.insert(name.getText().toString(),
                    address.getText().toString(), type,
                    notes.getText().toString(),
                    feed.getText().toString());
    }
    else {
      helper.update(restaurantId, name.getText().toString(),
                    address.getText().toString(), type,
                    notes.getText().toString(),
                    feed.getText().toString());
    }
  }
}
```

Then, add an implementation of `onPause()` to `DetailForm` that calls `save()`:

```
@Override
public void onPause() {
  save();

  super.onPause();
}
```

Step #3: Add a TextView and Options Menu Item for Location

Given that we have made the Save button obsolete, we can remove it from our layouts, putting in place a spot to display the GPS coordinates (when we have them). We also need to allow the user to request a location fix from GPS, and the easiest way to do that is to add another options menu item.

In res/layout/detail_form.xml, remove the Save button and add in another TableRow that has two TextView widgets, one with a "Location:" caption and one (named location) that will hold our actual GPS coordinates. The resulting layout file should look something like this:

```
<ScrollView xmlns:android="http://schemas.android.com/apk/res/android"
  android:layout_width="match_parent"
  android:layout_height="wrap_content">
  <TableLayout
    android:layout_width="match_parent"
    android:layout_height="wrap_content"
    android:stretchColumns="1"
    android:shrinkColumns="1"
    >
    <TableRow>
      <TextView android:text="Name:" />
      <EditText android:id="@+id/name" />
    </TableRow>
    <TableRow>
      <TextView android:text="Address:" />
      <EditText android:id="@+id/addr" />
    </TableRow>
    <TableRow>
      <TextView android:text="Type:" />
      <RadioGroup android:id="@+id/types">
        <RadioButton android:id="@+id/take_out"
          android:text="Take-Out"
          android:checked="true"
        />
        <RadioButton android:id="@+id/sit_down"
          android:text="Sit-Down"
        />
        <RadioButton android:id="@+id/delivery"
          android:text="Delivery"
        />
      </RadioGroup>
    </TableRow>
    <TableRow>
      <TextView android:text="Location:" />
      <TextView android:id="@+id/location" android:text="(not set)" />
```

```
    </TableRow>
    <EditText android:id="@+id/notes"
      android:inputType="textMultiLine"
      android:gravity="top"
      android:lines="2"
      android:scrollHorizontally="false"
      android:maxLines="2"
      android:layout_span="2"
      android:hint="Notes"
      android:layout_marginTop="4dip"
    />
    <EditText android:id="@+id/feed"
      android:layout_span="2"
      android:hint="Feed URL"
    />
  </TableLayout>
</ScrollView>
```

Eclipse users can accomplish this by:

1. Double-clicking on the res/layout/detail_form.xml file in the Package Manager to bring it up in the graphical editor

2. Right-clicking over the Save button and choosing Delete from the context menu

3. Dragging a TableRow widget from the Layouts section of the tool palette into the TableLayout after the row containing the RadioGroup

4. Dragging a TextView widget from the "Form Widgets" section of the tool palette into the left-hand column of the new TableRow

5. Right-clicking over the new TextView widget, choosing Properties > Text... from the context menu, filling in Location: as the value, and clicking OK

6. Dragging a TextView widget from the "Form Widgets" section of the tool palette into the right-hand column of the new TableRow

7. Right-clicking over the new TextView widget, choosing Properties > Text... from the context menu, filling in (not set) as the value, and clicking OK

8. Right-clicking over the new TextView widget, choosing Edit ID from the context menu, filling in location as the value, and clicking OK

9. Saving your changes (e.g., <Ctrl>-<S>)

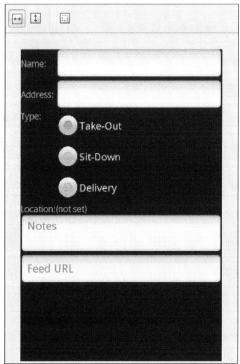

Figure 73. The detail form in the Eclipse graphical editor, with the new table row

Similarly, in res/layout-land/detail_form.xml, replace the Save button with a nested horizontal LinearLayout holding onto the same two TextView widgets:

```
<ScrollView xmlns:android="http://schemas.android.com/apk/res/android"
  android:layout_width="match_parent"
  android:layout_height="wrap_content">
  <TableLayout
    android:layout_width="match_parent"
    android:layout_height="wrap_content"
    android:stretchColumns="2"
    android:shrinkColumns="2"
  >
  <TableRow>
    <TextView android:text="Name:" />
    <EditText android:id="@+id/name"
      android:layout_span="2"
  />
  </TableRow>
  <TableRow>
```

```
      <TextView android:text="Address:" />
      <EditText android:id="@+id/addr"
        android:layout_span="2"
      />
    </TableRow>
    <TableRow>
      <TextView android:text="Type:" />
      <RadioGroup android:id="@+id/types">
        <RadioButton android:id="@+id/take_out"
          android:text="Take-Out"
          android:checked="true"
        />
        <RadioButton android:id="@+id/sit_down"
          android:text="Sit-Down"
        />
        <RadioButton android:id="@+id/delivery"
          android:text="Delivery"
        />
      </RadioGroup>
      <LinearLayout android:orientation="vertical">
        <EditText android:id="@+id/notes"
          android:inputType="textMultiLine"
          android:gravity="top"
          android:lines="2"
          android:scrollHorizontally="false"
          android:maxLines="2"
          android:layout_width="match_parent"
          android:layout_height="wrap_content"
          android:hint="Notes"
        />
        <EditText android:id="@+id/feed"
          android:layout_width="match_parent"
          android:layout_height="wrap_content"
          android:hint="Feed URL"
        />
        <LinearLayout
          android:layout_width="wrap_content"
          android:layout_height="wrap_content"
          android:orientation="horizontal"
          >
          <TextView android:text="Location:"
            android:layout_width="wrap_content"
            android:layout_height="wrap_content"
          />
          <TextView android:id="@+id/location"
            android:text="(not set)"
            android:layout_width="wrap_content"
            android:layout_height="wrap_content"
          />
        </LinearLayout>
      </LinearLayout>
    </TableRow>
  </TableLayout>
</ScrollView>
```

Eclipse users can accomplish this by:

1. Double-clicking on the `res/layout-and/detail_form.xml` file in the Package Manager to bring it up in the graphical editor

2. Right-clicking over the Save button and choosing Delete from the context menu

3. Dragging a `LinearLayout (Horizontal)` widget from the Layouts section of the tool palette into the vertical `LinearLayout` holding the notes and feed URL fields (drag it on top of the feed URL field)

4. Dragging a `TextView` widget from the "Form Widgets" section of the tool palette into the new `LinearLayout`

5. Right-clicking over the new `TextView` widget, choosing Properties > Text... from the context menu, filling in `Location:` as the value, and clicking OK

6. Dragging a `TextView` widget from the "Form Widgets" section of the tool palette into the new `LinearLayout`

7. Right-clicking over the new `TextView` widget, choosing Properties > Text... from the context menu, filling in `(not set)` as the value, and clicking OK

8. Right-clicking over the new `TextView` widget, choosing Edit ID from the context menu, filling in `location` as the value, and clicking OK

9. Saving your changes (e.g., <Ctrl>-<S>)

Figure 74. The landscape detail form in the Eclipse graphical editor, with the new widgets

In DetailForm, add in a data member for the location TextView:

```
TextView location=null;
```

Also, we need to retrieve that widget in the onCreate() method of DetailForm, as we have with the other widgets we modify:

```
location=(TextView)findViewById(R.id.location);
```

Then, in the load() method of DetailForm, we can get our latitude and longitude from RestaurantHelper and pour them into the TextView:

```
private void load() {
  Cursor c=helper.getById(restaurantId);

  c.moveToFirst();
  name.setText(helper.getName(c));
  address.setText(helper.getAddress(c));
  notes.setText(helper.getNotes(c));
  feed.setText(helper.getFeed(c));

  if (helper.getType(c).equals("sit_down")) {
    types.check(R.id.sit_down);
  }
  else if (helper.getType(c).equals("take_out")) {
    types.check(R.id.take_out);
  }
```

```
else {
  types.check(R.id.delivery);
}

location.setText(String.valueOf(helper.getLatitude(c))
                 +", "
                 +String.valueOf(helper.getLongitude(c)));

c.close();
}
```

We also need to add a `location` options menu item to our `res/menu/details_option.xml` file, for the user to request collecting the GPS location for the restaurant. Grab some likely icon to go with the menu item, such as `ic_menu_compass.png` from the Android SDK. Then, modify that file to resemble:

```xml
<?xml version="1.0" encoding="utf-8"?>
<menu xmlns:android="http://schemas.android.com/apk/res/android">
  <item android:id="@+id/feed"
    android:title="RSS Feed"
    android:icon="@drawable/ic_menu_friendslist"
  />
  <item android:id="@+id/location"
    android:title="Save Location"
    android:icon="@drawable/ic_menu_compass"
  />
</menu>
```

Eclipse users can make this change by:

1. Double-clicking on the `res/menu/details_option.xml` file in the Package Explorer to bring it up in the graphical editor

2. Clicking the Add... button to the right of the list of menu items

3. Choosing Item in the dialog box and clicking OK to add a blank menu item

4. Specifying `@+id/location` as the Id of the new menu item

5. Setting the title of the new menu item to be `Save Location`

6. Setting the icon of the new menu item to be `@drawable/ic_menu_compass` (or whatever icon it is that you are using)

7. Saving the changes (e.g., <Ctrl>-<S>)

Step #4: Update the Permissions

To use GPS, we will need to add the ACCESS_FINE_LOCATION permission to our AndroidManifest.xml file. The resulting file should look a bit like:

```xml
<?xml version="1.0" encoding="utf-8"?>
<manifest android:versionCode="1"
          android:versionName="1.0"
          package="apt.tutorial"
          xmlns:android="http://schemas.android.com/apk/res/android">

  <uses-permission android:name="android.permission.INTERNET" />
  <uses-permission android:name="android.permission.ACCESS_NETWORK_STATE" />
  <uses-permission android:name="android.permission.ACCESS_FINE_LOCATION" />
  <supports-screens android:largeScreens="true"
                    android:normalScreens="true"
                    android:smallScreens="false" />
  <application android:label="@string/app_name">
    <activity android:label="@string/app_name"
              android:name=".LunchList">
      <intent-filter>
        <action android:name="android.intent.action.MAIN" />
        <category android:name="android.intent.category.LAUNCHER" />
      </intent-filter>
    </activity>
    <activity android:name=".DetailForm"></activity>
    <activity android:name=".EditPreferences"></activity>
    <activity android:name=".FeedActivity"></activity>
    <service android:name=".FeedService"></service>
  </application>
</manifest>
```

Eclipse users can add this by:

1. Double-clicking on the AndroidManifest.xml file in the Package Explorer to bring it up in the graphical editor

2. Clicking on the Permissions sub-tab

3. Clicking the Add... button to the right of the list of permissions, then choosing "Uses Permission" in the dialog and clicking OK to create a new <uses-permission> element

4. Assigning that element the android.permission.ACCESS_FINE_LOCATION value via the drop-down

5. Saving the changes (e.g., <Ctrl>-<S>)

Step #5: Find Our Location Using GPS

Now, we need to actually figure out where we are, when the user asks. Since the GPS radio is normally not on, to save power, we cannot just ask Android, "hey, where are we?" Instead, we will need to request location updates, long enough to get a fix.

First, add a data member to `DetailForm` for `LocationManager`, the system service that is our gateway to location information:

```
LocationManager locMgr=null;
```

Next, we need to initialize this data member by calling `getSystemService()`, asking for the `LOCATION_SERVICE`. `onCreate()` of `DetailForm` is a likely place to do this, so add that call somewhere in `onCreate()`:

```
locMgr=(LocationManager)getSystemService(LOCATION_SERVICE);
```

Then, we need to detect when the user taps our location options menu item. What we can do is ask the `LocationManager` to turn on GPS and start fetching fixes, letting us know when they arrive. This is done via the `requestLocationUpdates()` method. So, amend the `onOptionsItemSelected()` method in `DetailsForm` to add in the `requestLocationUpdates()` call:

```
@Override
public boolean onOptionsItemSelected(MenuItem item) {
  if (item.getItemId()==R.id.feed) {
    if (isNetworkAvailable()) {
      Intent i=new Intent(this, FeedActivity.class);

      i.putExtra(FeedActivity.FEED_URL, feed.getText().toString());
      startActivity(i);
    }
    else {
      Toast
        .makeText(this, "Sorry, the Internet is not available",
                  Toast.LENGTH_LONG)
        .show();
    }

    return(true);
  }
  else if (item.getItemId()==R.id.location) {
```

```
    locMgr.requestLocationUpdates(LocationManager.GPS_PROVIDER,
                            0, 0, onLocationChange);

    return(true);
  }

  return(super.onOptionsItemSelected(item));
}
```

The second and third parameters to requestLocationUpdates() are the desired frequency of updates and the minimum distance moved to let us know of a position change – we set these both to zero, so we get fixes as soon as they arrive. The fourth parameter is a LocationListener object, here named onLocationChange, which will be called with onLocationChanged() when GPS fixes arrive. When a GPS fix arrives, we need to:

- Update the UI with the GPS coordinates

- Save those GPS coordinates in the database for this restaurant

- Stop requesting updates, since we only need the one

With that in mind, add the onLocationChange data member to DetailForm:

```
LocationListener onLocationChange=new LocationListener() {
  public void onLocationChanged(Location fix) {
    helper.updateLocation(restaurantId, fix.getLatitude(),
                        fix.getLongitude());
    location.setText(String.valueOf(fix.getLatitude())
                        +", "
                        +String.valueOf(fix.getLongitude()));
    locMgr.removeUpdates(onLocationChange);

    Toast
      .makeText(DetailForm.this, "Location saved",
              Toast.LENGTH LONG)
      .show();
  }

  public void onProviderDisabled(String provider) {
    // required for interface, not used
  }

  public void onProviderEnabled(String provider) {
    // required for interface, not used
  }

  public void onStatusChanged(String provider, int status,
                        Bundle extras) {
```

```
    // required for interface, not used
  }
};
```

Note that we also display a Toast, just to let the user know that we successfully collected the location. There are other methods on LocationListener that, for the purposes of this tutorial, we will ignore.

However, it is possible that the user will have left the activity while we are still waiting on a GPS fix. In that case, it is safest to abandon the GPS request – otherwise, we may leave the GPS radio on indefinitely, particularly if we are in a large building where we cannot get a GPS fix. So, amend onPause() in DetailForm to remove our request for updates:

```
@Override
public void onPause() {
  save();
  locMgr.removeUpdates(onLocationChange);

  super.onPause();
}
```

You will also need to add imports for:

*   android.location.Location
*   android.location.LocationListener
*   android.location.LocationManager

Step #6: Only Enable Options Menu Item If Saved

The updateLocation() method on RestaurantHelper does a SQL UPDATE to add our latitude and longitude to a restaurant. However, this only works if the restaurant exists in the database. Right now, it is possible for the user to start adding a new restaurant, then request saving the GPS coordinates – that will not work. To combat this threat, we should disable the location options menu item if the restaurant is not saved in the database. We can tell whether or not it is saved by checking to see if restaurantId – the key of our restaurant – is null or not. A non-null restaurantId means the restaurant exists in the database.

One way to make this change is to add an `onPrepareOptionsMenu()` method to `DetailForm`, such as this one:

```
@Override
public boolean onPrepareOptionsMenu(Menu menu) {
  if (restaurantId==null) {
    menu.findItem(R.id.location).setEnabled(false);
  }

  return(super.onPrepareOptionsMenu(menu));
}
```

Here, we retrieve the menu item and disable it if `restaurantId` is `null`. `onPrepareOptionsMenu()` is called every time the MENU button is pressed, not just the first time.

The entire `DetailForm` class, incorporating all changes in this tutorial, should look something like this:

```
package apt.tutorial;

import android.app.Activity;
import android.content.Intent;
import android.database.Cursor;
import android.location.Location;
import android.location.LocationListener;
import android.location.LocationManager;
import android.net.ConnectivityManager;
import android.net.NetworkInfo;
import android.os.Bundle;
import android.view.Menu;
import android.view.MenuInflater;
import android.view.MenuItem;
import android.view.View;
import android.widget.EditText;
import android.widget.RadioGroup;
import android.widget.TextView;
import android.widget.Toast;

public class DetailForm extends Activity {
  EditText name=null;
  EditText address=null;
  EditText notes=null;
  EditText feed=null;
  RadioGroup types=null;
  RestaurantHelper helper=null;
  String restaurantId=null;
  TextView location=null;
  LocationManager locMgr=null;
```

```
@Override
public void onCreate(Bundle savedInstanceState) {
  super.onCreate(savedInstanceState);
  setContentView(R.layout.detail_form);

  locMgr=(LocationManager)getSystemService(LOCATION_SERVICE);
  helper=new RestaurantHelper(this);

  name=(EditText)findViewById(R.id.name);
  address=(EditText)findViewById(R.id.addr);
  notes=(EditText)findViewById(R.id.notes);
  types=(RadioGroup)findViewById(R.id.types);
  feed=(EditText)findViewById(R.id.feed);
  location=(TextView)findViewById(R.id.location);

  restaurantId=getIntent().getStringExtra(LunchList.ID_EXTRA);

  if (restaurantId!=null) {
    load();
  }
}

@Override
public void onPause() {
  save();
  locMgr.removeUpdates(onLocationChange);

  super.onPause();
}

@Override
public void onDestroy() {
  helper.close();

  super.onDestroy();
}

@Override
public boolean onCreateOptionsMenu(Menu menu) {
  new MenuInflater(this).inflate(R.menu.details_option, menu);

  return(super.onCreateOptionsMenu(menu));
}

@Override
public boolean onPrepareOptionsMenu(Menu menu) {
  if (restaurantId==null) {
    menu.findItem(R.id.location).setEnabled(false);
  }

  return(super.onPrepareOptionsMenu(menu));
}
```

```
@Override
public boolean onOptionsItemSelected(MenuItem item) {
  if (item.getItemId()==R.id.feed) {
    if (isNetworkAvailable()) {
      Intent i=new Intent(this, FeedActivity.class);

      i.putExtra(FeedActivity.FEED_URL, feed.getText().toString());
      startActivity(i);
    }
    else {
      Toast
        .makeText(this, "Sorry, the Internet is not available",
                  Toast.LENGTH_LONG)
        .show();
    }

    return(true);
  }
  else if (item.getItemId()==R.id.location) {
    locMgr.requestLocationUpdates(LocationManager.GPS_PROVIDER,
                                  0, 0, onLocationChange);

    return(true);
  }

  return(super.onOptionsItemSelected(item));
}

private boolean isNetworkAvailable() {
  ConnectivityManager
cm=(ConnectivityManager)getSystemService(CONNECTIVITY_SERVICE);
  NetworkInfo info=cm.getActiveNetworkInfo();

  return(info!=null);
}

private void load() {
  Cursor c=helper.getById(restaurantId);

  c.moveToFirst();
  name.setText(helper.getName(c));
  address.setText(helper.getAddress(c));
  notes.setText(helper.getNotes(c));
  feed.setText(helper.getFeed(c));

  if (helper.getType(c).equals("sit_down")) {
    types.check(R.id.sit_down);
  }
  else if (helper.getType(c).equals("take_out")) {
    types.check(R.id.take_out);
  }
  else {
    types.check(R.id.delivery);
  }
```

```
   location.setText(String.valueOf(helper.getLatitude(c))
                 +", "
                 +String.valueOf(helper.getLongitude(c)));

   c.close();
}

private void save() {
  if (name.getText().toString().length()>0) {
    String type=null;

    switch (types.getCheckedRadioButtonId()) {
      case R.id.sit_down:
        type="sit_down";
        break;
      case R.id.take_out:
        type="take_out";
        break;
      default:
        type="delivery";
        break;
    }

    if (restaurantId==null) {
      helper.insert(name.getText().toString(),
                  address.getText().toString(), type,
                  notes.getText().toString(),
                  feed.getText().toString());
    }
    else {
      helper.update(restaurantId, name.getText().toString(),
                  address.getText().toString(), type,
                  notes.getText().toString(),
                  feed.getText().toString());
    }
  }
}

LocationListener onLocationChange=new LocationListener() {
  public void onLocationChanged(Location fix) {
    helper.updateLocation(restaurantId, fix.getLatitude(),
                        fix.getLongitude());
    location.setText(String.valueOf(fix.getLatitude())
                  +", "
                  +String.valueOf(fix.getLongitude()));
    locMgr.removeUpdates(onLocationChange);

    Toast
      .makeText(DetailForm.this, "Location saved",
              Toast.LENGTH_LONG)
      .show();
  }
```

```
  public void onProviderDisabled(String provider) {
    // required for interface, not used
  }

  public void onProviderEnabled(String provider) {
    // required for interface, not used
  }

  public void onStatusChanged(String provider, int status,
                              Bundle extras) {
    // required for interface, not used
  }
};
}
```

At this point, if you compile and install the application, on the detail form, you will see a place for the restaurant GPS coordinates:

Figure 75. The detail form, with default GPS coordinates

Pressing the MENU button will bring up the new options menu item:

Figure 76. The detail form and its new options menu

To test it, if you are running it on actual hardware, just tap the menu item and wait for the Toast to appear. If you are running the application on an emulator, you will need to use DDMS to send a fake GPS fix, after tapping the menu item to "turn on the GPS radio", as it were. The Emulator Controls tab of DDMS will have a spot for you to supply a longitude and latitude, plus a Send button to push the fake fix over to LunchList.

Extra Credit

Here are some things you can try beyond those step-by-step instructions:

- Use the Criteria object to remove the hard-wired dependency on GPS. However, in this case, we would still want ACCURACY_FINE locations – we are trying to fix the position of a restaurant, which would be useless if off by half a kilometer or more.

- Tie into a geocoding service to allow the user to fill in the address of the restaurant from the GPS coordinates, rather than having to ask somebody, let alone having to type it in. Note that while Android has a Geocoder, it appears to be somewhat buggy, so while you are welcome to experiment with it, do not be shocked if you encounter some problems.

• Add a "reset" or "revert" options menu item that allows the user to restore the values that are in the database, in case they made edits and do not want to save them. If the restaurant is not in the database (i.e., has never been saved), this options menu item should blank the detail form.

• If you have not added options for deleting a restaurant, this might be a good time. After all, if the user accidentally taps on the add options menu item in the LunchList activity, they are forced to save a restaurant in our current UI. Add a "delete" options menu item on DetailForm (preferably with an AlertDialog for confirmation) and/or a "delete" context menu item on LunchList itself.

• Since the restaurant is either in or not in the database at the start of DetailForm, and that state does not change while the activity is on-screen, we would not need to use onPrepareOptionsMenu() – we could disable the menu item in onCreateOptionsMenu(), after inflating the menu. Make this change and experiment with the results.

Further Reading

Location tracking, via GPS or other technologies, is covered in the "Accessing Location-Based Services" chapter of The Busy Coder's Guide to Android Development[50].

---

50 http://commonsware.com/Android

Putting Lunch on the Map

Now that we have GPS coordinates for our restaurants, it might be useful to show where those locations are on a map, so that the user can remember how to get there. The simple way do to that would be to launch the built-in maps application, via a `geo:` URL and an `ACTION_VIEW` Intent. However, we cannot draw a marker on that sort of map, which might be interesting. So, here, we will do things the hard way, by integrating `MapActivity` and `MapView` into LunchList.

Step-By-Step Instructions

First, you need to have completed the previous tutorial. If you are beginning the tutorials here, or if you wish to not use your existing work, you can download a ZIP file with all of the tutorial results, and you can copy the `17-Location` edition of `LunchList` to use as a starting point. If you are using Eclipse, these instructions will help you load the project into a workspace.

Step #1: Make Sure You Are Ready

You will need to register for an API key to use with the mapping services and set it up in your development environment with your debug certificate. Full instructions for generating API keys, for development and production use, can be found on the Android Google Maps Add-On Web site[51]. In the

---

51   http://code.google.com/android/add-ons/google-apis/mapkey.html

interest of brevity, let's focus on the narrow case of getting your app running in your emulator. Doing this requires the following steps:

1. Visit the API key signup page[52] and review the terms of service

2. Re-read those terms of service and make really really sure you want to agree to them, then check the "I have read and agree..." checkbox

3. Find the MD5 digest of the certificate used for signing your debug-mode applications (described in detail below)

4. On the API key signup page, paste in that MD5 signature and submit the form

5. On the resulting page, save the API key that you are given

The trickiest part is finding the MD5 signature of the certificate used for signing your debug-mode applications... and much of the complexity is merely in making sense of the concept.

All Android applications are signed using a digital signature generated from a certificate. You are automatically given a debug certificate when you set up the SDK, and there is a separate process for creating a self-signed certificate for use in your production applications. This signature process involves the use of the Java keytool and jarsigner utilities. For the purposes of getting your API key, you only need to worry about keytool. You will find this in your Java SDK. Since it runs from the command line, it helps if you put the Java SDK's bin/ directory in your PATH.

To get your MD5 digest of your debug certificate, if you are on OS X or Linux, use the following command:

```
keytool -list -alias androiddebugkey -keystore ~/.android/debug.keystore
-storepass android -keypass android
```

On other development platforms, you will need to replace the value of the -keystore switch with the location for your platform and user account:

- XP: C:\Documents and Settings\<user>\.android\debug.keystore

---

52 http://code.google.com/android/maps-api-signup.html

- Vista/Windows 7: `C:\Users\<user>\.android\debug.keystore`

(where `<user>` is your account name)

The second line of the output contains your MD5 digest, as a series of pairs of hex digits separated by colons.

You will also need to be testing on an AVD or device that has Google Maps installed. If the Google Maps application is available via the home screen's launcher, then you should be good to go.

And, you need to make sure that your build target is set to an Android edition that has the Google APIs, so you can compile your application with references to Google Maps. In Eclipse, you will find this on the Android entry in the project properties; outside of Eclipse, ensure that your `default.properties` file has a "target" property set to one with the Google APIs, such as:

```
# This file is automatically generated by Android Tools.
# Do not modify this file - YOUR CHANGES WILL BE ERASED!
#
# This file must be checked in Version Control Systems.
#
# To customize properties used by the Ant build system use,
# "build.properties", and override values to adapt the script to your
# project structure.

# Project target.
target=Google Inc.:Google APIs:8
```

Step #2: Add an Options Menu Item for Map

First, we need to give the user a way to request a map of the restaurant. The simplest solution: add another options menu item.

You will need an icon for this new menu item, perhaps the `ic_menu_mapmode.png` file from the Android SDK, which you can copy into the `res/drawable/` directory of your project.

Then, add a map `<item>` element to the `res/menu/details_option.xml` file:

```xml
<?xml version="1.0" encoding="utf-8"?>
<menu xmlns:android="http://schemas.android.com/apk/res/android">
  <item android:id="@+id/feed"
    android:title="RSS Feed"
    android:icon="@drawable/ic_menu_friendslist"
  />
  <item android:id="@+id/location"
    android:title="Save Location"
    android:icon="@drawable/ic_menu_compass"
  />
  <item android:id="@+id/map"
    android:title="Show on Map"
    android:icon="@drawable/ic_menu_mapmode"
  />
</menu>
```

Eclipse users can do this by:

1. Double-clicking on the `res/menu/details_option.xml` file in the Package Explorer to bring it up in the graphical editor

2. Clicking the Add... button to the right of the list of menu items

3. Choosing Item in the dialog box and clicking OK to add a blank menu item

4. Specifying `@+id/map` as the Id of the new menu item

5. Setting the title of the new menu item to be `Show on Map`

6. Setting the icon of the new menu item to be `@drawable/ic_menu_mapmode` (or whatever icon it is that you are using)

7. Saving the changes (e.g., <Ctrl>-<S>)

Also, modify `onPrepareOptionsMenu()` in `DetailForm` to disable this menu item if the restaurant is not saved (and therefore definitely lacks a location):

```java
@Override
public boolean onPrepareOptionsMenu(Menu menu) {
  if (restaurantId==null) {
    menu.findItem(R.id.location).setEnabled(false);
    menu.findItem(R.id.map).setEnabled(false);
  }
```

```
      return(super.onPrepareOptionsMenu(menu));
}
```

Step #3: Create and Use a MapActivity

Next, let us integrate a basic MapActivity.

First, we need to tell Android that we intend to use the Google Maps capability. This is accomplished via a <uses-library> element in the manifest, indicating that we plan to use com.google.android.maps. This will cause that firmware library to be loaded into our process when the application starts up, and it makes classes like MapActivity available to us.

So, modify AndroidManifest.xml to add the <uses-library> element:

```
<?xml version="1.0" encoding="utf-8"?>
<manifest android:versionCode="1"
          android:versionName="1.0"
          package="apt.tutorial"
          xmlns:android="http://schemas.android.com/apk/res/android">

  <uses-permission android:name="android.permission.INTERNET" />
  <uses-permission android:name="android.permission.ACCESS_NETWORK_STATE" />
  <uses-permission android:name="android.permission.ACCESS_FINE_LOCATION" />
  <supports-screens android:largeScreens="true"
                    android:normalScreens="true"
                    android:smallScreens="false" />
  <application android:label="@string/app_name">
    <uses-library android:name="com.google.android.maps" />
    <activity android:label="@string/app_name"
              android:name=".LunchList">
      <intent-filter>
        <action android:name="android.intent.action.MAIN" />
        <category android:name="android.intent.category.LAUNCHER" />
      </intent-filter>
    </activity>
    <activity android:name=".DetailForm"></activity>
    <activity android:name=".EditPreferences"></activity>
    <activity android:name=".FeedActivity"></activity>
    <activity android:name=".RestaurantMap"></activity>
    <service android:name=".FeedService"></service>
  </application>
</manifest>
```

Eclipse users can make this change by:

1. Double-clicking on the `AndroidManifest.xml` file to bring it up in the graphical editor

2. Clicking on the Application sub-tab

3. Clicking the Add... button to the right of the Application Nodes list

4. Choosing Uses Library in the dialog and clicking OK

5. Choosing `com.google.android.maps` for the "name" in the drop-down for the new element on the right

6. Setting the "required" value to be `true` via the drop-down for the new element on the right

7. Saving your changes (e.g., <Ctrl>-<S>)

Next, add a rudimentary `RestaurantMap` class to the LunchList project, in the `apt.tutorial` package, inheriting from `MapActivity`, and loading in the `R.layout.map` layout resource. Eclipse users can do this by right-clicking over the `apt.tutorial` package in Package Explorer, choosing New > Class from the context menu, then specifying `MapActivity` as the class name and `com.google.android.maps.MapActivity` as the superclass.

You will also need to add that activity to the manifest, with an appropriate `<activity>` element, akin to the other activities that we have added. Eclipse users can add this element by:

1. Double-clicking on the `AndroidManifest.xml` file in Package Explorer to bring it up in the editor

2. Clicking on the Application sub-tab

3. Clicking on the Add... button next to the Application Nodes list

4. Choosing Activity in the node type dialog and clicking OK

5. Clicking the Browse... button next to the Name field and choosing `MapActivity`

6. Saving changes (e.g., <Ctrl>-<S>)

In addition to onCreate(), the initial cut of RestaurantMap will need to override isRouteDisplayed(), as that is an abstract method – just return false. Here is what this class should look like at the outset:

```
package apt.tutorial;

import android.os.Bundle;
import com.google.android.maps.MapActivity;

public class RestaurantMap extends MapActivity {
  @Override
  public void onCreate(Bundle savedInstanceState) {
    super.onCreate(savedInstanceState);
    setContentView(R.layout.map);
  }

  @Override
  protected boolean isRouteDisplayed() {
    return(false);
  }
}
```

Now, we need to tie that into the DetailForm class, so when the user clicks on the map options menu item, we launch RestaurantMap. That is merely a matter of adding another condition to onOptionsItemSelected() and calling startActivity():

```
@Override
public boolean onOptionsItemSelected(MenuItem item) {
  if (item.getItemId()==R.id.feed) {
    if (isNetworkAvailable()) {
      Intent i=new Intent(this, FeedActivity.class);

      i.putExtra(FeedActivity.FEED_URL, feed.getText().toString());
      startActivity(i);
    }
    else {
      Toast
        .makeText(this, "Sorry, the Internet is not available",
                  Toast.LENGTH_LONG)
        .show();
    }

    return(true);
  }
  else if (item.getItemId()==R.id.location) {
    locMgr.requestLocationUpdates(LocationManager.GPS_PROVIDER,
                                  0, 0, onLocationChange);

    return(true);
```

```
  }
  else if (item.getItemId()==R.id.map) {
    Intent i=new Intent(this, RestaurantMap.class);

    startActivity(i);

    return(true);
  }

  return(super.onOptionsItemSelected(item));
}
```

We also need a layout file, res/layout/map.xml. It can just be a full-screen MapView. However, there are three tricks:

1. Because MapView is not part of android.widget, you must fully-qualify it as com.google.android.maps.MapView

2. You will need to have an android:apiKey attribute containing *your* API key

3. You probably want to have android:clickable="true", so the user can pan and zoom around the map by themselves

Here is a layout file that fits those requirements (though you will need to replace the API key shown here with your own):

```
<?xml version="1.0" encoding="utf-8"?>
<com.google.android.maps.MapView
  xmlns:android="http://schemas.android.com/apk/res/android"
  android:id="@+id/map"
  android:layout_width="match_parent"
  android:layout_height="match_parent"
  android:apiKey="00yHj0k7_7vxbuQ9zwyXI4bNMJrAjYrJ9KKHgbQ"
  android:clickable="true" />
```

Eclipse users will need to create this layout by manually editing the XML – as do non-Eclipse users – as MapView is not a widget available in the tool palette at this time.

Step #4: Create an ItemizedOverlay

If we want to display a marker where the restaurant is, we are going to need to get our latitude and longitude to the RestaurantMap, then use that with an ItemizedOverlay to render our marker.

To get the latitude and longitude from DetailForm to RestaurantMap, we will use Intent extras once again. So, define some public static String data members to use as Intent extra keys in RestaurantMap:

```
public static final String EXTRA_LATITUDE="apt.tutorial.EXTRA_LATITUDE";
public static final String EXTRA_LONGITUDE="apt.tutorial.EXTRA_LONGITUDE";
public static final String EXTRA_NAME="apt.tutorial.EXTRA_NAME";
```

Then...we have a problem.

In DetailForm, the only point where we have the Cursor for loading our data is in the load() method. By the time we get to onOptionsItemSelected() to launch the RestaurantMap, we no longer have that Cursor. We could parse it out of the TextView displaying those coordinates, but that would be a hassle.

So, in DetailForm, add a pair of data members to cache the latitude and longitude:

```
double latitude=0.0d;
double longitude=0.0d;
```

Then, populate those in the load() method of DetailForm:

```
private void load() {
  Cursor c=helper.getById(restaurantId);

  c.moveToFirst();
  name.setText(helper.getName(c));
  address.setText(helper.getAddress(c));
  notes.setText(helper.getNotes(c));
  feed.setText(helper.getFeed(c));

  if (helper.getType(c).equals("sit_down")) {
    types.check(R.id.sit_down);
  }
  else if (helper.getType(c).equals("take_out")) {
```

```
      types.check(R.id.take_out);
    }
    else {
      types.check(R.id.delivery);
    }

    latitude=helper.getLatitude(c);
    longitude=helper.getLongitude(c);

    location.setText(String.valueOf(latitude)
                        +", "
                        +String.valueOf(longitude));

    c.close();
}
```

Now, we can modify `onOptionsItemSelected()` to put the latitude and longitude in as `Intent` extras, along with the name of the restaurant for good measure:

```
@Override
public boolean onOptionsItemSelected(MenuItem item) {
  if (item.getItemId()==R.id.feed) {
    if (isNetworkAvailable()) {
      Intent i=new Intent(this, FeedActivity.class);

      i.putExtra(FeedActivity.FEED_URL, feed.getText().toString());
      startActivity(i);
    }
    else {
      Toast
        .makeText(this, "Sorry, the Internet is not available",
                Toast.LENGTH_LONG)
        .show();
    }

    return(true);
  }
  else if (item.getItemId()==R.id.location) {
    locMgr.requestLocationUpdates(LocationManager.GPS_PROVIDER,
                              0, 0, onLocationChange);

    return(true);
  }
  else if (item.getItemId()==R.id.map) {
    Intent i=new Intent(this, RestaurantMap.class);

    i.putExtra(RestaurantMap.EXTRA_LATITUDE, latitude);
    i.putExtra(RestaurantMap.EXTRA_LONGITUDE, longitude);
    i.putExtra(RestaurantMap.EXTRA_NAME, name.getText().toString());

    startActivity(i);
```

```
      return(true);
    }

    return(super.onOptionsItemSelected(item));
  }
}
```

The complete `DetailForm` class, with all the modifications for this tutorial, should resemble:

```
package apt.tutorial;

import android.app.Activity;
import android.content.Intent;
import android.database.Cursor;
import android.location.Location;
import android.location.LocationListener;
import android.location.LocationManager;
import android.net.ConnectivityManager;
import android.net.NetworkInfo;
import android.os.Bundle;
import android.view.Menu;
import android.view.MenuInflater;
import android.view.MenuItem;
import android.view.View;
import android.widget.EditText;
import android.widget.RadioGroup;
import android.widget.TextView;
import android.widget.Toast;

public class DetailForm extends Activity {
  EditText name=null;
  EditText address=null;
  EditText notes=null;
  EditText feed=null;
  RadioGroup types=null;
  RestaurantHelper helper=null;
  String restaurantId=null;
  TextView location=null;
  LocationManager locMgr=null;
  double latitude=0.0d;
  double longitude=0.0d;

  @Override
  public void onCreate(Bundle savedInstanceState) {
    super.onCreate(savedInstanceState);
    setContentView(R.layout.detail_form);

    locMgr=(LocationManager)getSystemService(LOCATION_SERVICE);
    helper=new RestaurantHelper(this);

    name=(EditText)findViewById(R.id.name);
```

```
    address=(EditText)findViewById(R.id.addr);
    notes=(EditText)findViewById(R.id.notes);
    types=(RadioGroup)findViewById(R.id.types);
    feed=(EditText)findViewById(R.id.feed);
    location=(TextView)findViewById(R.id.location);

    restaurantId=getIntent().getStringExtra(LunchList.ID_EXTRA);

    if (restaurantId!=null) {
      load();
    }
  }

  @Override
  public void onPause() {
    save();

    super.onPause();
  }

  @Override
  public void onDestroy() {
    helper.close();
    locMgr.removeUpdates(onLocationChange);

    super.onDestroy();
  }

  @Override
  public boolean onCreateOptionsMenu(Menu menu) {
    new MenuInflater(this).inflate(R.menu.details_option, menu);

    return(super.onCreateOptionsMenu(menu));
  }

  @Override
  public boolean onPrepareOptionsMenu(Menu menu) {
    if (restaurantId==null) {
      menu.findItem(R.id.location).setEnabled(false);
      menu.findItem(R.id.map).setEnabled(false);
    }

    return(super.onPrepareOptionsMenu(menu));
  }

  @Override
  public boolean onOptionsItemSelected(MenuItem item) {
    if (item.getItemId()==R.id.feed) {
      if (isNetworkAvailable()) {
        Intent i=new Intent(this, FeedActivity.class);

        i.putExtra(FeedActivity.FEED_URL, feed.getText().toString());
        startActivity(i);
      }
```

```
      else {
        Toast
          .makeText(this, "Sorry, the Internet is not available",
                    Toast.LENGTH_LONG)
          .show();
      }

      return(true);
    }
    else if (item.getItemId()==R.id.location) {
      locMgr.requestLocationUpdates(LocationManager.GPS_PROVIDER,
                                    0, 0, onLocationChange);

      return(true);
    }
    else if (item.getItemId()==R.id.map) {
      Intent i=new Intent(this, RestaurantMap.class);

      i.putExtra(RestaurantMap.EXTRA_LATITUDE, latitude);
      i.putExtra(RestaurantMap.EXTRA_LONGITUDE, longitude);
      i.putExtra(RestaurantMap.EXTRA_NAME, name.getText().toString());

      startActivity(i);

      return(true);
    }

    return(super.onOptionsItemSelected(item));
  }

  private boolean isNetworkAvailable() {
    ConnectivityManager
cm=(ConnectivityManager)getSystemService(CONNECTIVITY_SERVICE);
    NetworkInfo info=cm.getActiveNetworkInfo();

    return(info!=null);
  }

  private void load() {
    Cursor c=helper.getById(restaurantId);

    c.moveToFirst();
    name.setText(helper.getName(c));
    address.setText(helper.getAddress(c));
    notes.setText(helper.getNotes(c));
    feed.setText(helper.getFeed(c));

    if (helper.getType(c).equals("sit_down")) {
      types.check(R.id.sit_down);
    }
    else if (helper.getType(c).equals("take_out")) {
      types.check(R.id.take_out);
    }
    else {
```

```
      types.check(R.id.delivery);
    }

  latitude=helper.getLatitude(c);
  longitude=helper.getLongitude(c);

  location.setText(String.valueOf(latitude)
                   +", "
                   +String.valueOf(longitude));

  c.close();
}

private void save() {
  if (name.getText().toString().length()>0) {
    String type=null;

    switch (types.getCheckedRadioButtonId()) {
      case R.id.sit_down:
        type="sit_down";
        break;
      case R.id.take_out:
        type="take_out";
        break;
      default:
        type="delivery";
        break;
    }

    if (restaurantId==null) {
      helper.insert(name.getText().toString(),
                    address.getText().toString(), type,
                    notes.getText().toString(),
                    feed.getText().toString());
    }
    else {
      helper.update(restaurantId, name.getText().toString(),
                    address.getText().toString(), type,
                    notes.getText().toString(),
                    feed.getText().toString());
    }
  }
}

LocationListener onLocationChange=new LocationListener() {
  public void onLocationChanged(Location fix) {
    helper.updateLocation(restaurantId, fix.getLatitude(),
                          fix.getLongitude());
    location.setText(String.valueOf(fix.getLatitude())
                     +", "
                     +String.valueOf(fix.getLongitude()));
    locMgr.removeUpdates(onLocationChange);

    Toast
```

```
        .makeText(DetailForm.this, "Location saved",
                  Toast.LENGTH_LONG)
      .show();
  }

  public void onProviderDisabled(String provider) {
    // required for interface, not used
  }

  public void onProviderEnabled(String provider) {
    // required for interface, not used
  }

  public void onStatusChanged(String provider, int status,
                              Bundle extras) {
    // required for interface, not used
  }
};
}
```

In RestaurantMap, we can retrieve these extras by adding a couple of lines to onCreate():

```
double lat=getIntent().getDoubleExtra(EXTRA_LATITUDE, 0);
double lon=getIntent().getDoubleExtra(EXTRA_LONGITUDE, 0);
```

It might be nice to center the map on this location, so we know the marker will be visible. And, we can set the zoom level of the map to a reasonable level, so we are not viewing a map of the world or something at the outset. To do these things, we will need to access our MapView and its accompanying MapController. And, we will need to convert our latitude and longitude into a GeoPoint, which stores the latitude and longitude in microdegrees (10 times the number of degrees), so Google Maps can do all its necessary calculations using fixed-point math.

To do all that, add a MapView data member named map:

```
private MapView map=null;
```

Then, add these few lines to onCreate(), after the lines you added above to retrieve the latitude and longitude:

```
map=(MapView)findViewById(R.id.map);
```

```
map.getController().setZoom(17);

GeoPoint status=new GeoPoint((int)(lat*1000000.0),
                             (int)(lon*1000000.0));

map.getController().setCenter(status);
map.setBuiltInZoomControls(true);
```

Of course, we still do not have our overlay.

While there is an Overlay class as part of the Google Maps add-on for Android, ItemizedOverlay will be far simpler for our use case – Overlay is for drawing lines and shaded areas, while ItemizedOverlay is for placing markers on discrete points. Here is a minimalist ItemizedOverlay subclass, named RestaurantOverlay, which we can use as an inner class of RestaurantMap:

```
private class RestaurantOverlay extends ItemizedOverlay<OverlayItem> {
  private OverlayItem item=null;

  public RestaurantOverlay(Drawable marker, GeoPoint point,
                           String name) {
    super(marker);

    boundCenterBottom(marker);

    item=new OverlayItem(point, name, name);

    populate();
  }

  @Override
  protected OverlayItem createItem(int i) {
    return(item);
  }

  @Override
  public int size() {
    return(1);
  }
}
```

In the constructor, we are receiving as parameters our GeoPoint, plus the restaurant's name, and a Drawable image to use for the actual map marker. The constructor calls boundCenterBottom() – if the marker's "point" is centered on the bottom of the image, boundCenterBottom() will set up our drop shadow for us. It also creates an OverlayItem for our restaurant, passing it the `GeoPoint`, plus the name as both the name of the item and the item's "snippet".

At this point, `RestaurantOverlay` calls `populate()`, which triggers Android to call `size()` on the overlay (which returns 1, the sum total of points we are drawing), and then `getItem()` for each item (which returns the `OverlayItem` created in the constructor).

To use this, we need to add a few more lines to the bottom of `onCreate()` of `RestaurantMap`:

```
Drawable marker=getResources().getDrawable(R.drawable.marker);

marker.setBounds(0, 0, marker.getIntrinsicWidth(),
                 marker.getIntrinsicHeight());

map
  .getOverlays()
  .add(new RestaurantOverlay(marker, status,
                        getIntent().getStringExtra(EXTRA_NAME)));
```

Here, we load a `Drawable` resource (you will need a corresponding file in `res/drawable/` culled from somewhere) and tell the map to add our `RestaurantOverlay` to its roster of overlays.

You will need to add a handful of imports:

- `android.graphics.drawable.Drawable`
- `com.google.android.maps.GeoPoint`
- `com.google.android.maps.ItemizedOverlay`
- `com.google.android.maps.MapView`
- `com.google.android.maps.OverlayItem`

Step #5: Handle Marker Taps

The last piece of the puzzle is to respond when the user taps on the restaurant... just for fun. To do this, add an `onTap()` method to `RestaurantOverlay`:

```
@Override
protected boolean onTap(int i) {
  Toast.makeText(RestaurantMap.this,
                 item.getSnippet(),
                 Toast.LENGTH_SHORT).show();

  return(true);
}
```

We are passed in the index of the marker the user tapped, which in this case will always be 0 since there is but one marker. Here, we just display a Toast, containing the name of the restaurant, stashed in the OverlayItem's "snippet". You will need to add an import for android.widget.Toast, though.

The complete RestaurantMap class should look a wee bit like:

```
package apt.tutorial;

import android.graphics.drawable.Drawable;
import android.os.Bundle;
import android.widget.Toast;
import com.google.android.maps.GeoPoint;
import com.google.android.maps.ItemizedOverlay;
import com.google.android.maps.MapActivity;
import com.google.android.maps.MapController;
import com.google.android.maps.MapView;
import com.google.android.maps.OverlayItem;

public class RestaurantMap extends MapActivity {
  public static final String EXTRA_LATITUDE="apt.tutorial.EXTRA_LATITUDE";
  public static final String EXTRA_LONGITUDE="apt.tutorial.EXTRA_LONGITUDE";
  public static final String EXTRA_NAME="apt.tutorial.EXTRA_NAME";
  private MapView map=null;

  @Override
  public void onCreate(Bundle savedInstanceState) {
    super.onCreate(savedInstanceState);
    setContentView(R.layout.map);

    double lat=getIntent().getDoubleExtra(EXTRA_LATITUDE, 0);
    double lon=getIntent().getDoubleExtra(EXTRA_LONGITUDE, 0);

    map=(MapView)findViewById(R.id.map);

    map.getController().setZoom(17);

    GeoPoint status=new GeoPoint((int)(lat*1000000.0),
                                 (int)(lon*1000000.0));

    map.getController().setCenter(status);
```

```
    map.setBuiltInZoomControls(true);

    Drawable marker=getResources().getDrawable(R.drawable.marker);

    marker.setBounds(0, 0, marker.getIntrinsicWidth(),
                    marker.getIntrinsicHeight());

    map
      .getOverlays()
      .add(new RestaurantOverlay(marker, status,
                            getIntent().getStringExtra(EXTRA_NAME)));
  }

  @Override
  protected boolean isRouteDisplayed() {
    return(false);
  }

  private class RestaurantOverlay extends ItemizedOverlay<OverlayItem> {
    private OverlayItem item=null;

    public RestaurantOverlay(Drawable marker, GeoPoint point,
                            String name) {
      super(marker);

      boundCenterBottom(marker);

      item=new OverlayItem(point, name, name);

      populate();
    }

    @Override
    protected OverlayItem createItem(int i) {
      return(item);
    }

    @Override
    protected boolean onTap(int i) {
      Toast.makeText(RestaurantMap.this,
                    item.getSnippet(),
                    Toast.LENGTH_SHORT).show();

      return(true);
    }

    @Override
    public int size() {
      return(1);
    }
  }
}
```

If you compile and run this project, in the detail form for a restaurant, you will see the new options menu item:

Figure 77. The detail form, with the new Map options menu item

Tapping it will bring up the map on the stated location:

Figure 78. The "restaurant" location shown on the map

And tapping on the marker displays the Toast:

Figure 79. The "restaurant" name in a Toast

If all you see is your marker floating atop a grey screen with gridlines, here are the possible problems:

- You forgot your API key in the res/layout/map.xml file.

- Your device or emulator does not have Internet access (e.g., the emulator shows zero bars of signal strength). In the case of the emulator, if your development machine has Internet access, try simply restarting the emulator. If that does not help, there may be firewall issues at your location.

Extra Credit

Here are some things you can try beyond those step-by-step instructions:

- Give the user some means of opening the actual Google Maps application on the location, instead of our own MapActivity. For example, that way they can get driving directions to the restaurant.

- Experiment with different zoom levels as the starting point.

300

- Add an options menu item on the LunchList activity to launch `RestaurantMap` with no extras. When `RestaurantMap` detects the lack of extras in `onCreate()`, it can use `RestaurantHelper` to load all the restaurants that have a latitude and longitude and display all of them on the map.

Further Reading

Integration with Google Maps is covered in the "Mapping with MapView and MapActivity" chapter of The Busy Coder's Guide to Android Development[53].

Also, bear in mind that the documentation for Android's mapping code is not found in the Android developer guide directly, but rather at the site for the Google add-on for Android[54].

---

53 http://commonsware.com/Android
54 http://code.google.com/android/add-ons/google-apis

Is It Lunchtime Yet?

Now that we are keeping tabs on possible places to go to lunch, we still have only addressed the "space" portion of "the space-time continuum". There is a matter of time, especially lunchtime, to consider. If we help the user choose *where* to go to lunch, we can also help remind the user *when* it is time to go to lunch.

Of course, some users would just use whatever "alarm clock" application exists on their device. Such users are boring, and we will not consider them further.

Hence, in this tutorial, we will add some preferences related to alerting the user when lunch is, then use `AlarmManager` – which, despite its name, has nothing to do with alarm clocks – to let us know when that time arrives, so we can in turn let the user know.

Step-By-Step Instructions

First, you need to have completed the previous tutorial. If you are beginning the tutorials here, or if you wish to not use your existing work, you can download a ZIP file with all of the tutorial results, and you can copy the `18-Map` edition of `LunchList` to use as a starting point. If you are using Eclipse, these instructions will help you load the project into a workspace.

Note that if you are importing existing code, you will need to replace the Maps API key found in the map layout file, since the "answers" to this and future tutorials have an API key that is not yours.

Step #1: Create a TimePreference

We want the user to specify a time when we should remind them to go have lunch. We could have a whole activity dedicated to this. However, this feels like an application setting, so it would be nice if we could collect our alarm information via SharedPreferences and our existing EditPreferences activity.

However, there is no TimePreference designed for collecting a time. Fortunately, building one is not too difficult.

Add a new class, TimePreference.java, to the LunchList project, in the apt.tutorial package, extending DialogPreference, that looks like this:

```java
package apt.tutorial;

import android.content.Context;
import android.content.res.TypedArray;
import android.preference.DialogPreference;
import android.util.AttributeSet;
import android.view.View;
import android.widget.TimePicker;

public class TimePreference extends DialogPreference {
  private int lastHour=0;
  private int lastMinute=0;
  private TimePicker picker=null;

  public static int getHour(String time) {
    String[] pieces=time.split(":");

    return(Integer.parseInt(pieces[0]));
  }

  public static int getMinute(String time) {
    String[] pieces=time.split(":");

    return(Integer.parseInt(pieces[1]));
  }

  public TimePreference(Context ctxt, AttributeSet attrs) {
    super(ctxt, attrs);
```

```
    setPositiveButtonText("Set");
    setNegativeButtonText("Cancel");
}

@Override
protected View onCreateDialogView() {
  picker=new TimePicker(getContext());

  return(picker);
}

@Override
protected void onBindDialogView(View v) {
  super.onBindDialogView(v);

  picker.setCurrentHour(lastHour);
  picker.setCurrentMinute(lastMinute);
}

@Override
protected void onDialogClosed(boolean positiveResult) {
  super.onDialogClosed(positiveResult);

  if (positiveResult) {
    lastHour=picker.getCurrentHour();
    lastMinute=picker.getCurrentMinute();

    String time=String.valueOf(lastHour)+":"+String.valueOf(lastMinute);

    if (callChangeListener(time)) {
      persistString(time);
    }
  }
}

@Override
protected Object onGetDefaultValue(TypedArray a, int index) {
  return(a.getString(index));
}

@Override
protected void onSetInitialValue(boolean restoreValue, Object defaultValue) {
  String time=null;

  if (restoreValue) {
    if (defaultValue==null) {
      time=getPersistedString("00:00");
    }
    else {
      time=getPersistedString(defaultValue.toString());
    }
  }
  else {
```

```
    time=defaultValue.toString();
  }

  lastHour=getHour(time);
  lastMinute=getMinute(time);
  }
}
```

Eclipse users can right-click over apt.tutorial in the Package Explorer and choose New > Class from the context menu to bring up the new class dialog. Set the class name to be TimePreference and set the parent class to be android.preference.DialogPreference. Then, click OK and fill in the implementation shown above.

There is a fair amount of code here. Let's review what the various methods are for:

- getHour() and getMinute() are static helper methods, to extract the hour and minute, as integers, from a string encoded in HH:MM format. We have to store our time collected by TimePreference as a single piece of data in the SharedPreferences, so storing it as an HH:MM formatted string seems like a reasonable choice.

- We have a Preference constructor, where we indicate what captions should be for the positive and negative buttons at the bottom of the dialog.

- onCreateDialogView() will be called as part of the dialog box being displayed. We need to return a View that represents the content of the dialog. We could inflate a layout here, if we wanted. However, for simplicity, we are simply using a TimePicker widget constructed directly in Java.

- onBindDialogView() will be called after onCreateDialogView(), and our job is to fill in whatever preference data should go into that dialog. Some other methods described later in this list will have been called first, populating a lastHour and lastMinute pair of data members with the hour and minute from the SharedPreferences. We just turn around and pop those into the TimePicker.

- onDialogClosed() will be called when the user clicks either the positive or negative button, or clicks the BACK button (same as clicking the negative button). If they clicked the positive button, we assemble a new HH:MM string from the values in the TimePicker, then tell DialogPreference to persist that value to the SharedPreferences.

- onGetDefaultValue() will be called when Android needs us to convert an android:defaultValue attribute into an object of the appropriate data type. For example, an integer preference would need to convert the android:defaultValue String to an Integer. In our case, our preference is being stored as a String, so we can extract the String from the TypedArray that represents all of the attributes on this preference in the preference XML resource.

- Finally, onSetInitialValue() will be called before onBindDialogView(), where we are told the actual preference value to start with. That could be an actual saved preference value from before, or the android:defaultValue value, or nothing at all (in which case, we start with "00:00"). Wherever the string comes from, we parse it into the lastHour and lastMinute integer data members for use by onBindDialogView().

Step #2: Collect Alarm Preferences

Now that we have a TimePreference, we can use it to find out when the user wants to be alerted for lunchtime. However, users might not want to be alerted at all, so we should really add two preferences: a CheckBoxPreference to enable lunchtime alerts, plus the TimePreference to find out when that alert should show.

So, add a couple of new elements to res/xml/preferences.xml in your LunchList project:

```
<PreferenceScreen
  xmlns:android="http://schemas.android.com/apk/res/android">
  <ListPreference
    android:key="sort_order"
    android:title="Sort Order"
    android:summary="Choose the order the list uses"
    android:entries="@array/sort_names"
    android:entryValues="@array/sort_clauses"
    android:dialogTitle="Choose a sort order" />
  <CheckBoxPreference
```

```
    android:key="alarm"
    android:title="Sound a Lunch Alarm"
    android:summary="Check if you want to know when it is time for lunch" />
 <apt.tutorial.TimePreference
    android:key="alarm_time"
    android:title="Lunch Alarm Time"
    android:defaultValue="12:00"
    android:summary="Set your desired time for the lunch alarm"
    android:dependency="alarm" />
</PreferenceScreen>
```

Since there is no decent graphical editor for preferences, Eclipse users will want to edit the XML directly.

The CheckBoxPreference, keyed as alarm, is not particularly unusual. Our TimePreference, keyed as alarm_time, has a few things worth mentioning:

- Since our custom class is not a standard preference class, the element name is the fully-qualified class name (apt.tutorial.TimePreference).

- It has android:defaultValue set to "12:00" (the ANSI standard time for lunch), in case the user toggles on the CheckBoxPreference but fails to update the time itself.

- By having android:dependency="alarm", the TimePreference will be disabled if the CheckBoxPreference is unchecked. Since that preference starts off unchecked, the TimePreference starts off disabled.

To collect these preferences from the user, all we have to do is adjust this resource. EditPreferences will automatically start collecting the new information. However, for other reasons, we will be making some modifications to EditPreferences, later in this tutorial.

Step #3: Set Up a Boot-Time Receiver

We are going to use AlarmManager for returning control to us every day when the user's specified lunchtime arrives. However, AlarmManager has one serious limitation when compared with cron or Windows Scheduled Tasks: on a reboot, the alarm schedule is wiped clean. Hence, many applications that intend to use `AlarmManager` will also need to get control at boot time, simply to set up the alarm again. So, we will add that logic to LunchList.

Create a new Java class, `OnBootReceiver.java`, in the `apt.tutorial` package, inheriting from `BroadcastReceiver`, that looks like this:

```
package apt.tutorial;

import android.content.BroadcastReceiver;
import android.content.Context;
import android.content.Intent;

public class OnBootReceiver extends BroadcastReceiver {
  @Override
  public void onReceive(Context ctxt, Intent intent) {
    // do something
  }
}
```

Eclipse users can right-click over `apt.tutorial` in the Package Explorer and choose New > Class from the context menu to bring up the new class dialog. Set the class name to be `OnBootReceiver` and set the parent class to be `android.content.BroadcastReceiver`. Then, click OK and fill in the implementation shown above.

The "real" work for a `BroadcastReceiver` is in the `onReceive()` method. In our case, that is a placeholder for the moment, to be addressed in the next step.

We also need to add a `<receiver>` element to the manifest, identifying that `OnBootReceiver` should get control when the system broadcasts the `BOOT_COMPLETED` event. However, to be able to register such a receiver, we need to hold the `RECEIVE_BOOT_COMPLETED` permission, so users know that we are trying to get control at boot time.

So, add that permission and the corresponding `<receiver>` element to `AndroidManifest.xml`, resulting in a file that should resemble:

```
<?xml version="1.0" encoding="utf-8"?>
<manifest xmlns:android="http://schemas.android.com/apk/res/android"
      package="apt.tutorial"
      android:versionCode="1"
      android:versionName="1.0">
```

```
    <uses-permission android:name="android.permission.INTERNET" />
    <uses-permission android:name="android.permission.ACCESS_NETWORK_STATE" />
    <uses-permission android:name="android.permission.ACCESS_FINE_LOCATION" />
    <uses-permission android:name="android.permission.RECEIVE_BOOT_COMPLETED"/>
    <application android:label="@string/app_name">
        <uses-library android:name="com.google.android.maps" />
        <activity android:name=".LunchList"
                android:label="@string/app_name">
            <intent-filter>
                <action android:name="android.intent.action.MAIN" />
                <category android:name="android.intent.category.LAUNCHER" />
            </intent-filter>
        </activity>
        <activity android:name=".DetailForm">
        </activity>
        <activity android:name=".EditPreferences">
        </activity>
        <activity android:name=".FeedActivity">
        </activity>
        <activity android:name=".RestaurantMap">
        </activity>
        <service android:name=".FeedService">
        </service>
        <receiver android:name=".OnBootReceiver" android:enabled="false">
            <intent-filter>
                <action android:name="android.intent.action.BOOT_COMPLETED"/>
            </intent-filter>
        </receiver>
    </application>
</manifest>
```

If you look closely, you will notice something a bit unusual about that `<receiver>` element: we have `android:enabled="false"`, meaning that the `BroadcastReceiver` is disabled by default. There is a reason for that, which we'll see in the next step.

Eclipse users can add this element by:

1. Double-clicking on the `AndroidManifest.xml` file to bring it up in the graphical editor

2. Clicking on the Application sub-tab

3. Clicking the Add... button to the right of the Application Nodes list

4. Choosing Receiver in the dialog and clicking OK

5. Clicking the Browse... button next to the Name field on the right and choosing `OnBootReceiver` as the implementation

6. Setting the "enabled" value to be `false` via the drop-down for the new element on the right

7. Saving your changes (e.g., <Ctrl>-<S>)

Step #4: Manage Preference Changes

When the user toggles on the alarm `CheckBoxPreference`, we want to set up `AlarmManager` to wake us up daily at the requested time.

If the user changes the alarm time (e.g., from 12:00 to 12:30), we want to cancel the existing alarm and set up a new one with `AlarmManager`.

If the user toggles off the alarm `CheckBoxPreference`, we want to cancel the existing alarm.

And, on a reboot, if the alarm was requested, we want to set up `AlarmManager`.

That sounds like a fair amount of work, but it is not really all that bad. There are two major operations (set and cancel alarms) and two major triggers (preference changes and a reboot).

First, let us set up the code to set and cancel the alarms. Since we need this both from whatever detects the preference changes and `OnBootReceiver`, we should have these methods be reachable from both places. The easiest way to do that is to make them static methods, and lacking a better spot, we may as well tuck those static methods on `OnBootReceiver`.

So, add these methods to `OnBootReceiver`:

```
public static void setAlarm(Context ctxt) {
  AlarmManager mgr=(AlarmManager)ctxt.getSystemService(Context.ALARM_SERVICE);
  Calendar cal=Calendar.getInstance();
  SharedPreferences prefs=PreferenceManager.getDefaultSharedPreferences(ctxt);
  String time=prefs.getString("alarm_time", "12:00");

  cal.set(Calendar.HOUR_OF_DAY, TimePreference.getHour(time));
```

```
  cal.set(Calendar.MINUTE, TimePreference.getMinute(time));
  cal.set(Calendar.SECOND, 0);
  cal.set(Calendar.MILLISECOND, 0);

  if (cal.getTimeInMillis()<System.currentTimeMillis()) {
    cal.add(Calendar.DAY_OF_YEAR, 1);
  }

  mgr.setRepeating(AlarmManager.RTC_WAKEUP, cal.getTimeInMillis(),
                   AlarmManager.INTERVAL_DAY,
                   getPendingIntent(ctxt));
}

public static void cancelAlarm(Context ctxt) {
  AlarmManager mgr=(AlarmManager)ctxt.getSystemService(Context.ALARM_SERVICE);

  mgr.cancel(getPendingIntent(ctxt));
}

private static PendingIntent getPendingIntent(Context ctxt) {
  Intent i=new Intent(ctxt, OnAlarmReceiver.class);

  return(PendingIntent.getBroadcast(ctxt, 0, i, 0));
}
```

Also, update onReceive() of OnBootReceiver to call our setAlarm() method:

```
@Override
public void onReceive(Context ctxt, Intent intent) {
  setAlarm(ctxt);
}
```

Now, let's take a look at what we have added.

setAlarm() will be called from onReceive(). Here, we get access to AlarmManager via getSystemService(), plus access our SharedPreferences. We find the alarm_time preference and create a Calendar object that has the requested hour and minute. However, we may need to adjust the day – if it is before the alarm time today, we want the next alarm to be today's; if it is after today's alarm should have gone off, we want the next alarm to be tomorrow's.

Then, we call setRepeating() on AlarmManager to actually schedule the alarm. We specify an RTC_WAKEUP alarm, meaning that we will get control at the time specified by the Calendar object, even if the device is asleep at the time. We specify INTERVAL_DAY, so the alarm will go off every 24 hours after the first one. And, we call our getPendingIntent() method to say what we are going to do when the alarm goes off – here, we are going to send a broadcast to another BroadcastReceiver, OnAlarmReceiver, that we will set up in the next step.

cancelAlarm() simply creates an equivalent PendingIntent and calls cancel() on AlarmManager. This can be called blindly, since if the alarm is not scheduled, AlarmManager will simply ignore the cancel request.

You will need to add the following imports:

- android.app.AlarmManager
- android.app.PendingIntent
- android.content.SharedPreferences
- android.preference.PreferenceManager
- java.util.Calendar

The complete OnBootReceiver class, with these changes, should look a bit like:

```
package apt.tutorial;

import android.app.AlarmManager;
import android.app.PendingIntent;
import android.content.BroadcastReceiver;
import android.content.Context;
import android.content.Intent;
import android.content.SharedPreferences;
import android.preference.PreferenceManager;
import java.util.Calendar;

public class OnBootReceiver extends BroadcastReceiver {
  public static void setAlarm(Context ctxt) {
    AlarmManager mgr=(AlarmManager)ctxt.getSystemService(Context.ALARM_SERVICE);
    Calendar cal=Calendar.getInstance();
    SharedPreferences prefs=PreferenceManager.getDefaultSharedPreferences(ctxt);
    String time=prefs.getString("alarm_time", "12:00");

    cal.set(Calendar.HOUR_OF_DAY, TimePreference.getHour(time));
    cal.set(Calendar.MINUTE, TimePreference.getMinute(time));
    cal.set(Calendar.SECOND, 0);
    cal.set(Calendar.MILLISECOND, 0);
```

```
    if (cal.getTimeInMillis()<System.currentTimeMillis()) {
      cal.add(Calendar.DAY_OF_YEAR, 1);
    }

    mgr.setRepeating(AlarmManager.RTC_WAKEUP, cal.getTimeInMillis(),
                    AlarmManager.INTERVAL_DAY,
                    getPendingIntent(ctxt));
  }

  public static void cancelAlarm(Context ctxt) {
    AlarmManager mgr=(AlarmManager)ctxt.getSystemService(Context.ALARM_SERVICE);

    mgr.cancel(getPendingIntent(ctxt));
  }

  private static PendingIntent getPendingIntent(Context ctxt) {
    Intent i=new Intent(ctxt, OnAlarmReceiver.class);

    return(PendingIntent.getBroadcast(ctxt, 0, i, 0));
  }

  @Override
  public void onReceive(Context ctxt, Intent intent) {
    setAlarm(ctxt);
  }
}
```

You will notice that we are blindly setting up the alarm via onReceive(). This would seem to be a mistake – after all, if the user has not requested the alarm, we should not be setting it up. Conversely, if you recall from the previous step that OnBootReceiver is initially disabled, that too would seem to be a bug, since we will never set up the alarm on a reboot. In truth, we will be toggling whether or not OnBootReceiver is enabled based upon preference changes, so it will only get control if it is needed. This means that users who elect to have alarms will have them even after a reboot, but users who skip the alarms get a slightly faster reboot, since our code will not be executed.

We also need to get control when the user changes their preferences. The standard way to do this is to register an OnSharedPreferenceChangeListener, which will be notified on SharedPreferences changes. Since the only place we are actually changing the SharedPreferences is from the EditPreferences activity, we may as well use OnSharedPreferenceChangeListener there.

Add the following code to EditPreferences:

```
@Override
public void onResume() {
  super.onResume();

  prefs=PreferenceManager.getDefaultSharedPreferences(this);
  prefs.registerOnSharedPreferenceChangeListener(onChange);
}

@Override
public void onPause() {
  prefs.unregisterOnSharedPreferenceChangeListener(onChange);

  super.onPause();
}

SharedPreferences.OnSharedPreferenceChangeListener onChange=
  new SharedPreferences.OnSharedPreferenceChangeListener() {
  public void onSharedPreferenceChanged(SharedPreferences prefs,
                                        String key) {
    if ("alarm".equals(key)) {
      boolean enabled=prefs.getBoolean(key, false);
      int flag=(enabled ?
                PackageManager.COMPONENT_ENABLED_STATE_ENABLED :
                PackageManager.COMPONENT_ENABLED_STATE_DISABLED);
      ComponentName component=new ComponentName(EditPreferences.this,
                                      OnBootReceiver.class);

      getPackageManager()
        .setComponentEnabledSetting(component,
                            flag,
                            PackageManager.DONT_KILL_APP);

      if (enabled) {
        OnBootReceiver.setAlarm(EditPreferences.this);
      }
      else {
        OnBootReceiver.cancelAlarm(EditPreferences.this);
      }
    }
    else if ("alarm_time".equals(key)) {
      OnBootReceiver.cancelAlarm(EditPreferences.this);
      OnBootReceiver.setAlarm(EditPreferences.this);
    }
  }
};
```

You will also need to add a `SharedPreferences` data member named `prefs`:

```
SharedPreferences prefs=null;
```

And, you will need to add some imports:

- android.content.ComponentName

- android.content.SharedPreferences

- android.content.pm.PackageManager

- android.preference.PreferenceManager

In onResume(), we get at the SharedPreferences and call registerOnSharedPreferenceChangeListener(), registering our OnSharedPreferenceChangeListener (named onChange). We unregister this in onPause(). That way, while the user has the activity up and is interacting with it, we will find out about changes in preferences.

Our OnSharedPreferenceChangeListener will be called with onSharedPreferenceChanged() whenever the user changes any of the preferences. If they toggle the alarm preference, we find out what the current setting is. Then, we call setComponentEnabledSetting() on the PackageManager to enable or disable OnBootReceiver. Since our alarm preference is set to be off by default, and our <receiver> element said that OnBootReceiver was disabled by default, we should remain in sync. Also, we call setAlarm() or cancelAlarm() depending on the state of the alarm preference. If they change the alarm_time preference, we know that the alarm preference must be on (otherwise, they cannot change alarm_time), so we cancel the old alarm and schedule a new one for the new time.

The complete edition of EditPreferences, with these changes, should resemble:

```
package apt.tutorial;

import android.app.Activity;
import android.content.ComponentName;
import android.content.SharedPreferences;
import android.content.pm.PackageManager;
import android.os.Bundle;
import android.preference.PreferenceActivity;
import android.preference.PreferenceManager;

public class EditPreferences extends PreferenceActivity {
  SharedPreferences prefs=null;

  @Override
  public void onCreate(Bundle savedInstanceState) {
    super.onCreate(savedInstanceState);
```

```
    addPreferencesFromResource(R.xml.preferences);
  }

  @Override
  public void onResume() {
    super.onResume();

    prefs=PreferenceManager.getDefaultSharedPreferences(this);
    prefs.registerOnSharedPreferenceChangeListener(onChange);
  }

  @Override
  public void onPause() {
    prefs.unregisterOnSharedPreferenceChangeListener(onChange);

    super.onPause();
  }

  SharedPreferences.OnSharedPreferenceChangeListener onChange=
    new SharedPreferences.OnSharedPreferenceChangeListener() {
    public void onSharedPreferenceChanged(SharedPreferences prefs,
                                  String key) {
      if ("alarm".equals(key)) {
        boolean enabled=prefs.getBoolean(key, false);
        int flag=(enabled ?
                  PackageManager.COMPONENT_ENABLED_STATE_ENABLED :
                  PackageManager.COMPONENT_ENABLED_STATE_DISABLED);
        ComponentName component=new ComponentName(EditPreferences.this,
                                  OnBootReceiver.class);

        getPackageManager()
          .setComponentEnabledSetting(component,
                                  flag,
                                  PackageManager.DONT_KILL_APP);

        if (enabled) {
          OnBootReceiver.setAlarm(EditPreferences.this);
        }
        else {
          OnBootReceiver.cancelAlarm(EditPreferences.this);
        }
      }
      else if ("alarm_time".equals(key)) {
        OnBootReceiver.cancelAlarm(EditPreferences.this);
        OnBootReceiver.setAlarm(EditPreferences.this);
      }
    }
  };
}
```

What is still missing is OnAlarmReceiver, which we will implement in the
next step.

Step #5: Display the Alarm

Given all the work done in the previous step, our `PendingIntent` scheduled with `AlarmManager` should be invoked at the specified time each day, if the user has enabled alarms.

Now, we just need to do something at that time.

The code above has the `PendingIntent` send a broadcast to trigger an `OnAlarmReceiver` class. That will not be able to directly display anything to the user, since a `BroadcastReceiver` has no direct access to the UI. However, it can start an activity. So, let's create an `AlarmActivity` that will be what we display to the user.

First, we need a layout, so create a `res/layout/alarm.xml` file that contains something like this:

```xml
<?xml version="1.0" encoding="utf-8"?>
<TextView
  xmlns:android="http://schemas.android.com/apk/res/android"
  android:layout_width="wrap_content"
  android:layout_height="wrap_content"
  android:text="It's time for lunch!"
  android:textSize="30sp"
  android:textStyle="bold"
/>
```

The `AlarmActivity` itself – another `Activity` subclass in the `apt.tutorial` package – can be very trivial:

```java
package apt.tutorial;

import android.app.Activity;
import android.os.Bundle;

public class AlarmActivity extends Activity {
  @Override
  public void onCreate(Bundle savedInstanceState) {
    super.onCreate(savedInstanceState);
    setContentView(R.layout.alarm);
  }
}
```

Eclipse users can create this activity this by right-clicking over the apt.tutorial package in Package Explorer, choosing New > Class from the context menu, then specifying AlarmActivity as the class name and android.app.Activity as the superclass.

Also create an OnAlarmReceiver subclass of BroadcastReceiver in the apt.tutorial package, and have it call startActivity() to bring up AlarmActivity:

```
package apt.tutorial;

import android.content.BroadcastReceiver;
import android.content.Context;
import android.content.Intent;

public class OnAlarmReceiver extends BroadcastReceiver {
  @Override
  public void onReceive(Context ctxt, Intent intent) {
    Intent i=new Intent(ctxt, AlarmActivity.class);

    i.setFlags(Intent.FLAG_ACTIVITY_NEW_TASK);

    ctxt.startActivity(i);
  }
}
```

Eclipse users can create this activity this by right-clicking over the apt.tutorial package in Package Explorer, choosing New > Class from the context menu, then specifying OnAlarmReceiver as the class name and android.content.BroadcastReceiver as the superclass.

We need to add FLAG_ACTIVITY_NEW_TASK to the Intent, because if we do not, our startActivity() call will fail with an error telling us to add FLAG_ACTIVITY_NEW_TASK. Calling startActivity() from someplace other than an activity typically requires this flag, though sometimes it is automatically added for you.

Finally, we need to add both of these to the manifest, via an <activity> and <receiver> element, respectively:

```
<?xml version="1.0" encoding="utf-8"?>
<manifest android:versionCode="1"
```

```
        android:versionName="1.0"
        package="apt.tutorial"
        xmlns:android="http://schemas.android.com/apk/res/android">

  <uses-permission android:name="android.permission.INTERNET" />
  <uses-permission android:name="android.permission.ACCESS_NETWORK_STATE" />
  <uses-permission android:name="android.permission.ACCESS_FINE_LOCATION" />
  <uses-permission android:name="android.permission.RECEIVE_BOOT_COMPLETED" />
  <supports-screens android:largeScreens="true"
                    android:normalScreens="true"
                    android:smallScreens="false" />
  <application android:label="@string/app_name">
    <uses-library android:name="com.google.android.maps" />
    <activity android:label="@string/app_name"
              android:name=".LunchList">
      <intent-filter>
        <action android:name="android.intent.action.MAIN" />
        <category android:name="android.intent.category.LAUNCHER" />
      </intent-filter>
    </activity>
    <activity android:name=".DetailForm"></activity>
    <activity android:name=".EditPreferences"></activity>
    <activity android:name=".FeedActivity"></activity>
    <activity android:name=".RestaurantMap"></activity>
    <activity android:name=".AlarmActivity"></activity>
    <service android:name=".FeedService"></service>
    <receiver android:enabled="false"
              android:name=".OnBootReceiver">
      <intent-filter>
        <action android:name="android.intent.action.BOOT_COMPLETED" />
      </intent-filter>
    </receiver>
    <receiver android:name=".OnAlarmReceiver"></receiver>
  </application>
</manifest>
```

Eclipse users can make this change by:

1. Double-clicking on the AndroidManifest.xml file to bring it up in the graphical editor

2. Clicking on the Application sub-tab

3. Clicking the Add... button to the right of the Application Nodes list

4. Choosing Activity in the dialog and clicking OK

5. Clicking the Browse... button next to the Name field and choosing AlarmActivity as the activity implementation

6. Clicking the Add... button again

7. Choosing Receiver in the dialog and clicking OK

8. Clicking the Browse... button next to the Name field and choosing `OnAlarmReceiver` as the `BroadcastReceiver` implementation

9. Saving your changes (e.g., <Ctrl>-<S>)

The net effect is that when the `AlarmManager` alarm "sounds", `OnAlarmReceiver` will get control and call `startActivity()` to open up `AlarmActivity`. We could have bypassed `OnAlarmReceiver`, by using a `getActivity()` `PendingIntent` and have it open `AlarmActivity` directly. The fact that we added `OnAlarmReceiver` suggests that maybe – just maybe – we will be doing something more in this area in a future tutorial.

If you compile and install LunchList, the preference screen will have our two new preferences:

Figure 80. The preferences, including a pair of new ones

Toggling the alarm on will enable the time preference:

Figure 81. The preferences, all enabled this time

Tapping on the time preference will bring up our TimePreference dialog with the TimePicker:

Figure 82. The TimePreference in action

When lunchtime rolls around, our AlarmActivity will appear out of nowhere:

Figure 83. The extremely bland AlarmActivity

Extra Credit

Here are some things you can try beyond those step-by-step instructions:

- Rather than rolling our own alarm, use `android.provider.AlarmClock` to set an alarm in the alarm clock app on the device.

- Give the user some way to dismiss today's alarm in advance – for example, they may have a lunch meeting scheduled before their normal time.

- Allow the user to specify the time not via a `TimePreference`, but via an `EditTextPreference`. Grumble as you work your way through parsing algorithms for various ways the user might encode the time. Curse under your breath when you realize that some users might try typing in "half past noon". Realize why we went through the trouble to create `TimePreference` in the first place.

- Use the curiously-named `Vibrator` system service to shake the phone when the alarm activity is displayed. You will need to hold the VIBRATE permission, and you will need a device that has a vibration motor (e.g., not the emulator and not some tablets like the Motorola XOOM).

• Make the alarm activity look more interesting.

Further Reading

You can learn more about the AlarmManager in the "Advanced Service Patterns" chapter of The Busy Coder's Guide to *Advanced* Android Development[55]. You can read more about creating custom preferences in "Creating Custom Dialogs and Preferences", also found in The Busy Coder's Guide to *Advanced* Android Development[56].

---

55 http://commonsware.com/AdvAndroid
56 http://commonsware.com/AdvAndroid

More Subtle Lunch Alarms

Displaying the lunchtime alarm via a full-screen activity certainly works, and if the user is looking at the screen, it will get their attention. However, it is also rather disruptive if they happen to be using the phone right that instant. For example, if they are typing a text message while driving, your alarm activity popping up out of nowhere might distract them enough to cause an accident.

So, in the interest of public safety, we should give the user an option to have a more subtle way to remind them to have lunch.

The best solution for this sort of a notification is a Notification, strangely enough, so this tutorial will have us tie into NotificationManager when the user asks for that style of lunch alarm.

Step-By-Step Instructions

First, you need to have completed the previous tutorial. If you are beginning the tutorials here, or if you wish to not use your existing work, you can download a ZIP file with all of the tutorial results, and you can copy the 19-Alarm edition of LunchList to use as a starting point. If you are using Eclipse, these instructions will help you load the project into a workspace.

Step #1: Collect Alarm Style Preference

Since we need to give the users a choice between displaying `AlarmActivity` or a `Notification`, and since we are collecting other alarm data via `SharedPreferences`, it seems like a good idea to simply add another preference, this time for alarm style.

Edit `res/xml/preferences.xml` to add a new `CheckBoxPreference` named `use_notification`. Make it depend upon the `alarm` preference (as does `alarm_time`), and have it default to `true`, just to be safe:

```xml
<PreferenceScreen
  xmlns:android="http://schemas.android.com/apk/res/android">
  <ListPreference
    android:key="sort_order"
    android:title="Sort Order"
    android:summary="Choose the order the list uses"
    android:entries="@array/sort_names"
    android:entryValues="@array/sort_clauses"
    android:dialogTitle="Choose a sort order" />
  <CheckBoxPreference
    android:key="alarm"
    android:title="Sound a Lunch Alarm"
    android:summary="Check if you want to know when it is time for lunch" />
  <apt.tutorial.TimePreference
    android:key="alarm_time"
    android:title="Lunch Alarm Time"
    android:defaultValue="12:00"
    android:summary="Set your desired time for the lunch alarm"
    android:dependency="alarm" />
  <CheckBoxPreference
    android:key="use_notification"
    android:title="Use a Notification"
    android:defaultValue="true"
    android:summary="Check if you want a status bar icon at lunchtime, or
uncheck for a full-screen notice"
    android:dependency="alarm" />
</PreferenceScreen>
```

Once again, Eclipse users should simply modify the XML directly.

There is nothing we need to do to the `EditPreferences` activity this time.

Step #2: Display the Alarm, Redux

The reason we set up the OnAlarmReceiver in the previous tutorial was to support alerting the user by either a Notification or AlarmActivity. OnAlarmReceiver can make the determination which approach to use, based on the use_notification preference value. If we want the Notification, it can raise that directly; otherwise, it can call startActivity() as before.

Modify onReceive() of OnAlarmReceiver as follows:

```
@Override
public void onReceive(Context ctxt, Intent intent) {
  SharedPreferences prefs=PreferenceManager.getDefaultSharedPreferences(ctxt);
  boolean useNotification=prefs.getBoolean("use_notification",
                                     true);

  if (useNotification) {
    NotificationManager mgr=
      (NotificationManager)ctxt.getSystemService(Context.NOTIFICATION_SERVICE);
    Notification note=new Notification(R.drawable.stat_notify_chat,
                               "It's time for lunch!",
                               System.currentTimeMillis());
    PendingIntent i=PendingIntent.getActivity(ctxt, 0,
                      new Intent(ctxt, AlarmActivity.class),
                                      0);

    note.setLatestEventInfo(ctxt, "LunchList",
                      "It's time for lunch! Aren't you hungry?",
                      i);
    note.flags|=Notification.FLAG_AUTO_CANCEL;

    mgr.notify(NOTIFY_ME_ID, note);
  }
  else {
    Intent i=new Intent(ctxt, AlarmActivity.class);

    i.setFlags(Intent.FLAG_ACTIVITY_NEW_TASK);

    ctxt.startActivity(i);
  }
}
```

You will also need a static data member for NOTIFY_ME_ID, a locally-unique integer to identify this Notification from any others we might raise:

```
private static final int NOTIFY_ME_ID=1337;
```

You will need a new drawable resource, res/drawable/stat_notify_chat.png, perhaps obtained from your Android SDK.

You will also need to add some imports:

- android.app.Notification
- android.app.NotificationManager
- android.app.PendingIntent
- android.content.SharedPreferences
- android.preference.PreferenceManager

First, we get the SharedPreferences and look up use_notification. If use_notification is false, we continue as before, calling startActivity().

If use_notification is true, however, we:

- Obtain access to the NotificationManager via getSystemService()

- Create a Notification object, indicating the icon, the "ticker text" (which appears briefly in the status bar when the Notification is displayed), and the timestamp associated with the event

- Create a getActivity() PendingIntent for our AlarmActivity

- Attaching that PendingIntent to the Notification via setLatestEventInfo(), where we also supply a title and description to go in the tile for this Notification in the status drawer

- Add the FLAG_AUTO_CANCEL flag to the Notification, so tapping on its tile will automatically dismiss the Notification

- Call notify() on NotificationManager with our Notification, to have it be displayed

The complete OnAlarmReceiver with these modifications should resemble:

```
package apt.tutorial;

import android.app.Notification;
import android.app.NotificationManager;
import android.app.PendingIntent;
import android.content.BroadcastReceiver;
```

```
import android.content.Context;
import android.content.Intent;
import android.content.SharedPreferences;
import android.preference.PreferenceManager;

public class OnAlarmReceiver extends BroadcastReceiver {
  private static final int NOTIFY_ME_ID=1337;

  @Override
  public void onReceive(Context ctxt, Intent intent) {
    SharedPreferences prefs=PreferenceManager.getDefaultSharedPreferences(ctxt);
    boolean useNotification=prefs.getBoolean("use_notification",
                                      true);

    if (useNotification) {
      NotificationManager mgr=
        (NotificationManager)ctxt.getSystemService(Context.NOTIFICATION_SERVICE)
;

      Notification note=new Notification(R.drawable.stat_notify_chat,
                                  "It's time for lunch!",
                                  System.currentTimeMillis());
      PendingIntent i=PendingIntent.getActivity(ctxt, 0,
                          new Intent(ctxt, AlarmActivity.class),
                                      0);

      note.setLatestEventInfo(ctxt, "LunchList",
                          "It's time for lunch! Aren't you hungry?",
                          i);
      note.flags|=Notification.FLAG_AUTO_CANCEL;

      mgr.notify(NOTIFY_ME_ID, note);
    }
    else {
      Intent i=new Intent(ctxt, AlarmActivity.class);

      i.setFlags(Intent.FLAG_ACTIVITY_NEW_TASK);

      ctxt.startActivity(i);
    }
  }
}
```

If you compile and install the application, the preference screen will show the new preference:

Figure 84. The new notification style preference

If you choose the Notification mode, when lunchtime arrives, your Notification will appear in the status bar:

Figure 85. The notification, right as it is being added, showing the "ticker text"

Sliding down the drawer will show the entry for the Notification:

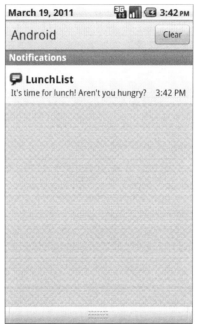

Figure 86. The notification drawer, showing the full notification

Tapping that entry will bring up `AlarmActivity`, as if `OnAlarmReceiver` had launched it directly.

On an Android 3.x device, though, the look will be somewhat different. The `Notification` will appear initially as a bubble:

Figure 87. The notification on an Android 3.0 tablet

The drawer now appears when tapping on the clock in the lower-right corner:

Figure 88. The notification drawer on an Android 3.0 tablet

Tapping on either the bubble or the item in the drawer will trigger `AlarmActivity`.

Extra Credit

Here are some things you can try beyond those step-by-step instructions:

- Experiment with the LED options with a `Notification` (e.g., `ledARGB`). Note, though, that not all devices have LEDs, and those that do may not support third-party applications playing with the LEDs. You will need to add the `FLAG_SHOW_LIGHTS` flag as well for this to work.

- Play with the sound field on `Notification`, pointing it to a file on external storage containing an MP3 that you want to have played when the `Notification` is displayed.

Further Reading

Notifications are covered in the "Alerting Users Via Notifications" chapter of The Busy Coder's Guide to Android Development[57].

---

57 http://commonsware.com/Android

A Restaurant In Your Own Home

In this tutorial, we will create an "app widget", the term Android uses for interactive elements a user can add to their home screen. In particular, we will create an app widget that shows a random restaurant out of the LunchList database. It will also have a button to choose another random restaurant. Also, if the user taps on the name of the restaurant, we will open up the detail form activity for that restaurant.

Step-By-Step Instructions

First, you need to have completed the previous LunchList tutorial. If you are starting the tutorials here, or if you wish to not use your existing work, you can download a ZIP file with all of the tutorial results, and you can copy the 20-Notification edition of LunchList to use as a starting point. If you are using Eclipse, these instructions will help you load the project into a workspace.

Step #1: Find An App Widget Background and Some Icons

We are going to need a background to use for our app widget, so its contents do not seem to float in empty space in the home screen. Ideally, this background is resizeable, so we have a choice of using an XML-defined drawable resource, or a nine-patch PNG.

If you examine the `21-AppWidget` project in the book's source code repository, you will see that there is a `widget_frame.9.png` file in `LunchList/res/drawable`. That nine-patch image works nicely for your app widget. It is actually a clone of the nine-patch used as the background for the `Toast` class, culled from the Android open source project. You are welcome to use this image or find (or create) another of your choosing. If you wish to download it directly, here is the link[58].

You will also need an icon, which will go alongside the `LunchList` name in Android's list of available widgets. Find some likely icon (32px square or so) and add it as `LunchList/res/drawable/icon.png`. You will also need a similarly-sized icon for our choose-another-random-restaurant `ImageButton`, named `LunchList/res/drawable/ff.png`. You are welcome to copy these icons from the `21-AppWidget` project from the book's source code as well, if you wish, or here is a link to icon.png[59] and ff.png[60] respectively.

Step #2: Design the App Widget Layout

Next, we need to define a layout for our app widgets. App widgets are created via layout files, no different than activities, `ListView` rows, and the like. Right now, all we want is to show the name of the app widget, inside of something to serve as the widget's background.

So, create a `LunchList/res/layout/widget.xml` file with the following content:

```
<?xml version="1.0" encoding="utf-8"?>
<RelativeLayout xmlns:android="http://schemas.android.com/apk/res/android"
  android:layout_width="match_parent"
  android:layout_height="match_parent"
  android:background="@drawable/widget_frame"
```

---

58 https://github.com/commonsguy/cw-lunchlist/raw/master/21-
    AppWidget/LunchList/res/drawable/widget_frame.9.png
59 https://github.com/commonsguy/cw-lunchlist/raw/master/21-
    AppWidget/LunchList/res/drawable/icon.png
60 https://github.com/commonsguy/cw-lunchlist/raw/master/21-
    AppWidget/LunchList/res/drawable/ff.png

```
>
  <TextView android:id="@+id/name"
    android:layout_width="wrap_content"
    android:layout_height="wrap_content"
    android:layout_centerVertical="true"
    android:layout_alignParentLeft="true"
    android:layout_toLeftOf="@+id/next"
    android:textSize="10pt"
    android:textColor="#FFFFFFFF"
  />
  <ImageButton android:id="@id/next"
    android:layout_width="wrap_content"
    android:layout_height="wrap_content"
    android:layout_centerVertical="true"
    android:layout_alignParentRight="true"
    android:src="@drawable/ff"
  />
</RelativeLayout>
```

Here we have a RelativeLayout wrapping around a TextView (to hold the name of the restaurant) and an ImageButton (to let the user pick another random restaurant). The RelativeLayout has our background image, to ensure that the TextView and ImageButton have a consistent background, as opposed to whatever might be on the home screen's wallpaper.

Unfortunately for Eclipse users, the drag-and-drop support for RelativeLayout is fairly broken, and so you will need to edit the XML directly. Eclipse users can create the empty file by right-clicking over res/layout/ in the Package Explorer, choosing New > File from the context menu, giving the new file a name of widget.xml, and clicking Finish.

Step #3: Add an (Empty) AppWidgetProvider

Next, we need to create an AppWidgetProvider. AppWidgetProvider, a subclass of BroadcastReceiver, provides the base implementation for an app widget and gives us lifecycle methods like onUpdate() we can override to add custom behavior.

For now, though, just create an empty AppWidgetProvider implementation, with the truly unique name of AppWidget:

```
package apt.tutorial;

import android.appwidget.AppWidgetProvider;

public class AppWidget extends AppWidgetProvider {
}
```

Eclipse users can right-click over `apt.tutorial` in the Package Explorer and choose New > Class from the context menu to bring up the new class dialog. Set the class name to be `AppWidget` and set the parent class to be `android.appwidget.AppWidgetProvider`. Then, click OK and fill in the implementation shown above.

Step #4: Add the Widget Metadata

As part of wiring our app widget into our application, we need to create a "widget metadata" XML document. This file provides additional configuration definitions for the app widget, for things that cannot readily go into the manifest.

So, create a `LunchList/res/xml/widget_provider.xml` file with the following content:

```
<?xml version="1.0" encoding="utf-8"?>
<appwidget-provider xmlns:android="http://schemas.android.com/apk/res/android"
  android:minWidth="300dip"
  android:minHeight="79dip"
  android:updatePeriodMillis="1800000"
  android:initialLayout="@layout/widget"
/>
```

Eclipse users can create the empty file by right-clicking over `res/xml/` in the Package Explorer, choosing New > File from the context menu, giving the new file a name of `widget_provider.xml`, and clicking Finish. Then, give that newly-created file the content shown above.

Here, we provide a height and width suggestion, which Android will convert into a number of "cells" given the actual screen size and density. Our height and width will give us a 4x1 cell widget, which means it will take up the entire width of a portrait mode screen.

The metadata also indicates the starting layout to use (the one we created earlier in this tutorial) and an "update period", which tells Android how frequently to ask us to update the app widget's contents (set to 30 minutes, in milliseconds).

Step #5: Update the Manifest

Now, we can add our widget to the manifest file. Edit AndroidManifest.xml to look like the following:

```xml
<?xml version="1.0" encoding="utf-8"?>
<manifest xmlns:android="http://schemas.android.com/apk/res/android"
      package="apt.tutorial"
      android:versionCode="1"
      android:versionName="1.0">
  <uses-permission android:name="android.permission.INTERNET" />
  <uses-permission android:name="android.permission.ACCESS_NETWORK_STATE" />
  <uses-permission android:name="android.permission.ACCESS_FINE_LOCATION" />
  <uses-permission android:name="android.permission.RECEIVE_BOOT_COMPLETED"/>
  <supports-screens
        android:xlargeScreens="true"
        android:largeScreens="true"
        android:normalScreens="true"
        android:smallScreens="false"
  />
  <application android:label="@string/app_name">
      <uses-library android:name="com.google.android.maps" />
      <activity android:name=".LunchList"
                android:label="@string/app_name">
          <intent-filter>
              <action android:name="android.intent.action.MAIN" />
              <category android:name="android.intent.category.LAUNCHER" />
          </intent-filter>
      </activity>
      <activity android:name=".DetailForm">
      </activity>
      <activity android:name=".EditPreferences">
      </activity>
      <activity android:name=".FeedActivity">
      </activity>
      <activity android:name=".RestaurantMap">
      </activity>
      <activity android:name=".AlarmActivity">
      </activity>

      <service android:name=".FeedService">
      </service>

      <receiver android:name=".OnBootReceiver" android:enabled="false">
```

```
                    <intent-filter>
                        <action android:name="android.intent.action.BOOT_COMPLETED"/>
                    </intent-filter>
                </receiver>
                <receiver android:name=".OnAlarmReceiver">
                </receiver>
                <receiver android:name=".AppWidget"
                    android:label="@string/app_name"
                    android:icon="@drawable/icon">
                    <intent-filter>
                        <action android:name="android.appwidget.action.APPWIDGET_UPDATE"
/>
                    </intent-filter>
                    <meta-data
                        android:name="android.appwidget.provider"
                        android:resource="@xml/widget_provider"
                    />
                </receiver>
            </application>
</manifest>
```

In particular, note the new `<receiver>` element towards the bottom – that is where we are teaching Android where our code and metadata resides for this app widget. The filter for APPWIDGET_UPDATE means that we will get control when Android wants us to update the app widget's contents, such as when the app widget is first added to the home screen.

Eclipse users can add this element by:

1. Double-clicking on the `AndroidManifest.xml` file to bring it up in the graphical editor

2. Clicking on the Application sub-tab

3. Clicking the Add... button to the right of the Application Nodes list

4. Choosing Receiver in the dialog and clicking OK

5. Clicking the Browse... button next to the Name field on the right and choosing `AppWidget` as the implementation

6. With the `AppWidget` receiver item selected in the Application Nodes list, click the Add... button and choose "Intent Filter" in the selection dialog

7. With the newly-added `Intent` filter selected in the Application Nodes list, click the Add... button and choose Action in the selection dialog

8. Type the value `android.appwidget.action.APPWIDGET_UPDATE` in the Name combobox, since it may not be one of the choices available in the drop-down

9. Saving your changes (e.g., <Ctrl>-<S>)

At this point, you can compile and install the updated version of the application. Then, long-tap somewhere on the background of your home screen, to bring up the list of options for things to add to it:

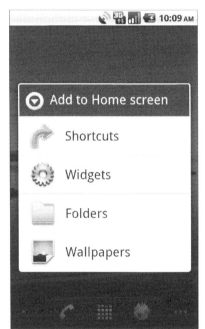

Figure 89. The list of things to add to the home screen

Choose Widgets, to bring up the list of available widgets:

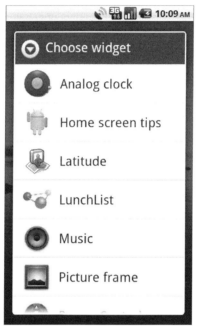

Figure 90. The list of available widgets

Then, choose our LunchList widget. It will show up, but have no contents, because we have not defined any contents yet.

Step #6: Delegate to an IntentService

For simple app widgets, you can update the app widget's UI just in onUpdate() of your AppWidgetProvider.

However, in order to load the random restaurant, we need to query the database to find such a restaurant. Ideally, we do not do this on the main application thread, yet onUpdate() will be called on the main application thread.

For app widgets that have slow operations like flash I/O or network I/O, the recommended pattern is to have the AppWidgetProvider delegate to an IntentService to do the real work. That way, the work will automatically be performed on a background thread.

Modify `AppWidget` to look like this:

```
package apt.tutorial;

import android.appwidget.AppWidgetManager;
import android.appwidget.AppWidgetProvider;
import android.content.Context;
import android.content.Intent;

public class AppWidget extends AppWidgetProvider {
  @Override
  public void onUpdate(Context ctxt,
                       AppWidgetManager mgr,
                       int[] appWidgetIds) {
    ctxt.startService(new Intent(ctxt, WidgetService.class));
  }
}
```

Here, we are simply calling `startService()` on our `IntentService`, so it will wake up and do what is needed.

You will need to add imports for:

- `android.appwidget.AppWidgetManager`
- `android.appwidget.AppWidgetProvider`
- `android.content.Context`
- `android.content.Intent`

Step #7: Show a Random Restaurant

Finally, we need to implement the `WidgetService` that will actually display a random restaurant in the app widget. To do this, we will override the `onUpdate()` method in our `AppWidget` class and have it do the database I/O to find a random restaurant.

With that in mind, add the following `WidgetService` class to the LunchList project, in the `apt.tutorial` package:

```
package apt.tutorial;

import android.app.IntentService;
import android.app.PendingIntent;
```

```
import android.appwidget.AppWidgetManager;
import android.content.ComponentName;
import android.content.Context;
import android.content.Intent;
import android.database.Cursor;
import android.database.sqlite.SQLiteDatabase;
import android.widget.RemoteViews;

public class WidgetService extends IntentService {
  public WidgetService() {
    super("WidgetService");
  }

  @Override
  public void onHandleIntent(Intent intent) {
    ComponentName me=new ComponentName(this, AppWidget.class);
    RemoteViews updateViews=new RemoteViews("apt.tutorial",
                                    R.layout.widget);
    RestaurantHelper helper=new RestaurantHelper(this);
    AppWidgetManager mgr=AppWidgetManager.getInstance(this);

    try {
      Cursor c=helper
                .getReadableDatabase()
                .rawQuery("SELECT COUNT(*) FROM restaurants", null);

      c.moveToFirst();

      int count=c.getInt(0);

      c.close();

      if (count>0) {
        int offset=(int)(count*Math.random());
        String args[]={String.valueOf(offset)};

        c=helper
            .getReadableDatabase()
            .rawQuery("SELECT _ID, name FROM restaurants LIMIT 1 OFFSET ?",
args);
        c.moveToFirst();
        updateViews.setTextViewText(R.id.name, c.getString(1));

        Intent i=new Intent(this, DetailForm.class);

        i.putExtra(LunchList.ID_EXTRA, c.getString(0));

        PendingIntent pi=PendingIntent.getActivity(this, 0, i,
                                            PendingIntent.FLAG_UPDATE_CURR
ENT);

        updateViews.setOnClickPendingIntent(R.id.name, pi);

        c.close();
```

```
    }
    else {
      updateViews.setTextViewText(R.id.title,
                            this.getString(R.string.empty));
    }
  }
  finally {
    helper.close();
  }

  Intent i=new Intent(this, WidgetService.class);
  PendingIntent pi=PendingIntent.getService(this, 0, i, 0);

  updateViews.setOnClickPendingIntent(R.id.next, pi);
  mgr.updateAppWidget(me, updateViews);
  }
}
```

Eclipse users can right-click over in the Package Explorer and choose New > Class from the context menu to bring up the new class dialog. Set the class name to be WidgetService and set the parent class to be android.app.IntentService. Then, click OK and fill in the implementation shown above.

Here, we:

- Create a RemoteViews object, which represents a set of GUI "commands" to invoke on the home screen that defines how to modify the app widget

- Get access to an AppWidgetManager, which is the bridge between our application and the home screen hosting the app widget

- Open up a database connection

- Find out how many restaurants there are via a SQL query

- Load a random restaurant via another SQL query

- Set the name TextView in the app widget (via the RemoteViews) to have either the name of the restaurant or an error message

- If there is a restaurant, set up a PendingIntent to be triggered when the user taps on the name of the restaurant, set to start up the DetailForm with the ID_EXTRA in place to bring up the proper restaurant

- Set up a `PendingIntent` to be triggered when the user taps on the `ImageButton` that will simply invoke `WidgetService` again, thereby updating the app widget with a random restaurant again

- Update the app widget itself

You will also need to add a new string resource, named `empty`, that will go into the app widget if there is no restaurant available (e.g., the database is empty):

```xml
<?xml version="1.0" encoding="utf-8"?>
<resources>
    <string name="app_name">LunchList</string>
    <string name="empty">No restaurants!</string>
</resources>
```

Then, update the `AndroidManifest.xml` again, this time adding in a `<service>` element for a to-be-defined `WidgetService`:

```xml
<?xml version="1.0" encoding="utf-8"?>
<manifest android:versionCode="1"
          android:versionName="1.0"
          package="apt.tutorial"
          xmlns:android="http://schemas.android.com/apk/res/android">

 <uses-permission android:name="android.permission.INTERNET" />
 <uses-permission android:name="android.permission.ACCESS_NETWORK_STATE" />
 <uses-permission android:name="android.permission.ACCESS_FINE_LOCATION" />
 <uses-permission android:name="android.permission.RECEIVE_BOOT_COMPLETED" />
 <supports-screens android:largeScreens="true"
                    android:normalScreens="true"
                    android:smallScreens="false" />
 <application android:label="@string/app_name">
   <uses-library android:name="com.google.android.maps" />
   <activity android:label="@string/app_name"
             android:name=".LunchList">
     <intent-filter>
       <action android:name="android.intent.action.MAIN" />
       <category android:name="android.intent.category.LAUNCHER" />
     </intent-filter>
   </activity>
   <activity android:name=".DetailForm"></activity>
   <activity android:name=".EditPreferences"></activity>
   <activity android:name=".FeedActivity"></activity>
   <activity android:name=".RestaurantMap"></activity>
   <activity android:name=".AlarmActivity"></activity>
   <service android:name=".FeedService"></service>
   <service android:name=".WidgetService"></service>
   <receiver android:enabled="false"
```

```
                  android:name=".OnBootReceiver">
    <intent-filter>
      <action android:name="android.intent.action.BOOT_COMPLETED" />
    </intent-filter>
  </receiver>
  <receiver android:name=".OnAlarmReceiver"></receiver>
  <receiver android:icon="@drawable/icon"
            android:label="@string/app_name"
            android:name=".AppWidget">
    <intent-filter>
      <action android:name="android.appwidget.action.APPWIDGET_UPDATE" />
    </intent-filter>
    <meta-data android:name="android.appwidget.provider"
               android:resource="@xml/widget_provider" />
  </receiver>
 </application>
</manifest>
```

Eclipse users can add this element by:

1. Double-clicking on the `AndroidManifest.xml` file to bring it up in the graphical editor

2. Clicking on the Application sub-tab

3. Clicking the Add... button to the right of the Application Nodes list

4. Choosing Service in the dialog and clicking OK

5. Clicking the Browse... button next to the Name field on the right and choosing `WidgetService` as the implementation

6. Saving your changes (e.g., <Ctrl>-<S>)

Make sure you have at least two restaurants in `LunchList` – otherwise, clicking the button is guaranteed to have no visible effect. Even with two restaurants, there is a 50% chance that tapping the button will randomly choose the same restaurant again

At this point, compile and reinstall the application. Also, if you got rid of the empty app widget, add a new one to your home screen. You should see the name of one of your restaurants:

Figure 91. The app widget, showing the random restaurant

Tapping the name of the restaurant will launch the DetailForm activity, while tapping the ImageButton will update the app widget in place with a random restaurant (hopefully different than the one presently shown).

Extra Credit

Here are some things you can try beyond those step-by-step instructions:

- Add other widgets to the app widget layout, such as a logo icon

- Reduce the font size of the name and add a second TextView to the layout to show the restaurant's address

- Experiment with other widget sizes instead of the 4x1 cell format used in the widget metadata

- Rather than show a random restaurant, keep track of the last restaurant viewed and cycle through them in progression, looping back to the first in the list when you reach the end. Consider adding a second ImageButton to move backwards through the list.

- Add another button that, when clicked, displays a Toast of the notes for the currently-viewed restaurant.

Further Reading

App widgets are covered in a chapter of The Busy Coder's Guide to *Advanced* Android Development[61].

---

61 http://commonsware.com/AdvAndroid

A Lunch *List* At Home

The previous tutorial set up an app widget, showing one restaurant at a time. For quite a while, this was about as good as we could get with app widgets – there was no way to show the full list of restaurants right on the home screen.

In the words of Bob Dylan, "the times, they are a-changin'".

The new Honeycomb UI introduced with Android 3.0 now allows ListView to be used with app widgets. Of course, this only works on newer versions of Android, not older ones. So, if we want to take advantage of this, we will need two implementations of the app widget layout and logic: one for Android 1.x/2.x, and one for Android 3.0+.

On the other hand, it allows us to actually have a lunch *list* on the home screen, and portraying a list of restaurants is the point behind the app, so it would seem worthwhile to go through this effort.

Step-By-Step Instructions

First, you need to have completed the previous LunchList tutorial. If you are starting the tutorials here, or if you wish to not use your existing work, you can download a ZIP file with all of the tutorial results, and you can copy the 21-AppWidget edition of LunchList to use as a starting point. If you are using

Eclipse, these instructions will help you load the project into a workspace –
but *please* read through this tutorial first, particularly Step #1 below.

Step #1: Update Your Build Environment

Your build environment needs two things:

1. It needs an Android 3.x SDK, so you can use Android 3.x capabilities
   (carefully!) in your application

2. It needs something to test the resulting app upon, which could
   either be an Android 3.x device or an Android 3.x emulator

First, open up the Android SDK and AVD Manager. In Eclipse, this is in the
Window menu. Outside of Eclipse, run the android command. Check your
list of installed packages and see if you have:

- SDK Platform Android 3.0, API 11; or Android 3.1, API 12, or Android
  3.2, API 13

- Google APIs by Google Inc., Android API 11 or API 12 or API 13

If you are missing one or both, visit the Available Packages portion of the
SDK and AVD Manager and download the missing pieces. The plain
Android SDK will be in the "Android Repository", while the Google APIs
will be in the "Third party Add-ons" area. You will want the API levels to
match (i.e., if you have SDK Platform for API 13, you want the Google APIs
for API 13 as well).

Then, if you have a piece of Android 3.x hardware that you will be using for
these tutorials, skip ahead to Step #2. Otherwise, in the Android SDK and
AVD Manager (in Eclipse, available via Window | Android SDK and AVD
Manager from the main menu), click on the Virtual Devices option on the
right, and check your list of prepared AVDs. If you have one for "Google
APIs (Google Inc.)" for Android 3.x, that will be the AVD you will want to
use in an emulator for testing the app. If not, click the New... button and
define an AVD for "Google APIs (Google Inc.) - API Level 11" (or 12 or 13,
whichever you downloaded). Be sure to give it a small virtual SD card
(32MB should suffice) for use in later tutorials.

Note that the Android 3.x emulator is **extremely slow** as of the time of this writing. On most development hardware, it will be unusable. If you have access to Android 3.x hardware, using that is strongly encouraged.

Step #2: Update Your Provider and Widget Layout XML

If we want to have a version of our app widget that looks and works distinctly differently from the original app widget, we will need widget provider and widget layout XML resources to match. However, for any given device, we only want one app widget to be available – the "classic" app widget for Android 1.x and 2.x devices, and the new ListView-based app widget for Android 3.0. Hence, we do not want have two separate app widget definitions... yet we need two separate app widget definitions.

This conundrum is solved by version-specific resource sets.

You can add a -vNN suffix to a resource directory, where NN is an API level (e.g., 11). The resources contained in that resource directory will only be used on devices running that version of Android *or higher*. Hence, we can create -v11 resources for our Honeycomb-based app widget, with the same names as we used for the original resources for the original app widget. On an Android 3.x environment, the -v11 versions of the resources will be used. On an Android 1.x or 2.x device, the original versions of the resources will be used.

With that in mind, create a res/xml-v11/ directory in your project (Eclipse users: right-click on the res/ directory and choose New > Folder from the context menu), and create a widget_provider.xml file in there with the following content:

```
<?xml version="1.0" encoding="utf-8"?>
<appwidget-provider xmlns:android="http://schemas.android.com/apk/res/android"
  android:minWidth="220dip"
  android:minHeight="220dip"
  android:updatePeriodMillis="1800000"
  android:initialLayout="@layout/widget"
/>
```

Eclipse users can create the empty file by right-clicking over res/xmlv-11/ in the Package Explorer, choosing New > File from the context menu, giving the new file a name of widget_provider.xml, and clicking Finish. Then, give that newly-created file the content shown above.

Other than declaring the width and height to be 220dip (3 cells), the provider XML is no different than what we had originally.

Then, create a res/layout-v11/ directory in your project, and create a widget.xml file in there with the following content:

```
<?xml version="1.0" encoding="utf-8"?>
<ListView xmlns:android="http://schemas.android.com/apk/res/android"
  android:id="@+id/restaurants"
  android:layout_width="match_parent"
  android:layout_height="match_parent"
  android:layout_margin="3dp"
  android:background="@drawable/widget_frame"
/>
```

Here, we declare that the UI for our app widget will be a ListView. As with the original widget, we set up a background, so there is contrast between the ListView and whatever wallpaper the user may have on the home screen. Otherwise, this layout file is unremarkable... until we start trying to use it from the app widget code.

Eclipse users can create this new layout by:

1. Creating the res/layout-v11/ directory by right-clicking on the res/ directory and choose New > Folder from the context menu

2. Right-clicking over the res/layout-v11/ directory, choosing New > File from the context menu, giving the file the name of widget.xml, and clicking Finish

3. Dragging a ListView from the Composite section of the tool palette into the main editing area

4. Right-clicking over the ListView, choosing "Edit ID..." from the context menu, and giving it a value of restaurants

5. Right-clicking over the ListView, choosing Properties > Layout margin... from the context menu, and specifying a value of 3dp

6. Right-clicking over the ListView, choosing Properties > Background from the context menu, and choosing the widget_frame drawable resource

7. Saving your changes (e.g., <Ctrl>-<S>)

Also, change your build target to API Level 11 (or 12 or 13, whatever you downloaded). In Eclipse, the build target is in the Android section of the project properties, which you get to from the Project | Properties menu:

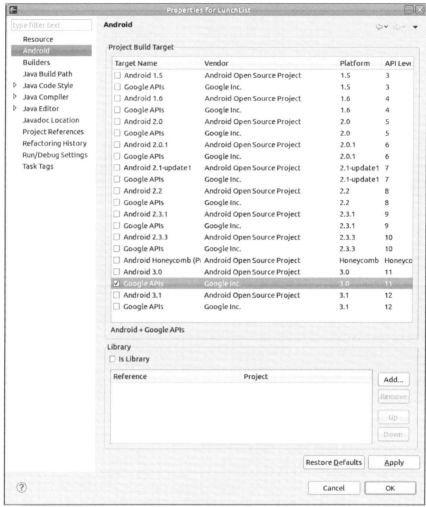

Figure 92. The Eclipse Project Properties dialog

Outside of Eclipse, change the `default.properties` file in the root of your project to have a target defined as:

```
target=Google Inc.:Google APIs:11
```

(substituting 12 or 13 if that is what you downloaded)

If you compile and install this version of LunchList on an Android 1.x or 2.x device or emulator, it should behave as it did before.

Step #3: Detect Which App Widget To Display

If we tried running this version of LunchList on an Android 3.x device or emulator, it will happily crash.

Why?

All our Java code is expecting the old widget layout. It will not be able to use the new widget layout with the ListView, yet that will be the layout that is loaded.

Hence, we need to route our Honeycomb-specific app widget logic through a different code path. The simplest way to do that is to add a bit of smarts to our onUpdate() method in AppWidget. Modify onUpdate() to look like this:

```
@Override
public void onUpdate(Context ctxt,
                     AppWidgetManager mgr,
                     int[] appWidgetIds) {
  if (Build.VERSION.SDK_INT>=Build.VERSION_CODES.HONEYCOMB) {
    onHCUpdate(ctxt, mgr, appWidgetIds);
  }
  else {
    ctxt.startService(new Intent(ctxt, WidgetService.class));
  }
}
```

Here, we use the Build class to detect if we are on HONEYCOMB or higher. If so, we route the update logic to an as-yet-unwritten onHCUpdate() method. Otherwise, we proceed as normal.

Step #4: Implement and Connect to the Remote-ViewsService

If you recall from earlier tutorials, providing the contents for a ListView came in the form of an Adapter. The Adapter was responsible for defining the rows in the ListView, on demand, based on various events (initial load of the list, user scrolling, etc.).

With a ListView-based app widget, the same basic needs exist. We somehow have to tell the ListView how many rows there are and supply the rows themselves as needed. However, just as writing a regular app widget is not nearly as straight-forward as is writing the same logic in an activity, using an AdapterView in an app widget is significantly more complex than is using an AdapterView in an activity.

However, if you have made it this far through the book, you are presumably up to the challenge. Or, possibly, you are simply a glutton for punishment.

In the previous step, we made a call to an onHCUpdate() method. Let's add the implementation of that method to the AppWidget class, as shown below:

```
public void onHCUpdate(Context ctxt, AppWidgetManager appWidgetManager,
                       int[] appWidgetIds) {
  for (int i=0; i<appWidgetIds.length; i++) {
    Intent svcIntent=new Intent(ctxt, ListWidgetService.class);

    svcIntent.putExtra(AppWidgetManager.EXTRA_APPWIDGET_ID, appWidgetIds[i]);
    svcIntent.setData(Uri.parse(svcIntent.toUri(Intent.URI_INTENT_SCHEME)));

    RemoteViews widget=new RemoteViews(ctxt.getPackageName(),
                                       R.layout.widget);

    widget.setRemoteAdapter(appWidgetIds[i], R.id.restaurants,
                            svcIntent);

    Intent clickIntent=new Intent(ctxt, DetailForm.class);
    PendingIntent clickPI=PendingIntent
                           .getActivity(ctxt, 0,
                                        clickIntent,
                                        PendingIntent.FLAG_UPDATE_CURRENT);

    widget.setPendingIntentTemplate(R.id.restaurants, clickPI);

    appWidgetManager.updateAppWidget(appWidgetIds[i], widget);
  }

  super.onUpdate(ctxt, appWidgetManager, appWidgetIds);
}
```

What this method does is:

- Iterates over all of the app widgets defined on the home screen that we are implementing (typically only one, but perhaps some user really likes lunch and therefore has several copies of the app widget)

- Creates an Intent, following the rules for AdapterView-based app widgets, that identifies a RemoteViewsService that we will implement shortly, named ListWidgetService

- Creates a RemoteViews for the app widget, attaching the Intent from the previous step as being the "remote adapter" for the AdapterView in our layout

- Creates a PendingIntent, identifying that we want clicks on items in the ListView to route to our DetailForm activity, and associate that as the "PendingIntent template" for the rows in the ListView

- Updates the app widget on the screen as with any other app widget

The entire AppWidget class, after all these changes, should resemble:

```
package apt.tutorial;

import android.app.PendingIntent;
import android.appwidget.AppWidgetManager;
import android.appwidget.AppWidgetProvider;
import android.content.Context;
import android.content.Intent;
import android.net.Uri;
import android.os.Build;
import android.widget.RemoteViews;

public class AppWidget extends AppWidgetProvider {
  @Override
  public void onUpdate(Context ctxt,
                       AppWidgetManager mgr,
                       int[] appWidgetIds) {
    if (Build.VERSION.SDK_INT>=Build.VERSION_CODES.HONEYCOMB) {
      onHCUpdate(ctxt, mgr, appWidgetIds);
    }
    else {
      ctxt.startService(new Intent(ctxt, WidgetService.class));
    }
  }

  public void onHCUpdate(Context ctxt, AppWidgetManager appWidgetManager,
                         int[] appWidgetIds) {
    for (int i=0; i<appWidgetIds.length; i++) {
      Intent svcIntent=new Intent(ctxt, ListWidgetService.class);
```

```
        svcIntent.putExtra(AppWidgetManager.EXTRA_APPWIDGET_ID, appWidgetIds[i]);
        svcIntent.setData(Uri.parse(svcIntent.toUri(Intent.URI_INTENT_SCHEME)));

        RemoteViews widget=new RemoteViews(ctxt.getPackageName(),
                                   R.layout.widget);

        widget.setRemoteAdapter(appWidgetIds[i], R.id.restaurants,
                        svcIntent);

        Intent clickIntent=new Intent(ctxt, DetailForm.class);
        PendingIntent clickPI=PendingIntent
                        .getActivity(ctxt, 0,
                                     clickIntent,
                                     PendingIntent.FLAG_UPDATE_CURRENT);

        widget.setPendingIntentTemplate(R.id.restaurants, clickPI);

        appWidgetManager.updateAppWidget(appWidgetIds[i], widget);
      }

    super.onUpdate(ctxt, appWidgetManager, appWidgetIds);
  }
}
```

Then, we need to create this ListWidgetService we reference in the Intent. So, add a new Java class for ListWidgetService to your project, in the apt.tutorial package, with the following implementation:

```
package apt.tutorial;

import android.content.Intent;
import android.widget.RemoteViewsService;

public class ListWidgetService extends RemoteViewsService {
  @Override
  public RemoteViewsFactory onGetViewFactory(Intent intent) {
    return(new ListViewsFactory(this.getApplicationContext(),
                          intent));
  }
}
```

Eclipse users can right-click over apt.tutorial in the Package Explorer and choose New > Class from the context menu to bring up the new class dialog. Set the class name to be ListWidgetService and set the parent class to be android.widget.RemoteViewsService. Then, click OK and fill in the implementation shown above.

A `RemoteViewsService` only needs to do one thing: return a `RemoteViewsFactory` from the `onGetViewFactory()` method. This will be called as soon as the app widget with the `AdapterView` is being put onto the screen, to supply the rows for the `AdapterView`. We will create the implementation of `RemoteViewsFactory` – here called `ListViewsFactory` – in the next step.

You will need to add imports for:

- `android.app.PendingIntent`
- `android.net.Uri`
- `android.os.Build`
- `android.widget.RemoteViews`

Since this is a new service, we also need to add the associated `<service>` element to the manifest, giving us a manifest akin to the one shown below:

```xml
<?xml version="1.0" encoding="utf-8"?>
<manifest android:versionCode="1"
          android:versionName="1.0"
          package="apt.tutorial"
          xmlns:android="http://schemas.android.com/apk/res/android">

  <uses-permission android:name="android.permission.INTERNET" />
  <uses-permission android:name="android.permission.ACCESS_NETWORK_STATE" />
  <uses-permission android:name="android.permission.ACCESS_FINE_LOCATION" />
  <uses-permission android:name="android.permission.RECEIVE_BOOT_COMPLETED" />
  <supports-screens android:largeScreens="true"
                     android:normalScreens="true"
                     android:smallScreens="false" />
  <application android:label="@string/app_name">
    <uses-library android:name="com.google.android.maps" />
    <activity android:label="@string/app_name"
              android:name=".LunchList">
      <intent-filter>
        <action android:name="android.intent.action.MAIN" />
        <category android:name="android.intent.category.LAUNCHER" />
      </intent-filter>
    </activity>
    <activity android:name=".DetailForm"></activity>
    <activity android:name=".EditPreferences"></activity>
    <activity android:name=".FeedActivity"></activity>
    <activity android:name=".RestaurantMap"></activity>
    <activity android:name=".AlarmActivity"></activity>
    <service android:name=".FeedService"></service>
    <service android:name=".WidgetService"></service>
    <service android:name=".ListWidgetService"
             android:permission="android.permission.BIND_REMOTEVIEWS">
```

```
    </service>
    <receiver android:enabled="false"
              android:name=".OnBootReceiver">
      <intent-filter>
        <action android:name="android.intent.action.BOOT_COMPLETED" />
      </intent-filter>
    </receiver>
    <receiver android:name=".OnAlarmReceiver"></receiver>
    <receiver android:icon="@drawable/icon"
              android:label="@string/app_name"
              android:name=".AppWidget">
      <intent-filter>
        <action android:name="android.appwidget.action.APPWIDGET_UPDATE" />
      </intent-filter>
      <meta-data android:name="android.appwidget.provider"
                 android:resource="@xml/widget_provider" />
    </receiver>
  </application>
</manifest>
```

Note that our service has an android:permission attribute, saying that the sender must hold the BIND_REMOTEVIEWS permission to talk to our service. This is so third parties do not try to call our RemoteViewsFactory and grab data they should not have access to. Only the firmware will be able to hold the BIND_REMOTEVIEWS permission.

Eclipse users can add this element by:

1. Double-clicking on the AndroidManifest.xml file to bring it up in the graphical editor

2. Clicking on the Application sub-tab

3. Clicking the Add... button to the right of the Application Nodes list

4. Choosing Service in the dialog and clicking OK

5. Clicking the Browse... button next to the Name field on the right and choosing ListWidgetService as the implementation

6. Type the value android.permission.BIND_REMOTEVIEWS in the Permission combobox, since it may not be one of the choices available in the drop-down

7. Saving your changes (e.g., <Ctrl>-<S>)

Step #5: Implement the RemoteViewsFactory

Now, we need to add the `ListViewsFactory` class – add the following to your project, in the `apt.tutorial` package:

```
package apt.tutorial;

import android.appwidget.AppWidgetManager;
import android.content.Context;
import android.content.Intent;
import android.database.Cursor;
import android.database.sqlite.SQLiteDatabase;
import android.os.Bundle;
import android.widget.RemoteViews;
import android.widget.RemoteViewsService;

public class ListViewsFactory
  implements RemoteViewsService.RemoteViewsFactory {
  private Context ctxt=null;
  private RestaurantHelper helper=null;
  private Cursor restaurants=null;

  public ListViewsFactory(Context ctxt, Intent intent) {
    this.ctxt=ctxt;
  }

  @Override
  public void onCreate() {
    helper=new RestaurantHelper(ctxt);
    restaurants=helper
                .getReadableDatabase()
                .rawQuery("SELECT _ID, name FROM restaurants", null);
  }

  @Override
  public void onDestroy() {
    restaurants.close();
    helper.close();
  }

  @Override
  public int getCount() {
    return(restaurants.getCount());
  }

  @Override
  public RemoteViews getViewAt(int position) {
    RemoteViews row=new RemoteViews(ctxt.getPackageName(),
                          R.layout.widget_row);

    restaurants.moveToPosition(position);
    row.setTextViewText(android.R.id.text1,
```

```
                    restaurants.getString(1));

  Intent i=new Intent();
  Bundle extras=new Bundle();

  extras.putString(LunchList.ID_EXTRA,
                   String.valueOf(restaurants.getInt(0)));
  i.putExtras(extras);
  row.setOnClickFillInIntent(android.R.id.text1, i);

  return(row);
}

@Override
public RemoteViews getLoadingView() {
  return(null);
}

@Override
public int getViewTypeCount() {
  return(1);
}

@Override
public long getItemId(int position) {
  restaurants.moveToPosition(position);

  return(restaurants.getInt(0));
}

@Override
public boolean hasStableIds() {
  return(true);
}

@Override
public void onDataSetChanged() {
  // no-op
}
}
```

Eclipse users can right-click over apt.tutorial in the Package Explorer and choose New > Class from the context menu to bring up the new class dialog. Set the class name to be ListViewsFactory and set the parent class to be android.widget.RemoteViewsService.RemoteViewsFactory. Then, click OK and fill in the implementation shown above.

A RemoteViewsFactory looks a lot like an Adapter. Many methods (e.g., getCount()) are direct analogues. Some of the noteworthy bits include:

- It has `onCreate()` and `onDestroy()` lifecycle methods, akin to an `Activity` or `Service`. Here, we query to find our restaurants in `onCreate()` and close up our `Cursor` and `DatabaseHelper` in `onDestroy()`.

- `getViewAt()` – the equivalent of `getView()` on an `Adapter` – populates a `RemoteViews` for the row, rather than a regular `View`. Notably, it creates an Intent just with a `LunchList.ID_EXTRA` extra, with our restaurant's primary key. That is then supplied to the `RemoteViews` via `setOnClickFillInIntent()`. The net effect is that when the user taps on one of our rows, the extra from this Intent will be merged into the "`PendingIntent` template" from before, to create the actual `PendingIntent` that will be used to perform whatever operation we requested.

- `getItemId()` returns a unique long value for the row; in this case, we use the primary key

We will also need our layout for the rows of the widget. You can copy the `android.R.layout.simple_list_item_1` resource from your SDK into `res/layout/widget_row.xml`, or use the version that appears below:

```
<?xml version="1.0" encoding="utf-8"?>
<!-- Copyright (C) 2006 The Android Open Source Project

    Licensed under the Apache License, Version 2.0 (the "License");
    you may not use this file except in compliance with the License.
    You may obtain a copy of the License at

         http://www.apache.org/licenses/LICENSE-2.0

    Unless required by applicable law or agreed to in writing, software
    distributed under the License is distributed on an "AS IS" BASIS,
    WITHOUT WARRANTIES OR CONDITIONS OF ANY KIND, either express or implied.
    See the License for the specific language governing permissions and
    limitations under the License.
-->

<TextView xmlns:android="http://schemas.android.com/apk/res/android"
    android:id="@android:id/text1"
    android:layout_width="match_parent"
    android:layout_height="wrap_content"
    android:textAppearance="?android:attr/textAppearanceLarge"
    android:gravity="center_vertical"
    android:paddingLeft="6dip"
```

```
     android:minHeight="?android:attr/listPreferredItemHeight"
/>
```

At this point, you can compile and install the updated version of the application into your Android 3.x emulator or device. Go into LunchList from the launcher and add a few restaurants – if this is the first time you have run the app on this device or emulator, your database will be empty. Then, tap on the + sign in the upper-right corner, or long-tap somewhere on the background, to bring up the app widget gallery:

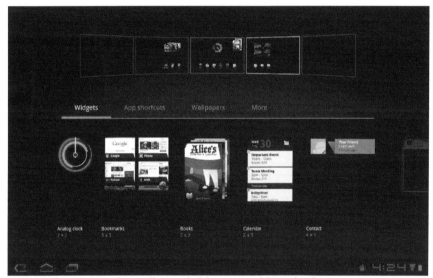

Figure 93. The gallery of things to add to the home screen

Scroll the gallery horizontally to find the LunchList app widget, with a fairly empty preview:

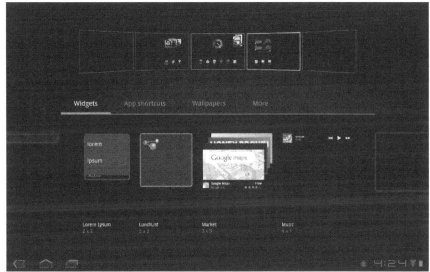

Figure 94. The gallery of available widgets, showing LunchList

Then, drag the LunchList app widget to one of your home screens. Tap on that home screen, and you should see your list of restaurants:

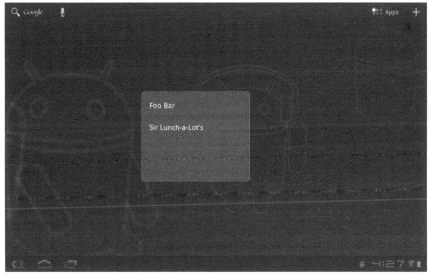

Figure 95. The LunchList Honeycomb app widget

The list should scroll up and down, assuming you have enough restaurants. Tapping on a restaurant should bring up the DetailForm activity on that restaurant.

Step #6: Set Up the Preview Image

When you added the app widget, while all the other app widgets had these nice previews showing what they would look like, the app widget for LunchList looked very plain and drab.

Clearly, this cannot stand.

We can add a reference to a preview image to our widget provider XML resource. The big question is: where do we get the preview image?

You have a few choices:

- You could use the screenshot feature of DDMS to take a picture of your home screen with the app widget on there, then crop to leave only the app widget behind

- You could create your own artwork from scratch, though this is certainly not the preferred approach

- You could use the Widget Preview app in the Android 3.x emulator (just very, very slowly)

If you wish to take the latter approach, in your Android 3.x emulator with the current LunchList installed, run the Widget Preview app. When it launches, it will bring up a list of the defined app widgets on your emulator:

Figure 96. The list of available widgets, in the Widget Preview app

Choose LunchList, and it will give you a preview of the app widget:

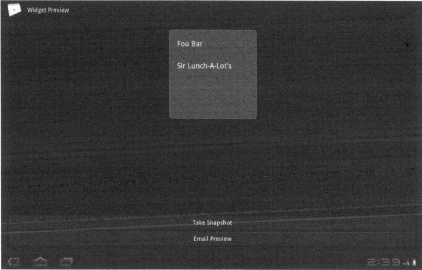

Figure 97. The Honeycomb LunchList app widget, as seen in the Widget Preview app

Then, click the "Take Snapshot" button at the bottom. You will find the image in the /mnt/sdcard/Download directory in DDMS.

Regardless of where you got your image, drop it in the `res/drawable/` directory in your project as `hc_widget_preview.png`, then add the `android:previewImage` attribute to your `res/xml-v11/widget_provider.xml` file:

```
<?xml version="1.0" encoding="utf-8"?>
<appwidget-provider xmlns:android="http://schemas.android.com/apk/res/android"
  android:minWidth="220dip"
  android:minHeight="220dip"
  android:updatePeriodMillis="1800000"
  android:initialLayout="@layout/widget"
  android:previewImage="@drawable/hc_widget_preview"
/>
```

Extra Credit

Here are some things you can try beyond those step-by-step instructions:

- Provide a button in the app widget to add a new restaurant, launching a blank `DetailForm`

- Create a more interesting layout to use for the rows in the list than just the name of the restaurant

- Switch from a `ListView` to a `StackView`, with a custom layout showing a restaurant as a "card" in the stack – you may need to consider a different widget size than the 3x3 cell format used presently

- Use `android:autoAdvanceViewId` to have the `StackView` switch to a new restaurant automatically

Further Reading

Honeycomb-powered app widgets are covered in a chapter of The Busy Coder's Guide to *Advanced* Android Development[62].

---

62 http://commonsware.com/AdvAndroid

A Fragment of Lunch at the Action Bar

The changes introduced in Android 3.0 (Honeycomb) do not stop with app widgets that can have a `ListView` in them. There is a new framework for interacting with the user. Part of this is the action bar, a combination of the old Android title bar, options menu, and a new toolbar feature. Part of this are fragments, which allow you to decompose your application into pieces that can be displayed in different combinations based upon screen size, to simplify handling of phones, tablets, TVs, etc.

This tutorial will experiment a bit with the action bar plus will move our existing `LunchList` and `DetailForm` logic into fragments. The benefit of the move to fragments will not truly be visible until the next tutorial, when we start providing a different UI for tablets than for phones.

Step-By-Step Instructions

First, you need to have completed the previous `LunchList` tutorial. If you are starting the tutorials here, or if you wish to not use your existing work, you can download a ZIP file with all of the tutorial results, and you can copy the `22-HCAppWidget` edition of `LunchList` to use as a starting point. If you are using Eclipse, these instructions will help you load the project into a workspace – but *please* read through this tutorial first, particularly Step #3 below.

Step #1: Set the Proper Target

In your manifest, update the `<uses-sdk>` element to declare that:

- The application overall supports Android 2.2 (API Level 8) and newer (`android:minSdkVersion="8"`)

- The application is targeting Android 3.0 (API Level 11), to get the new look and feel (`android:targetSdkVersion="11"`)

Eclipse users can accomplish this by:

1. Double-clicking on the `AndroidManifest.xml` file to bring it up in the graphical editor

2. Clicking on the Uses Sdk entry in the Manifest Extras list

3. Filling in 11 for the Target SDK Version

4. Saving your changes (e.g., <Ctrl>-<S>)

The resulting `AndroidManifest.xml` file will resemble:

```
<?xml version="1.0" encoding="utf-8"?>
<manifest android:versionCode="1"
          android:versionName="1.0"
          package="apt.tutorial"
          xmlns:android="http://schemas.android.com/apk/res/android">

  <uses-sdk android:minSdkVersion="4" android:targetSdkVersion="11" />
  <uses-permission android:name="android.permission.INTERNET" />
  <uses-permission android:name="android.permission.ACCESS_NETWORK_STATE" />
  <uses-permission android:name="android.permission.ACCESS_FINE_LOCATION" />
  <uses-permission android:name="android.permission.RECEIVE_BOOT_COMPLETED" />
  <supports-screens android:largeScreens="true"
                     android:normalScreens="true"
                     android:smallScreens="false" />
  <application android:label="@string/app_name">
    <uses-library android:name="com.google.android.maps" />
    <activity android:label="@string/app_name"
              android:name=".LunchList">
      <intent-filter>
        <action android:name="android.intent.action.MAIN" />
        <category android:name="android.intent.category.LAUNCHER" />
      </intent-filter>
    </activity>
    <activity android:name=".DetailForm"></activity>
    <activity android:name=".EditPreferences"></activity>
```

```
      <activity android:name=".FeedActivity"></activity>
      <activity android:name=".RestaurantMap"></activity>
      <activity android:name=".AlarmActivity"></activity>
      <service android:name=".FeedService"></service>
      <service android:name=".WidgetService"></service>
      <service android:name=".ListWidgetService"
              android:permission="android.permission.BIND_REMOTEVIEWS">
      </service>
      <receiver android:enabled="false"
                android:name=".OnBootReceiver">
        <intent-filter>
          <action android:name="android.intent.action.BOOT_COMPLETED" />
        </intent-filter>
      </receiver>
      <receiver android:name=".OnAlarmReceiver"></receiver>
      <receiver android:icon="@drawable/icon"
                android:label="@string/app_name"
                android:name=".AppWidget">
        <intent-filter>
          <action android:name="android.appwidget.action.APPWIDGET_UPDATE" />
        </intent-filter>
        <meta-data android:name="android.appwidget.provider"
                   android:resource="@xml/widget_provider" />
      </receiver>
    </application>
</manifest>
```

If you compile and run your project, it will look identical to the previous version for an Android 1.x or 2.x device or emulator. However, on an Android 3.x device or emulator, it will now have the action bar at the top, with the options menu items available via the menu button in the upper-right corner:

Figure 98. LunchList with the Honeycomb look and feel

Step #2: Promote "Add" to the Action Bar

The action bar looks a bit boring, with just the icon and name in the upper left and the options menu in the upper right. We have a lot of room, so it makes sense to do something with that room.

One easy thing to do – that works in a backwards-compatible fashion – is to selectively promote options menu items to be toolbar buttons.

Modify res/menu/option.xml to add an android:showAsAction attribute to the Add menu item:

```xml
<?xml version="1.0" encoding="utf-8"?>
<menu xmlns:android="http://schemas.android.com/apk/res/android">
  <item android:id="@+id/add"
    android:title="Add"
    android:icon="@drawable/ic_menu_add"
    android:showAsAction="ifRoom|withText"
  />
  <item android:id="@+id/prefs"
    android:title="Settings"
    android:icon="@drawable/ic_menu_preferences"
```

```
  />
</menu>
```

Eclipse users will need to make this change in the XML directly.

The value of "ifRoom|withText" means that the Add menu item should be promoted to a toolbar button if there is room in the action bar for it (ifRoom) and that it should show both the icon and the title, rather than just the icon (withText).

Without any other changes, if you compile and build this, you will once again see no change on an Android 1.x or 2.x device or emulator. But, on an Android 3.x device or emulator, Add should now appear as a toolbar button and no longer be in the options menu itself:

Figure 99. LunchList with the Add menu choice promoted to a toolbar button

Step #3: Add the ACL

It is possible to do more with the action bar and fragments, but to do so in a backwards-compatible fashion, we need the Android Compatibility Library

(ACL). This gives us access to a subset of the new classes introduced in Android 3.0 on older versions of Android.

First, open up the Android SDK and AVD Manager. In Eclipse, this is in the Window menu. Outside of Eclipse, run the android command. Check your list of installed packages and see if you have "Android Compatibility package". If not, install it from the "Android Repository" portion of the "Available packages" list.

Then, wherever you have your SDK installed, go into the extras/android/compatibility/v4 directory (note: that v4 portion may change over time). There should be an android-support-v4.jar in that directory (note: again, the v4 portion may be different). Copy that into the libs/ directory of your project.

Eclipse users will also need to add it to the build path. Eclipse users should right-click over the project name in the project explorer, then choose Build Path > Configure Build Path from the context menu. Click on the Libraries tab, then click the "Add JARs" button. Find the android-support-v4.jar file in your project's libs/ directory and select it. Then, you can close up this project properties window.

Step #4: Split LunchList Into a Fragment

When converting an existing application into one that uses fragments, one recipe is:

1. Clone an activity class into a fragment class

2. Update that fragment class as needed to actually be a fragment, inheriting from the proper class, updating lifecycle methods, and so on

3. Change the activity to one that hosts the fragment

4. Repeat steps 1-3 for each activity

5. Start to consider putting multiple fragments in a single activity when on larger-screen devices

In this tutorial, we will follow steps 1-4 from that list, starting first with the LunchList class. The next tutorial will get into step 5, where we really use fragments to their fullest extent.

Copy LunchList to LunchFragment

Create a copy of your current LunchList class into a LunchFragment.java file, in the apt.tutorial package. You will need to rename the class in the Java source, lest you get compiler complaints. Eclipse makes this easy: right-click over the LunchList class and choose Copy from the context menu, then right-click over the apt.tutorial package and choose Paste.

Just naming it LunchFragment does not make it a fragment, of course, which is what we get into next.

Reconfigure LunchFragment

While a fragment is reminiscent of an activity, they are certainly not the same. Hence, there is a fair bit of conversion work to be done to make LunchFragment work properly.

First, replace the import for ListActivity to one for android.support.v4.app.ListFragment, and have LunchFragment inherit from ListFragment. If you are using Eclipse, this will cause all sorts of warnings and errors, which we will progressively fix, so please do not panic.

The biggest change is that LunchFragment is no longer an Activity. Many places in the code use this to refer to a Context – Activity inherits from Context, but ListFragment does not. Hence, find and replace all this or LunchList.this occurrences and replace them with calls to getActivity(), such as in onOptionsItemSelected():

```
@Override
public boolean onOptionsItemSelected(MenuItem item) {
  if (item.getItemId()==R.id.add) {
    startActivity(new Intent(getActivity(), DetailForm.class));
```

```
    return(true);
  }
  else if (item.getItemId()==R.id.prefs) {
    startActivity(new Intent(getActivity(), EditPreferences.class));

    return(true);
  }

  return(super.onOptionsItemSelected(item));
}
```

Managed cursors have been deprecated in Android 3.0, but we can do a bit of "management" ourselves. Split the existing implementation of onCreate() into onCreate() and onResume(), also adding in setHasOptionsMenu() into onCreate() to let Android know that our fragment would like to contribute to the options menu:

```
@Override
public void onCreate(Bundle state) {
  super.onCreate(state);

  setHasOptionsMenu(true);
}

@Override
public void onResume() {
  super.onResume();

  helper=new RestaurantHelper(getActivity());
  prefs=PreferenceManager.getDefaultSharedPreferences(getActivity());
  initList();
  prefs.registerOnSharedPreferenceChangeListener(prefListener);
}
```

Also, convert onDestroy() into an equivalent onPause() implementation:

```
@Override
public void onPause() {
  helper.close();

  super.onPause();
}
```

And get rid of the startManagingCursor() and stopManagingCursor() calls from initList():

```
private void initList() {
  if (model!=null) {
    model.close();
  }

  model=helper.getAll(prefs.getString("sort_order", "name"));
  adapter=new RestaurantAdapter(model);
  setListAdapter(adapter);
}
```

The onCreateOptionsMenu() method is slightly different for a Fragment, in that we get a MenuInflater passed in as a parameter. So, modify onCreateOptionsMenu() to have the proper signature and use that MenuInflater:

```
@Override
public void onCreateOptionsMenu(Menu menu, MenuInflater inflater) {
  inflater.inflate(R.menu.option, menu);
}
```

In our RestaurantAdapter, we used to simply call getLayoutInflater(), but that no longer works, since that is not a method available on Fragment. So, call getLayoutInflater() on the Activity we get from getActivity():

```
class RestaurantAdapter extends CursorAdapter {
  RestaurantAdapter(Cursor c) {
    super(getActivity(), c);
  }

  @Override
  public void bindView(View row, Context ctxt,
                       Cursor c) {
    RestaurantHolder holder=(RestaurantHolder)row.getTag();

    holder.populateFrom(c, helper);
  }

  @Override
  public View newView(Context ctxt, Cursor c,
                      ViewGroup parent) {
    LayoutInflater inflater=getActivity().getLayoutInflater();
    View row=inflater.inflate(R.layout.row, parent, false);
    RestaurantHolder holder=new RestaurantHolder(row);

    row.setTag(holder);

    return(row);
  }
}
```

Finally, we need to do something different with our list item clicks. Before, LunchList would simply open up DetailForm. Now, though, we really want to delegate that to something else, probably the activity that is hosting the LunchFragment. Activities now serve as the orchestration layer, coordinating communication between fragments, whether those fragments are all in the same activity or are hosted by different activities, based upon screen size.

So, let's create a OnRestaurantListener inner interface declaration inside of LunchFragment:

```
public interface OnRestaurantListener {
  void onRestaurantSelected(long id);
}
```

Add a setOnRestaurantListener() setter method to supply an instance of that interface:

```
public void setOnRestaurantListener(OnRestaurantListener listener) {
  this.listener=listener;
}
```

You will also need to add a data member to LunchFragment named listener to hold onto this OnRestaurantListener object.

Finally, in onListItemClick(), instead of spawning an activity, just pass the Restaurant object's ID to the listener:

```
@Override
public void onListItemClick(ListView list, View view,
                            int position, long id) {
  if (listener!=null) {
    listener.onRestaurantSelected(id);
  }
}
```

The entire LunchFragment implementation, therefore, should resemble this:

```
package apt.tutorial;

import android.content.Context;
import android.content.Intent;
import android.content.SharedPreferences;
```

```java
import android.database.Cursor;
import android.os.Bundle;
import android.preference.PreferenceManager;
import android.support.v4.app.ListFragment;
import android.view.Menu;
import android.view.MenuInflater;
import android.view.MenuItem;
import android.view.View;
import android.view.ViewGroup;
import android.view.LayoutInflater;
import android.widget.AdapterView;
import android.widget.CursorAdapter;
import android.widget.ImageView;
import android.widget.ListView;
import android.widget.TextView;

public class LunchFragment extends ListFragment {
  public final static String ID_EXTRA="apt.tutorial._ID";
  Cursor model=null;
  RestaurantAdapter adapter=null;
  RestaurantHelper helper=null;
  SharedPreferences prefs=null;
  OnRestaurantListener listener=null;

  @Override
  public void onCreate(Bundle state) {
    super.onCreate(state);

    setHasOptionsMenu(true);
  }

  @Override
  public void onResume() {
    super.onResume();

    helper=new RestaurantHelper(getActivity());
    prefs=PreferenceManager.getDefaultSharedPreferences(getActivity());
    initList();
    prefs.registerOnSharedPreferenceChangeListener(prefListener);
  }

  @Override
  public void onPause() {
    helper.close();

    super.onPause();
  }

  @Override
  public void onListItemClick(ListView list, View view,
                              int position, long id) {
    if (listener!=null) {
      listener.onRestaurantSelected(id);
    }
```

```
}

@Override
public void onCreateOptionsMenu(Menu menu, MenuInflater inflater) {
  inflater.inflate(R.menu.option, menu);
}

@Override
public boolean onOptionsItemSelected(MenuItem item) {
  if (item.getItemId()==R.id.add) {
    startActivity(new Intent(getActivity(), DetailForm.class));

    return(true);
  }
  else if (item.getItemId()==R.id.prefs) {
    startActivity(new Intent(getActivity(), EditPreferences.class));

    return(true);
  }

  return(super.onOptionsItemSelected(item));
}

public void setOnRestaurantListener(OnRestaurantListener listener) {
  this.listener=listener;
}

private void initList() {
  if (model!=null) {
    model.close();
  }

  model=helper.getAll(prefs.getString("sort_order", "name"));
  adapter=new RestaurantAdapter(model);
  setListAdapter(adapter);
}

private SharedPreferences.OnSharedPreferenceChangeListener prefListener=
new SharedPreferences.OnSharedPreferenceChangeListener() {
  public void onSharedPreferenceChanged(SharedPreferences sharedPrefs,
                                        String key) {
    if (key.equals("sort_order")) {
      initList();
    }
  }
};

public interface OnRestaurantListener {
  void onRestaurantSelected(long id);
}

class RestaurantAdapter extends CursorAdapter {
  RestaurantAdapter(Cursor c) {
    super(getActivity(), c);
```

```
    }

    @Override
    public void bindView(View row, Context ctxt,
                          Cursor c) {
      RestaurantHolder holder=(RestaurantHolder)row.getTag();

      holder.populateFrom(c, helper);
    }

    @Override
    public View newView(Context ctxt, Cursor c,
                          ViewGroup parent) {
      LayoutInflater inflater=getActivity().getLayoutInflater();
      View row=inflater.inflate(R.layout.row, parent, false);
      RestaurantHolder holder=new RestaurantHolder(row);

      row.setTag(holder);

      return(row);
    }
  }

  static class RestaurantHolder {
    private TextView name=null;
    private TextView address=null;
    private ImageView icon=null;

    RestaurantHolder(View row) {
      name=(TextView)row.findViewById(R.id.title);
      address=(TextView)row.findViewById(R.id.address);
      icon=(ImageView)row.findViewById(R.id.icon);
    }

    void populateFrom(Cursor c, RestaurantHelper helper) {
      name.setText(helper.getName(c));
      address.setText(helper.getAddress(c));

      if (helper.getType(c).equals("sit_down")) {
        icon.setImageResource(R.drawable.ball_red);
      }
      else if (helper.getType(c).equals("take_out")) {
        icon.setImageResource(R.drawable.ball_yellow);
      }
      else {
        icon.setImageResource(R.drawable.ball_green);
      }
    }
  }
}
```

Make LunchList Host LunchFragment

With all the widgets and business logic moved into LunchFragment, there is not that much left for LunchList itself to do. It needs to:

- Arrange to have LunchFragment be displayed

- Arrange to find out when the user taps on a Restaurant in the list and do something with that event – in the short term, we will launch the DetailForm activity

With that in mind, change res/layout/main.xml to look like this:

```
<?xml version="1.0" encoding="utf-8"?>
<fragment xmlns:android="http://schemas.android.com/apk/res/android"
  class="apt.tutorial.LunchFragment"
  android:id="@+id/lunch"
  android:layout_width="match_parent"
  android:layout_height="match_parent"
/>
```

Eclipse users can delete the current res/layout/main.xml file and create a new one, dragging a Fragment from the Layouts section of the tool palette into the graphical editor. Set the Class property (Properties > Class from the context menu) to be apt.tutorial.LunchFragment, and set the ID (Edit ID... from the context menu) to be lunch.

Here, we declare that the contents of the activity simply consists of the LunchFragment itself, filling the screen.

Then, replace the existing LunchList code with the following:

```
package apt.tutorial;

import android.content.Intent;
import android.os.Bundle;
import android.support.v4.app.FragmentActivity;

public class LunchList extends FragmentActivity
    implements LunchFragment.OnRestaurantListener {
  public final static String ID_EXTRA="apt.tutorial._ID";

  @Override
```

```
public void onCreate(Bundle savedInstanceState) {
  super.onCreate(savedInstanceState);
  setContentView(R.layout.main);

  LunchFragment lunch
    =(LunchFragment)getSupportFragmentManager()
                      .findFragmentById(R.id.lunch);

  lunch.setOnRestaurantListener(this);
}

public void onRestaurantSelected(long id) {
  Intent i=new Intent(this, DetailForm.class);

  i.putExtra(ID_EXTRA, String.valueOf(id));
  startActivity(i);
}
}
```

Note that we now inherit from FragmentActivity, as opposed to ListActivity or Activity. This is a requirement of the ACL – applications using the Android 3.0 APIs directly would not necessarily need to inherit from any particular Activity class.

Our onCreate() method calls setContentView() as normal. Then, it finds our LunchFragment and registers itself as the OnRestaurantListener, since LunchList now implements that interface. That interface requires an onRestaurantSelected() method, which just invokes the DetailForm activity as before.

Step #5: Split DetailForm Into a Fragment

Just as we converted LunchList into LunchFragment and a hosting activity, so too must we convert DetailForm into DetailFragment and a hosting activity. And, as with LunchList, we will keep the activity name as DetailForm, so we do not need to change the manifest or any code that refers to DetailForm, such as our app widget implementations.

Copy DetailForm to DetailFragment

Create a copy of your current `DetailForm` class into a `DetailFragment.java` file, in the `apt.tutorial` package. You will need to rename the class in the Java source, lest you get compiler complaints. In Eclipse, right-click over the `DetailForm` class and choose Copy from the context menu, then right-click over the `apt.tutorial` package and choose Paste.

Reconfigure DetailFragment

First, replace the import for `Activity` to one for `android.support.v4.app.Fragment`, and have `DetailFragment` inherit from `Fragment`. Again, if you are using Eclipse, do not worry about all the errors this introduces.

Next, find and replace all `this` or `DetailForm.this` occurrences and replace them with calls to `getActivity()`, such as in `isNetworkAvailable()`:

```
private boolean isNetworkAvailable() {
  ConnectivityManager cm=(ConnectivityManager)getActivity().
                                    getSystemService(Context.CONNECTIV
ITY_SERVICE);
  NetworkInfo info=cm.getActiveNetworkInfo();

  return(info!=null);
}
```

Our `ListFragment` (`LunchFragment`) did not need a layout, as it simply needed a `ListView`. With `DetailFragment`, we need a layout. We will continue to use `res/layout/detail_form.xml` for the layout, using something else for the `DetailForm` activity later.

However, we now need to implement an `onCreateView()` method that we did not need with `LunchFragment`, to actually inflate the layout and return it:

```
@Override
public View onCreateView(LayoutInflater inflater, ViewGroup container,
                    Bundle savedInstanceState) {
  return(inflater.inflate(R.layout.detail_form, container, false));
}
```

Also, since we are not inflating the layout in onCreate() anymore, and therefore we cannot access the widgets in onCreate(), split some of the logic in onCreate() into an onActivityCreated() method, which is invoked after onCreateView():

```
@Override
public void onCreate(Bundle state) {
  super.onCreate(state);

  setHasOptionsMenu(true);
}

@Override
public void onActivityCreated(Bundle savedInstanceState) {
  super.onActivityCreated(savedInstanceState);

  locMgr=(LocationManager)getActivity().
                          getSystemService(Context.LOCATION_SERVICE);

  name=(EditText)getView().findViewById(R.id.name);
  address=(EditText)getView().findViewById(R.id.addr);
  notes=(EditText)getView().findViewById(R.id.notes);
  types=(RadioGroup)getView().findViewById(R.id.types);
  feed=(EditText)getView().findViewById(R.id.feed);
  location=(TextView)getView().findViewById(R.id.location);
}
```

Note that onCreate() also registers DetailFragment to participate in the options menu. For that to work, once again we need to adjust the onCreateOptionsMenu() method to reflect the new signature and use the supplied inflater:

```
@Override
public void onCreateOptionsMenu(Menu menu, MenuInflater inflater) {
  inflater.inflate(R.menu.details_option, menu);
}
```

Similarly, onPrepareOptionsMenu() now no longer needs to chain to the superclass or return a boolean:

```
@Override
public void onPrepareOptionsMenu(Menu menu) {
  if (restaurantId==null) {
    menu.findItem(R.id.location).setEnabled(false);
    menu.findItem(R.id.map).setEnabled(false);
  }
}
```

Some of the original onCreate() logic moves to onResume():

```
@Override
public void onResume() {
  super.onResume();

  helper=new RestaurantHelper(getActivity());
  restaurantId=getActivity().getIntent().getStringExtra(LunchList.ID_EXTRA);

  if (restaurantId!=null) {
    load();
  }
}
```

Also, fold the code from onDestroy() into onPause():

```
@Override
public void onPause() {
  save();
  helper.close();
  locMgr.removeUpdates(onLocationChange);

  super.onPause();
}
```

You will also need to add imports for android.content.Context,
android.view.LayoutInflater, and android.view.ViewGroup.

The resulting DetailFragment class should resemble:

```
package apt.tutorial;

import android.content.Context;
import android.content.Intent;
import android.database.Cursor;
import android.location.Location;
import android.location.LocationListener;
import android.location.LocationManager;
import android.net.ConnectivityManager;
import android.net.NetworkInfo;
import android.os.Bundle;
import android.support.v4.app.Fragment;
import android.view.LayoutInflater;
import android.view.Menu;
import android.view.MenuInflater;
import android.view.MenuItem;
import android.view.View;
import android.view.ViewGroup;
```

```
import android.widget.EditText;
import android.widget.RadioGroup;
import android.widget.TextView;
import android.widget.Toast;

public class DetailFragment extends Fragment {
  EditText name=null;
  EditText address=null;
  EditText notes=null;
  EditText feed=null;
  RadioGroup types=null;
  RestaurantHelper helper=null;
  String restaurantId=null;
  TextView location=null;
  LocationManager locMgr=null;
  double latitude=0.0d;
  double longitude=0.0d;

  @Override
  public void onCreate(Bundle state) {
    super.onCreate(state);

    setHasOptionsMenu(true);
  }

  @Override
  public View onCreateView(LayoutInflater inflater, ViewGroup container,
                           Bundle savedInstanceState) {
    return(inflater.inflate(R.layout.detail_form, container, false));
  }

  @Override
  public void onActivityCreated(Bundle savedInstanceState) {
    super.onActivityCreated(savedInstanceState);

    locMgr=(LocationManager)getActivity().
                             getSystemService(Context.LOCATION_SERVICE);

    name=(EditText)getView().findViewById(R.id.name);
    address=(EditText)getView().findViewById(R.id.addr);
    notes=(EditText)getView().findViewById(R.id.notes);
    types=(RadioGroup)getView().findViewById(R.id.types);
    feed=(EditText)getView().findViewById(R.id.feed);
    location=(TextView)getView().findViewById(R.id.location);
  }

  @Override
  public void onResume() {
    super.onResume();

    helper=new RestaurantHelper(getActivity());
    restaurantId=getActivity().getIntent().getStringExtra(LunchList.ID_EXTRA);

    if (restaurantId!=null) {
```

```
    load();
  }
}

@Override
public void onPause() {
  save();
  helper.close();
  locMgr.removeUpdates(onLocationChange);

  super.onPause();
}

@Override
public void onCreateOptionsMenu(Menu menu, MenuInflater inflater) {
  inflater.inflate(R.menu.details_option, menu);
}

@Override
public void onPrepareOptionsMenu(Menu menu) {
  if (restaurantId==null) {
    menu.findItem(R.id.location).setEnabled(false);
    menu.findItem(R.id.map).setEnabled(false);
  }
}

@Override
public boolean onOptionsItemSelected(MenuItem item) {
  if (item.getItemId()==R.id.feed) {
    if (isNetworkAvailable()) {
      Intent i=new Intent(getActivity(), FeedActivity.class);

      i.putExtra(FeedActivity.FEED_URL, feed.getText().toString());
      startActivity(i);
    }
    else {
      Toast
        .makeText(getActivity(), "Sorry, the Internet is not available",
                  Toast.LENGTH_LONG)
        .show();
    }

    return(true);
  }
  else if (item.getItemId()==R.id.location) {
    locMgr.requestLocationUpdates(LocationManager.GPS_PROVIDER,
                                  0, 0, onLocationChange);

    return(true);
  }
  else if (item.getItemId()==R.id.map) {
    Intent i=new Intent(getActivity(), RestaurantMap.class);

    i.putExtra(RestaurantMap.EXTRA_LATITUDE, latitude);
```

```
      i.putExtra(RestaurantMap.EXTRA_LONGITUDE, longitude);
      i.putExtra(RestaurantMap.EXTRA_NAME, name.getText().toString());

    startActivity(i);

    return(true);
  }

  return(super.onOptionsItemSelected(item));
}

private boolean isNetworkAvailable() {
  ConnectivityManager cm=(ConnectivityManager)getActivity().
                                        getSystemService(Context.CONNECT
IVITY_SERVICE);
  NetworkInfo info=cm.getActiveNetworkInfo();

  return(info!=null);
}

private void load() {
  Cursor c=helper.getById(restaurantId);

  c.moveToFirst();
  name.setText(helper.getName(c));
  address.setText(helper.getAddress(c));
  notes.setText(helper.getNotes(c));
  feed.setText(helper.getFeed(c));

  if (helper.getType(c).equals("sit_down")) {
    types.check(R.id.sit_down);
  }
  else if (helper.getType(c).equals("take_out")) {
    types.check(R.id.take_out);
  }
  else {
    types.check(R.id.delivery);
  }

  latitude=helper.getLatitude(c);
  longitude=helper.getLongitude(c);

  location.setText(String.valueOf(latitude)
                  +", "
                  +String.valueOf(longitude));

  c.close();
}

private void save() {
  if (name.getText().toString().length()>0) {
    String type=null;

    switch (types.getCheckedRadioButtonId()) {
```

```
      case R.id.sit_down:
        type="sit_down";
        break;
      case R.id.take_out:
        type="take_out";
        break;
      default:
        type="delivery";
        break;
    }

    if (restaurantId==null) {
      helper.insert(name.getText().toString(),
                    address.getText().toString(), type,
                    notes.getText().toString(),
                    feed.getText().toString());
    }
    else {
      helper.update(restaurantId, name.getText().toString(),
                    address.getText().toString(), type,
                    notes.getText().toString(),
                    feed.getText().toString());
    }
  }
}

LocationListener onLocationChange=new LocationListener() {
  public void onLocationChanged(Location fix) {
    helper.updateLocation(restaurantId, fix.getLatitude(),
                          fix.getLongitude());
    location.setText(String.valueOf(fix.getLatitude())
                    +", "
                    +String.valueOf(fix.getLongitude()));
    locMgr.removeUpdates(onLocationChange);

    Toast
      .makeText(getActivity(), "Location saved",
                Toast.LENGTH_LONG)
      .show();
  }

  public void onProviderDisabled(String provider) {
    // required for interface, not used
  }

  public void onProviderEnabled(String provider) {
    // required for interface, not used
  }

  public void onStatusChanged(String provider, int status,
                              Bundle extras) {
    // required for interface, not used
  }
```

```
    };
}
```

Make DetailForm Host DetailFragment

Now, we need to do something with this `DetailFragment`.

Create a new layout file, `res/layout/detail_activity.xml`, that loads in `DetailFragment`:

```xml
<?xml version="1.0" encoding="utf-8"?>
<fragment xmlns:android="http://schemas.android.com/apk/res/android"
  class="apt.tutorial.DetailFragment"
  android:id="@+id/details"
  android:layout_width="match_parent"
  android:layout_height="match_parent"
/>
```

Eclipse users can create an empty `res/layout/detail_activity.xml`, then drag a `Fragment` from the Layouts section of the tool palette into the graphical editor. Set the Class property (Properties > Class from the context menu) to be `apt.tutorial.DetailFragment`, and set the ID (Edit ID… from the context menu) to be `details`.

Then, replace the existing `DetailForm` logic with:

```java
package apt.tutorial;

import android.content.Intent;
import android.os.Bundle;
import android.support.v4.app.FragmentActivity;

public class DetailForm extends FragmentActivity {
  @Override
  public void onCreate(Bundle savedInstanceState) {
    super.onCreate(savedInstanceState);
    setContentView(R.layout.detail_activity);
  }
}
```

Here, all we do is load in the layout.

After having done all of that work, you should be able to compile and install your project onto a device or emulator... and see the exact same UI that you had after Step #2.

At this time, you may be tempted to hurt the author. The author would appreciate your restraint, as he bruises easily.

Besides, all of this work will pay off in the next tutorial, when we display LunchFragment and DetailFragment side-by-side on a tablet (or tablet-sized emulator).

Extra Credit

Here are some things you can try beyond those step-by-step instructions:

- Promote some of the options menu items from DetailFragment into the action bar.

- Create a copy of your project, remove the ACL from libs/ and your build path, and alter the project to use the native Honeycomb fragment and action bar classes and methods. This will only work on an Android 3.x device or emulator, since you are no longer backwards-compatible.

Further Reading

Basic work with fragments and the action bar – the level shown in this tutorial – can be found in a chapter of The Busy Coder's Guide to Android Development[63].

---

63 http://commonsware.com/Android

Lunches, Large and Small

Now that we have fragments set up, we can leverage them in the way they were intended: to allow us to mix and match what fragments are displayed at any time. In the case of this sample application, on a tablet, it would seem to make sense to have the list of restaurants and the selected restaurant side-by-side when the tablet is in landscape mode. So, that's what we will do here.

Step-By-Step Instructions

First, you need to have completed the previous LunchList tutorial. If you are starting the tutorials here, or if you wish to not use your existing work, you can download a ZIP file with all of the tutorial results, and you can copy the 23-Honeycomb edition of LunchList to use as a starting point. If you are using Eclipse, these instructions will help you load the project into a workspace.

Step #1: Add a Large Landscape Layout

First, we need to specify a separate layout for use on large screens in the landscape orientation. This will serve two roles:

1. It will let us declare where the two fragments (LunchFragment and DetailFragment) will go and how big they will be

2. It will let us determine at runtime that we have a space for the DetailFragment in the layout being used by LunchList, so we know to

add that fragment as needed based upon the user's restaurant choice

With that in mind, create a `res/layout-large-land/` directory in your project, and in there put a new copy of main.xml that looks like this:

```xml
<?xml version="1.0" encoding="utf-8"?>
<LinearLayout xmlns:android="http://schemas.android.com/apk/res/android"
  android:layout_width="match_parent"
  android:layout_height="match_parent"
  android:orientation="horizontal"
>
  <fragment
    class="apt.tutorial.LunchFragment"
    android:id="@+id/lunch"
    android:layout_width="0dip"
    android:layout_height="match_parent"
    android:layout_weight="40"
  />
  <FrameLayout
    android:id="@+id/details"
    android:layout_width="0dip"
    android:layout_height="match_parent"
    android:layout_weight="60"
  />
</LinearLayout>
```

This simply lays out the two fragments side-by-side, with the `LunchFragment` getting 40% of the width and the rest going to... a `FrameLayout`?

The reason for the `FrameLayout` is that we do not want to show an empty `DetailFragment` when there is no restaurant selected, as that could get confusing. Hence, we will dynamically add the `DetailFragment` once a restaurant is selected, and to do that, we need a container to put it in. `FrameLayout` is ideal for this purpose.

Eclipse users can create this layout by:

1. Right-clicking over the `res/` directory and choosing New > Folder, giving the new folder the name `layout-large-land`

2. Right-clicking over the new `res/layout-large-land/` directory and choosing New > File, giving the new file the name `main.xml`

3. Entering the aforementioned XML code, as setting this up by drag-and-drop does not work especially well.

Step #2: Detect Large Landscape Mode

When the user clicks on a restaurant in the LunchFragment, which then notifies LunchList of the event, we need to now be aware of whether we are supposed to display the DetailFragment in LunchList itself or the "old way" of launching DetailForm. The determining factor is whether we have that FrameLayout (R.id.details) or not.

So, modify onRestaurantSelected() to look like this:

```
public void onRestaurantSelected(long id) {
  if (findViewById(R.id.details)==null) {
    Intent i=new Intent(this, DetailForm.class);

    i.putExtra(ID_EXTRA, String.valueOf(id));
    startActivity(i);
  }
  else {
    // ummm... do something!
  }
}
```

Here, we simply look to see if we have the R.id.details widget or not. If we do not, we go through the original logic of calling startActivity(). If we do have the FrameLayout, though, we have some more work to do.

Step #3: Pass the Restaurant ID to DetailFragment

Right now, DetailFragment makes an implicit assumption that is is being hosted by DetailForm. While you will not find any references to DetailForm in DetailFragment, DetailFragment *does* ask its activity for the LunchList.ID_EXTRA value. That will not be the case when DetailFragment is being hosted by LunchList – instead, LunchList will need to supply the restaurant to load as needed.

Setting this up is surprisingly annoying.

First, add an ARG_REST_ID static data member:

```
private static final String ARG_REST_ID="apt.tutorial.ARG_REST_ID";
```

Then, use it in a revised version of onActivityCreated():

```
@Override
public void onActivityCreated(Bundle savedInstanceState) {
  super.onActivityCreated(savedInstanceState);

  locMgr=(LocationManager)getActivity().
                          getSystemService(Context.LOCATION_SERVICE);

  name=(EditText)getView().findViewById(R.id.name);
  address=(EditText)getView().findViewById(R.id.addr);
  notes=(EditText)getView().findViewById(R.id.notes);
  types=(RadioGroup)getView().findViewById(R.id.types);
  feed=(EditText)getView().findViewById(R.id.feed);
  location=(TextView)getView().findViewById(R.id.location);

  Bundle args=getArguments();

  if (args!=null) {
    loadRestaurant(args.getString(ARG_REST_ID));
  }
}
```

Here, instead of asking the containing activity for the ID_EXTRA as before, we call getArguments(). This may return a Bundle, supplied to the fragment by the parent activity. If we have such a bundle, there should be an ARG_REST_ID value in it, which is the restaurant ID. If so, we can go load that restaurant into the form via a loadRestaurant() method that you will need to add to DetailFragment:

```
public void loadRestaurant(String restaurantId) {
  this.restaurantId=restaurantId;

  if (restaurantId!=null) {
    load();
  }
}
```

The arguments path will be used when DetailFragment is hosted by the LunchList activity. For when DetailFragment is hosted by DetailForm, we get no opportunity to pass in arguments – the fragment is "wired into" the layout. However, we can simply call loadRestaurant() directly, as you will see. We cannot do this in the `LunchList` host scenario, because the timing is off, as you will also see.

To assist `LunchList` in getting this right, add a static `newInstance()` factory method on `DetailFragment`:

```
public static DetailFragment newInstance(long id) {
  DetailFragment result=new DetailFragment();
  Bundle args=new Bundle();

  args.putString(ARG_REST_ID, String.valueOf(id));
  result.setArguments(args);

  return(result);
}
```

This gives `LunchList` a simple API for adding the fragment, encapsulating all the argument stuff.

Then, we need to get rid of the old extra-based way of loading the restaurant, presently in `onResume()`. Convert `onResume()` into a `getHelper()` lazy-creator method:

```
private RestaurantHelper getHelper() {
  if (helper==null) {
    helper=new RestaurantHelper(getActivity());
  }

  return(helper);
}
```

Then, replace all spots where we are using helper directly to call `getHelper()` instead, such as:

```
private void load() {
  Cursor c=getHelper().getById(restaurantId);

  c.moveToFirst();
  name.setText(getHelper().getName(c));
  address.setText(getHelper().getAddress(c));
  notes.setText(getHelper().getNotes(c));
  feed.setText(getHelper().getFeed(c));

  if (getHelper().getType(c).equals("sit_down")) {
    types.check(R.id.sit_down);
```

```
  }
  else if (getHelper().getType(c).equals("take_out")) {
    types.check(R.id.take_out);
  }
  else {
    types.check(R.id.delivery);
  }

  latitude=getHelper().getLatitude(c);
  longitude=getHelper().getLongitude(c);

  location.setText(String.valueOf(latitude)
                    +", "
                    +String.valueOf(longitude));

  c.close();
}
```

DetailForm has to change as well – here, we need to extra that extra value and use it with loadRestaurant(). So, add an onResume() method to DetailForm, as follows:

```
@Override
public void onResume() {
  super.onResume();

  String restaurantId=getIntent().getStringExtra(LunchList.ID_EXTRA);

  if (restaurantId!=null) {
    DetailFragment details=(DetailFragment)getSupportFragmentManager()
                                      .findFragmentById(R.id.details);

    if (details!=null) {
      details.loadRestaurant(restaurantId);
    }
  }
}
```

So, if we are hosting DetailFragment via DetailForm, DetailForm will get the Intent extra, find the DetailFragment (inflated via the layout), and call loadRestaurant() on it, causing it to populate the form with the restaurant information.

The entire DetailFragment class after these changes should resemble:

```
package apt.tutorial;

import android.content.Context;
```

```
import android.content.Intent;
import android.database.Cursor;
import android.location.Location;
import android.location.LocationListener;
import android.location.LocationManager;
import android.net.ConnectivityManager;
import android.net.NetworkInfo;
import android.os.Bundle;
import android.support.v4.app.Fragment;
import android.view.LayoutInflater;
import android.view.Menu;
import android.view.MenuInflater;
import android.view.MenuItem;
import android.view.View;
import android.view.ViewGroup;
import android.widget.EditText;
import android.widget.RadioGroup;
import android.widget.TextView;
import android.widget.Toast;

public class DetailFragment extends Fragment {
  private static final String ARG_REST_ID="apt.tutorial.ARG_REST_ID";
  EditText name=null;
  EditText address=null;
  EditText notes=null;
  EditText feed=null;
  RadioGroup types=null;
  RestaurantHelper helper=null;
  String restaurantId=null;
  TextView location=null;
  LocationManager locMgr=null;
  double latitude=0.0d;
  double longitude=0.0d;

  public static DetailFragment newInstance(long id) {
    DetailFragment result=new DetailFragment();
    Bundle args=new Bundle();

    args.putString(ARG_REST_ID, String.valueOf(id));
    result.setArguments(args);

    return(result);
  }

  @Override
  public void onCreate(Bundle state) {
    super.onCreate(state);

    setHasOptionsMenu(true);
  }

  @Override
  public View onCreateView(LayoutInflater inflater, ViewGroup container,
                           Bundle savedInstanceState) {
```

```
      return(inflater.inflate(R.layout.detail_form, container, false));
}

@Override
public void onActivityCreated(Bundle savedInstanceState) {
  super.onActivityCreated(savedInstanceState);

  locMgr=(LocationManager)getActivity().
                          getSystemService(Context.LOCATION_SERVICE);

  name=(EditText)getView().findViewById(R.id.name);
  address=(EditText)getView().findViewById(R.id.addr);
  notes=(EditText)getView().findViewById(R.id.notes);
  types=(RadioGroup)getView().findViewById(R.id.types);
  feed=(EditText)getView().findViewById(R.id.feed);
  location=(TextView)getView().findViewById(R.id.location);

  Bundle args=getArguments();

  if (args!=null) {
    loadRestaurant(args.getString(ARG_REST_ID));
  }
}

@Override
public void onPause() {
  save();
  getHelper().close();
  locMgr.removeUpdates(onLocationChange);

  super.onPause();
}

@Override
public void onCreateOptionsMenu(Menu menu, MenuInflater inflater) {
  inflater.inflate(R.menu.details_option, menu);
}

@Override
public void onPrepareOptionsMenu(Menu menu) {
  if (restaurantId==null) {
    menu.findItem(R.id.location).setEnabled(false);
    menu.findItem(R.id.map).setEnabled(false);
  }
}

@Override
public boolean onOptionsItemSelected(MenuItem item) {
  if (item.getItemId()==R.id.feed) {
    if (isNetworkAvailable()) {
      Intent i=new Intent(getActivity(), FeedActivity.class);

      i.putExtra(FeedActivity.FEED_URL, feed.getText().toString());
      startActivity(i);
```

```
      }
      else {
        Toast
          .makeText(getActivity(), "Sorry, the Internet is not available",
                    Toast.LENGTH_LONG)
          .show();
      }

      return(true);
    }
    else if (item.getItemId()==R.id.location) {
      locMgr.requestLocationUpdates(LocationManager.GPS_PROVIDER,
                                    0, 0, onLocationChange);

      return(true);
    }
    else if (item.getItemId()==R.id.map) {
      Intent i=new Intent(getActivity(), RestaurantMap.class);

      i.putExtra(RestaurantMap.EXTRA_LATITUDE, latitude);
      i.putExtra(RestaurantMap.EXTRA_LONGITUDE, longitude);
      i.putExtra(RestaurantMap.EXTRA_NAME, name.getText().toString());

      startActivity(i);

      return(true);
    }

    return(super.onOptionsItemSelected(item));
  }

  public void loadRestaurant(String restaurantId) {
    this.restaurantId=restaurantId;

    if (restaurantId!=null) {
      load();
    }
  }

  private boolean isNetworkAvailable() {
    ConnectivityManager cm=(ConnectivityManager)getActivity()
                                       getSystemService(Context.CONNECT
IVITY_SERVICE);
    NetworkInfo info=cm.getActiveNetworkInfo();

    return(info!=null);
  }

  private RestaurantHelper getHelper() {
    if (helper==null) {
      helper=new RestaurantHelper(getActivity());
    }

    return(helper);
```

```
}

private void load() {
  Cursor c=getHelper().getById(restaurantId);

  c.moveToFirst();
  name.setText(getHelper().getName(c));
  address.setText(getHelper().getAddress(c));
  notes.setText(getHelper().getNotes(c));
  feed.setText(getHelper().getFeed(c));

  if (getHelper().getType(c).equals("sit_down")) {
    types.check(R.id.sit_down);
  }
  else if (getHelper().getType(c).equals("take_out")) {
    types.check(R.id.take_out);
  }
  else {
    types.check(R.id.delivery);
  }

  latitude=getHelper().getLatitude(c);
  longitude=getHelper().getLongitude(c);

  location.setText(String.valueOf(latitude)
                   +", "
                   +String.valueOf(longitude));

  c.close();
}

private void save() {
  if (name.getText().toString().length()>0) {
    String type=null;

    switch (types.getCheckedRadioButtonId()) {
      case R.id.sit_down:
        type="sit_down";
        break;
      case R.id.take_out:
        type="take_out";
        break;
      default:
        type="delivery";
        break;
    }

    if (restaurantId==null) {
      getHelper().insert(name.getText().toString(),
                         address.getText().toString(), type,
                         notes.getText().toString(),
                         feed.getText().toString());
    }
    else {
```

```
        getHelper().update(restaurantId, name.getText().toString(),
                            address.getText().toString(), type,
                            notes.getText().toString(),
                            feed.getText().toString());
      }
    }
  }

  LocationListener onLocationChange=new LocationListener() {
    public void onLocationChanged(Location fix) {
      getHelper().updateLocation(restaurantId, fix.getLatitude(),
                              fix.getLongitude());
      location.setText(String.valueOf(fix.getLatitude())
                    +", "
                    +String.valueOf(fix.getLongitude()));
      locMgr.removeUpdates(onLocationChange);

      Toast
        .makeText(getActivity(), "Location saved",
                Toast.LENGTH_LONG)
        .show();
    }

    public void onProviderDisabled(String provider) {
      // required for interface, not used
    }

    public void onProviderEnabled(String provider) {
      // required for interface, not used
    }

    public void onStatusChanged(String provider, int status,
                                Bundle extras) {
      // required for interface, not used
    }
  };
}
```

The entire `DetailForm` class after these changes should look a bit like:

```
package apt.tutorial;

import android.content.Intent;
import android.os.Bundle;
import android.support.v4.app.FragmentActivity;

public class DetailForm extends FragmentActivity {
  @Override
  public void onCreate(Bundle savedInstanceState) {
    super.onCreate(savedInstanceState);
    setContentView(R.layout.detail_activity);
  }
```

```
  @Override
  public void onResume() {
    super.onResume();

    String restaurantId=getIntent().getStringExtra(LunchList.ID_EXTRA);

    if (restaurantId!=null) {
      DetailFragment details=(DetailFragment)getSupportFragmentManager()
                                      .findFragmentById(R.id.details);

      if (details!=null) {
        details.loadRestaurant(restaurantId);
      }
    }
  }
}
```

Step #4: Dynamically Add DetailFragment

Now all that remains is to use the revised DetailFragment from within LunchList, when we have the placeholder FrameLayout for it. Modify onRestaurantSelected() in LunchList to look like this:

```
public void onRestaurantSelected(long id) {
  if (findViewById(R.id.details)==null) {
    Intent i=new Intent(this, DetailForm.class);

    i.putExtra(ID_EXTRA, String.valueOf(id));
    startActivity(i);
  }
  else {
    FragmentManager fragMgr=getSupportFragmentManager();
    DetailFragment
details=(DetailFragment)fragMgr.findFragmentById(R.id.details);

    if (details==null) {
      details=DetailFragment.newInstance(id);

      FragmentTransaction xaction=fragMgr.beginTransaction();

      xaction
        .add(R.id.details, details)
        .setTransition(FragmentTransaction.TRANSIT_FRAGMENT_OPEN)
        .addToBackStack(null)
        .commit();
    }
    else {
      details.loadRestaurant(String.valueOf(id));
    }
```

```
    }
}
```

We get a `FragmentManager` via `getSupportFragmentManager()`. That is the ACL approach – if we were using the Honeycomb APIs directly, we would simply use `getFragmentManager()`.

Then, we may need to create a `FragmentTransaction`. As the name suggests, this performs some sort of operation on the roster of dynamic fragments in the activity: add, replace, or remove. In this case, we want to add the `DetailFragment`... but only if it is not already there.

So, we call `findFragmentById()`, which takes the ID of the containing `FrameLayout` as a parameter. If this returns the `DetailFragment`, we do not need to create a new one, so we simply call `loadRestaurant()` on it. If, however, there is no `DetailFragment`, we create one via the static `newInstance()` factory method, and set up the `FragmentTransaction` to add it to the activity plus add it to the "back stack". The latter means that pressing the BACK button once, with the `DetailFragment` in the `LunchList`, will remove the `DetailFragment`. We also set the transition to be "open" (which may apply default animations), and wrap by committing the transaction, which means it will occur as soon as the main application thread gets around to it.

You will need to add imports for `android.support.v4.app.FragmentManager` and `android.support.v4.app.FragmentTransaction`.

The complete `LunchList` class should look something like:

```
package apt.tutorial;

import android.content.Intent;
import android.os.Bundle;
import android.support.v4.app.FragmentActivity;
import android.support.v4.app.FragmentManager;
import android.support.v4.app.FragmentTransaction;

public class LunchList extends FragmentActivity
    implements LunchFragment.OnRestaurantListener {
  public final static String ID_EXTRA="apt.tutorial._ID";
```

```
  @Override
  public void onCreate(Bundle savedInstanceState) {
    super.onCreate(savedInstanceState);
    setContentView(R.layout.main);

    LunchFragment lunch
      =(LunchFragment)getSupportFragmentManager()
                        .findFragmentById(R.id.lunch);

    lunch.setOnRestaurantListener(this);
  }

  public void onRestaurantSelected(long id) {
    if (findViewById(R.id.details)==null) {
      Intent i=new Intent(this, DetailForm.class);

      i.putExtra(ID_EXTRA, String.valueOf(id));
      startActivity(i);
    }
    else {
      FragmentManager fragMgr=getSupportFragmentManager();
      DetailFragment
details=(DetailFragment)fragMgr.findFragmentById(R.id.details);

      if (details==null) {
        details=DetailFragment.newInstance(id);

        FragmentTransaction xaction=fragMgr.beginTransaction();

        xaction
          .add(R.id.details, details)
          .setTransition(FragmentTransaction.TRANSIT_FRAGMENT_OPEN)
          .addToBackStack(null)
          .commit();
      }
      else {
        details.loadRestaurant(String.valueOf(id));
      }
    }
  }
}
```

If you compile and install this on an phone-sized device or emulator, you should see no difference. If you compile and install this on a tablet-sized device or emulator, you will start off with the LunchFragment on the left:

Figure 100. LunchList on a XOOM, with restaurants on the left

Then, tapping a restaurant will bring up the DetailFragment on the right:

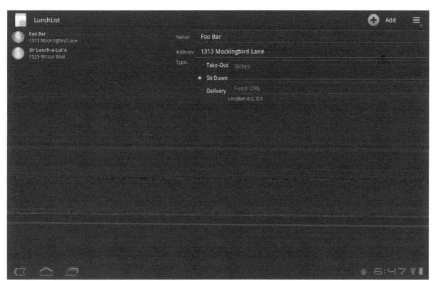

Figure 101. LunchList on a XOOM, with details on the right

Tapping a different restaurant changes the `DetailFragment` contents. Tapping the BACK button will remove the `DetailFragment`; tapping it again will close the `LunchList` activity.

Extra Credit

Here are some things you can try beyond those step-by-step instructions:

- Experiment with having the list of restaurants be in the action bar in the so-called "list" navigation mode (`NAVIGATION_MODE_LIST`). This will be a bit silly for tablets, but it might make sense for smaller devices, if and when they get the action bar and fragments. The techniques for this are found in a chapter of The Busy Coder's Guide to *Advanced* Android Development[64].

- We have lost our ability to save changes to the restaurant, except by using the BACK button to get rid of the `DetailFragment`. This makes for an awkward user experience. Come up with something better, such as automatically saving changes if we are loading a new restaurant into the existing fragment.

- Normally, when having a `ListFragment` on-screen along with a dynamic fragment tied to that list, the user's choice in the `ListFragment` is "activated". This is a persistent highlight, reminding the user the context of whatever the dynamic fragment is showing. Add this capability to `LunchFragment`, in the form of a `CHOICE_MODE_SINGLE` ListView and a row that supports the "activated" state... but only on API Level 11 or higher. The techniques for this are found in a chapter of The Busy Coder's Guide to *Advanced* Android Development[65].

Further Reading

Dynamic fragments via `FragmentTransaction` can be found in a chapter of The Busy Coder's Guide to *Advanced* Android Development[66].

64 http://commonsware.com/AdvAndroid
65 http://commonsware.com/AdvAndroid
66 http://commonsware.com/AdvAndroid

Getting Some Help With Lunch

We already arranged to display Web content using the user's default Web browser, as part of our rudimentary feed reader. Now, let us turn to WebView for Web content, in this case some basic online help.

Step-By-Step Instructions

First, you need to have completed the previous tutorial. If you are beginning the tutorials here, or if you wish to not use your existing work, you can download a ZIP file with all of the tutorial results, and you can copy the 24-MultScreenSizes edition of LunchList to use as a starting point. If you are using Eclipse, these instructions will help you load the project into a workspace.

Step #1: Draft and Package the Help HTML

Next, we need some placeholder HTML to serve as our help prose. This does not need to be terribly fancy – in fact, simpler HTML works better, simply because it loads faster.

So, write a Web page that will serve as the placeholder for the LunchList help. The key is where you put the page: create an assets/ directory in your project and store it as help.html in there. That will line up with the URL we will use in the next section to reference that help file.

Step #2: Create a Help Activity

Now, we can create a help activity class that will load our Web page and do some other useful things.

First, create `LunchList/res/layout/help.xml` with the following content:

```xml
<?xml version="1.0" encoding="utf-8"?>
<LinearLayout xmlns:android="http://schemas.android.com/apk/res/android"
  android:orientation="vertical"
  android:layout_width="match_parent"
  android:layout_height="match_parent"
  >
  <WebView android:id="@+id/webkit"
    android:layout_width="match_parent"
    android:layout_height="0px"
    android:layout_weight="1"
  />
</LinearLayout>
```

Then, create `LunchList/src/apt/tutorial/HelpPage.java` with the following code:

```java
package apt.tutorial.two;

import android.app.Activity;
import android.content.Intent;
import android.os.Bundle;
import android.webkit.WebView;

public class HelpPage extends Activity {
  private WebView browser;

  @Override
  public void onCreate(Bundle icicle) {
    super.onCreate(icicle);
    setContentView(R.layout.help);

    browser=(WebView)findViewById(R.id.webkit);
    browser.loadUrl("file:///android_asset/help.html");
  }
}
```

Note how we use `file:///android_asset/help.html` as the URL syntax to reach into our APK's assets to load the desired Web page.

Finally, as normal, we need to add another `<activity>` element to our `AndroidManifest.xml` file:

```
<activity android:name=".HelpPage"></activity>
```

Step #3: Splice In the Help Activity

Finally, we need to integrate `HelpPage` into the application, so users can display the help. As we have done in previous tutorials, we will accomplish this by extending the option menu with another menu item.

First, add the following `<item>` to `LunchList/res/menu/option.xml` and to `LunchList/res/menu/detail-option.xml`:

```
<item android:id="@+id/help"
  android:title="Help"
  android:icon="@drawable/ic_menu_help"
/>
```

You will also need a suitable menu icon, such as the `ic_menu_help.png` image from the Android SDK.

Then, update `onOptionsItemSelected()` in both `LunchFragment` and `DetailFragment` to launch `HelpPage` when our new help item is selected. The `else if` block you will need to add to both implementations of `onOptionsItemSelected()` is:

```
else if (item.getItemId()==R.id.help) {
  startActivity(new Intent(getActivity(), HelpPage.class));
}
```

For example, the complete `onOptionsItemSelected()` for `LunchFragment` should now look like:

```
@Override
public boolean onOptionsItemSelected(MenuItem item) {
  if (item.getItemId()==R.id.add) {
    startActivity(new Intent(getActivity(), DetailForm.class));

    return(true);
```

```
  }
  else if (item.getItemId()==R.id.prefs) {
    startActivity(new Intent(getActivity(), EditPreferences.class));

    return(true);
  }
  else if (item.getItemId()==R.id.help) {
    startActivity(new Intent(getActivity(), HelpPage.class));
  }

  return(super.onOptionsItemSelected(item));
}
```

Now, if you recompile and reinstall the application, clicking the help menu item from either activity brings up HelpPage with your help content:

Figure 102. The HelpPage activity

Extra Credit

Here are some things you can try beyond those step-by-step instructions:

- Support multiple pages of help text, by using `WebViewClient` and `shouldOverrideUrlLoading()`.

- Experiment with adding images or CSS stylesheets to the help page.

- When running on a larger-screen device, display the help in a `DialogFragment`

Further Reading

You can learn more about the basics of integrating a `WebView` widget into your activities in the "Embedding the WebKit Browser" chapter of The Busy Coder's Guide to Android Development[67].

---

67 http://commonsware.com/Android

Take a Monkey to Lunch

In this tutorial, we will use the Monkey utility to stress test the LunchList application.

Step-By-Step Instructions

First, you need to have completed the previous tutorial. If you are beginning the tutorials here, or if you wish to not use your existing work, you can download a ZIP file with all of the tutorial results, and you can copy the 25-WebKit edition of LunchList to use as a starting point. If you are using Eclipse, these instructions will help you load the project into a workspace.

Step #1: Prep LunchList

Ensure your LunchList has a few restaurants, of different types. Then, leave the LunchList at the LunchList activity itself (i.e., the list of available restaurants).

Step #2: Run the Monkey

Launch a command prompt or shell, and run the following command:

```
adb shell monkey -p apt.tutorial -v --throttle 100 600
```

Note that if you did not add your SDK's `platform-tools/` directory to your system PATH, you may need to change to that directory to get this command to execute properly.

This command indicates:

- You want to run the Monkey

- You want the Monkey to limit itself to testing your application (`-p apt.tutorial`), so if the Monkey attempts to do something that would exit your application (e.g., click the HOME button), that simulated input will be skipped

- You want the Monkey to execute one event every 100 milliseconds (`--throttle 100`)

- You want the Monkey to be verbose and report what events it simulates (`-v`)

- You want the Monkey to perform 600 simulated events

What you should see is the `LunchList` application running amok, as if some monkey were trying out different UI operations (clicking buttons, typing in fields, choosing menu options). If all goes well, `LunchList` will survive without errors. If something goes wrong, you will get an exception, and can use the log information (via DDMS or `adb logcat`) to see what failed and, possibly, how to fix it.

Your shell will show a running tally of what has been done, such as simulating screen taps or key presses.

Extra Credit

Here are some things you can try beyond those step-by-step instructions:

- Try updating your test process to be repeatable, so if you encounter some sort of exception, you can make it happen again. To do this, you will need to save your database file (stored in `/data/data/apt.tutorial/databases/lunchlist.db`) before running

Monkey with the -s switch to provide a known seed value. Each test run should back up the database, run Monkey with a fresh seed, and restore the database. If you got a crash or some other problem, re-run the process with the same seed, and you should be able to reproduce the failure.

- Experiment with additional options to configure the Monkey's operation, as described in the Monkey[68] documentation.

- Experiment with Android's built-in copy of the JUnit test framework to exercise the restaurant model class programmatically.

Further Reading

More about Android's test-related features, including more on the Monkey, can be found in the "Testing" chapter of The Busy Coder's Guide to *Advanced* Android Development[69].

68 http://developer.android.com/guide/developing/tools/monkey.html
69 http://commonsware.com/AdvAndroid

Ringing the Lunch Bell

Our time-for-lunch alarm is a visual alert, but right now we are not beeping the phone or otherwise audibly alerting the user to the fact that it is time for lunch. This feature might be useful, for users who have their phones in their pockets, purses, packs, ponchos, or parkas. So, in this tutorial, we will let the user choose a ringtone, then use it both with our Notification and with the full-activity alert.

Step-By-Step Instructions

First, you need to have completed the previous tutorial. If you are beginning the tutorials here, or if you wish to not use your existing work, you can download a ZIP file with all of the tutorial results, and you can copy the 25-WebKit edition of LunchList to use as a starting point. Note that the previous tutorial had no code changes.

Step #1: Add a Ringtone to the Emulator

If you are using a piece of hardware for developing and testing this application, you should already have ringtones available and can skip this step. However, the Android emulator does not come with any ringtones, for inexplicable reasons. So, we need to add one, so you can choose it during testing.

First, you need to find a likely piece of media for your ringtone and get it on your development machine.

Next, you need to upload that media to the external storage of the emulator. The easiest way to do this is to use the File Explorer in DDMS. In the Eclipse DDMS perspective, the File Explorer is a tab, by default in the upper-right main tab group. In the standalone DDMS, the File Explorer is obtained from the Device menu.

In DDMS, navigate into the /mnt/sdcard directory (note: this might be /sdcard in older Android emulators):

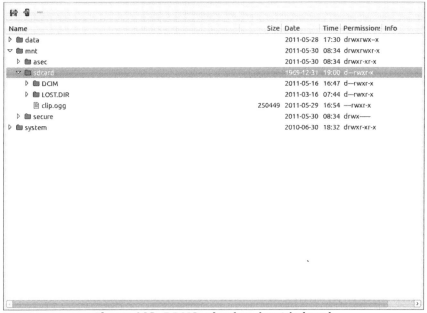

Figure 103. DDMS, viewing /mnt/sdcard

Then, click the to-phone toolbar icon, choose your ringtone file from the Open dialog, and upload it.

While this puts the file on the emulator, uploading a file from DDMS does not cause the MediaStore to index it. The simplest quick way to do this is to go into the Settings application, and from there into the "SD card & phone storage" screen:

Figure 104. The "SD card & phone storage" settings screen

Tap on the "Unmount SD card" entry, wait a bit, then tap on the "Mount SD card" entry when it appears.

At this point, you should be able to go into the Music application and see your ringtone as a song. Try playing the song – if you do not hear anything, and playing with the volume (back in the Settings application) does not help, then the emulator and your development machine are not getting along from an audio playback standpoint. That is not a major problem, though it will mean that you will be unable to hear the ringtones you are setting up in this tutorial.

Finally, long-press on the song in the Music app and choose it to be your ringtone.

Step #2: Set the Alarm Volume

Next, you will want to check the alarm volume on the emulator, to ensure that you will hear the media when it plays back. To do this, go into the Sound screen in the Settings application:

Figure 105. The Sound settings screen

Choose the Volume setting:

Figure 106. The Volume settings dialog

Make sure the "Alarm" volume is sufficiently high, then press OK.

Step #3: Add a RingtonePreference

Next, we need to add a preference to allow the user to choose the ringtone to associate with lunchtime.

To do this, add a RingtonePreference named alarm_ringtone to the res/xml/preferences.xml file:

```
<PreferenceScreen
  xmlns:android="http://schemas.android.com/apk/res/android">
  <ListPreference
    android:key="sort_order"
    android:title="Sort Order"
    android:summary="Choose the order the list uses"
    android:entries="@array/sort_names"
    android:entryValues="@array/sort_clauses"
    android:dialogTitle="Choose a sort order" />
  <CheckBoxPreference
```

```
      android:key="alarm"
      android:title="Sound a Lunch Alarm"
      android:summary="Check if you want to know when it is time for lunch" />
  <apt.tutorial.TimePreference
      android:key="alarm_time"
      android:title="Lunch Alarm Time"
      android:defaultValue="12:00"
      android:summary="Set your desired time for the lunch alarm"
      android:dependency="alarm" />
  <CheckBoxPreference
      android:key="use_notification"
      android:title="Use a Notification"
      android:defaultValue="true"
      android:summary="Check if you want a status bar icon at lunchtime, or
uncheck for a full-screen notice"
      android:dependency="alarm" />
  <RingtonePreference
      android:key="alarm_ringtone"
      android:title="Alarm Ringtone"
      android:summary="Indicate the ringtone to play when it is lunchtime"
      android:showSilent="true"
      android:dependency="alarm" />
</PreferenceScreen>
```

If you compile and reinstall the application, then go into the preferences via the options menu on the LunchList activity, you will see your new preference:

Figure 107. The new preferences, complete with ringtone

Tap on the Alarm Ringtone preference and choose the ringtone you want, such as the one set up in Step #1.

Step #4: Play the Ringtone... with the Notification

Now, we can start using the ringtone, beginning with the Notification.

A Notification already knows how to play a ringtone, by way of the sound data member. All we need to do is detect that the user wanted an alarm ringtone and use it.

With that in mind, update onReceive() of AlarmReceiver to add in a check of the alarm_ringtone preference and such, as shown below:

```
@Override
public void onReceive(Context ctxt, Intent intent) {
  SharedPreferences prefs=PreferenceManager.getDefaultSharedPreferences(ctxt);
  boolean useNotification=prefs.getBoolean("use_notification",
```

```
                                       true);

  if (useNotification) {
    NotificationManager mgr=
      (NotificationManager)ctxt.getSystemService(Context.NOTIFICATION_SERVICE);
    Notification note=new Notification(R.drawable.stat_notify_chat,
                                       "It's time for lunch!",
                                       System.currentTimeMillis());
    PendingIntent i=PendingIntent.getActivity(ctxt, 0,
                          new Intent(ctxt, AlarmActivity.class),
                                     0);

    note.setLatestEventInfo(ctxt, "LunchList",
                            "It's time for lunch! Aren't you hungry?",
                            i);
    note.flags|=Notification.FLAG_AUTO_CANCEL;

    String sound=prefs.getString("alarm_ringtone", null);

    if (sound!=null) {
      note.sound=Uri.parse(sound);
      note.audioStreamType=AudioManager.STREAM_ALARM;
    }

    mgr.notify(NOTIFY_ME_ID, note);
  }
  else {
    Intent i=new Intent(ctxt, AlarmActivity.class);

    i.setFlags(Intent.FLAG_ACTIVITY_NEW_TASK);

    ctxt.startActivity(i);
  }
}
```

Here, if there is a preference for the alarm, we convert the string representation into a Uri and put that in the sound data member of the Notification. We also set the audioStreamType data member to be AudioManager.STREAM_ALARM, meaning that the ringtone should be played at the alarm volume level (instead of, say, the media volume level).

You will need to add imports for android.media.AudioManager and android.net.Uri.

If you compile and install this version of the application, request lunchtime alerts via a Notification, and adjust your alarm time to be a minute or two from now, in a minute or two you will see the same Notification as before, but you will also hear the ringtone.

Step #5: Play the Ringtone... with the Activity

Finally, we can also arrange to play the same ringtone when the AlarmActivity appears. Our original AlarmActivity implementation did nothing but load the layout, so replace it entirely with the following:

```
package apt.tutorial;

import android.app.Activity;
import android.content.SharedPreferences;
import android.media.AudioManager;
import android.media.MediaPlayer;
import android.net.Uri;
import android.os.Bundle;
import android.preference.PreferenceManager;
import android.util.Log;

public class AlarmActivity extends Activity
  implements MediaPlayer.OnPreparedListener {
  MediaPlayer player=new MediaPlayer();

  @Override
  public void onCreate(Bundle savedInstanceState) {
    super.onCreate(savedInstanceState);
    setContentView(R.layout.alarm);

    SharedPreferences prefs=PreferenceManager.getDefaultSharedPreferences(this);
    String sound=prefs.getString("alarm_ringtone", null);

    if (sound!=null) {
      player.setAudioStreamType(AudioManager.STREAM_ALARM);

      try {
        player.setDataSource(sound);
        player.setOnPreparedListener(this);
        player.prepareAsync();
      }
      catch (Exception e) {
        Log.e("LunchList", "Exception in playing ringtone", e);
      }
    }
  }

  @Override
  public void onPause() {
    if (player.isPlaying()) {
      player.stop();
    }

    super.onPause();
  }
```

```
  public void onPrepared(MediaPlayer player) {
    player.start();
  }
}
```

Here, we do setContentView() as before, then check to see if we have a ringtone set for the alarm. If so, we create a new MediaPlayer object to play back that ringtone. Here, we:

- Set the volume stream to be STREAM_ALARM, as we did with the Notification

- Set the path to the ringtone via setDataSource()

- Indicate that the AlarmActivity itself should be notified after the MediaPlayer is "prepared" (i.e., metadata has been read in and buffers filled up enough to ensure smooth playback of the clip)

- Start the preparation process via prepareAsync()

The prepareAsync() method will do the I/O for loading in the initial clip data on an Android-supplied background thread. AlarmActivity will be notified when that is complete via the onPrepared() method, where we call start() on the MediaPlayer to begin playing the ringtone.

By default, the ringtone would play to completion, which might be a bit long. So, in onPause(), if the ringtone is still being played by the MediaPlayer, we stop it.

If you compile and install this version of the application, uncheck the "Use a Notification" checkbox in the settings , and adjust your alarm time to be a minute or two from now, in a minute or two you will see the AlarmActivity appear and hear your ringtone.

Extra Credit

Here are some things you can try beyond those step-by-step instructions:

- Add an option to allow the user to download a piece of media to serve as the ringtone.

- For `AlarmActivity`, try using `ToneGenerator` to emit a simple beep, as opposed to playing a ringtone.

Further Reading

More about Android's multimedia playback capabilities can be found in the "Media" chapter of The Busy Coder's Guide to *Advanced* Android Development[70].

---

70 http://commonsware.com/AdvAndroid

PART II – Hardware Tutorials

Asking Permission to Place a Call

In this tutorial, we will add a bit of code that asks permission to place a call, and we will add a phone number to our restaurant data model and detail form. Then, we will actually place the call.

Step-By-Step Instructions

First, you need to have completed the previous tutorial. If you are beginning the tutorials here, or if you wish to not use your existing work, you can download a ZIP file with all of the tutorial results, and you can copy the 27-Media edition of LunchList to use as a starting point. If you are using Eclipse, these instructions will help you load the project into a workspace.

Step #1: Add a Phone Number to the Database Schema

If we want our phone numbers to stick around, we need to put them in the database.

With that in mind, update RestaurantHelper to use the following implementation of onCreate():

```
@Override
public void onCreate(SQLiteDatabase db) {
  db.execSQL("CREATE TABLE restaurants (_id INTEGER PRIMARY KEY AUTOINCREMENT,
name TEXT, address TEXT, type TEXT, notes TEXT, feed TEXT, lat REAL, lon REAL,
phone TEXT);");
}
```

Any time you make a material modification to the schema, you also need to increment the schema version number. For RestaurantHelper, that is held in SCHEMA_VERSION, so increment to 4:

```
private static final int SCHEMA_VERSION=4;
```

Step #2: Intelligently Handle Database Updates

As before, when the schema version increments, onUpgrade() is called on RestaurantHelper rather than onCreate(). It is our job to update the schema, preferably without losing any user data. Here, we just use an ALTER TABLE SQL statement, since all we are doing is adding a column, to go along with all our other ALTER TABLE statements from previous schema upgrades:

```
@Override
public void onUpgrade(SQLiteDatabase db, int oldVersion, int newVersion) {
  if (oldVersion<2) {
    db.execSQL("ALTER TABLE restaurants ADD COLUMN feed TEXT");
  }

  if (oldVersion<3) {
    db.execSQL("ALTER TABLE restaurants ADD COLUMN lat REAL");
    db.execSQL("ALTER TABLE restaurants ADD COLUMN lon REAL");
  }

  if (oldVersion<4) {
    db.execSQL("ALTER TABLE restaurants ADD COLUMN phone TEXT");
  }
}
```

Step #3: Add Phone Number Support to the Rest of the Helper

We also need to update our insert() method on RestaurantHelper to accept a phone number:

```
public void insert(String name, String address,
                   String type, String notes,
                   String feed, String phone) {
  ContentValues cv=new ContentValues();

  cv.put("name", name);
  cv.put("address", address);
  cv.put("type", type);
  cv.put("notes", notes);
  cv.put("feed", feed);
  cv.put("phone", phone);

  getWritableDatabase().insert("restaurants", "name", cv);
}
```

and the corresponding update() method, also to accept a phone number:

```
public void update(String id, String name, String address,
                   String type, String notes, String feed,
                   String phone) {
  ContentValues cv=new ContentValues();
  String[] args={id};

  cv.put("name", name);
  cv.put("address", address);
  cv.put("type", type);
  cv.put("notes", notes);
  cv.put("feed", feed);
  cv.put("phone", phone);

  getWritableDatabase().update("restaurants", cv, "_ID=?",
                               args);
}
```

The two query methods, getAll() and getById(), also should return the phone number from each of their respective queries:

```
public Cursor getAll(String orderBy) {
  return(getReadableDatabase()
          .rawQuery("SELECT _id, name, address, type, notes, lat, lon, phone
FROM restaurants ORDER BY "+orderBy,
                    null));
}

public Cursor getById(String id) {
  String[] args={id};

  return(getReadableDatabase()
          .rawQuery("SELECT _id, name, address, type, notes, feed, lat, lon,
phone FROM restaurants WHERE _ID=?",
```

```
                             args));
}
```

Also, add a `getPhone()` method to `RestaurantHelper`, akin to the other methods that extract columns out of a Cursor:

```
public String getPhone(Cursor c) {
  return(c.getString(8));
}
```

The complete revised `RestaurantHelper` should now resemble:

```
package apt.tutorial;

import android.content.Context;
import android.content.ContentValues;
import android.database.Cursor;
import android.database.SQLException;
import android.database.sqlite.SQLiteOpenHelper;
import android.database.sqlite.SQLiteDatabase;
import android.database.sqlite.SQLiteQueryBuilder;

class RestaurantHelper extends SQLiteOpenHelper {
  private static final String DATABASE_NAME="lunchlist.db";
  private static final int SCHEMA_VERSION=4;

  public RestaurantHelper(Context context) {
    super(context, DATABASE_NAME, null, SCHEMA_VERSION);
  }

  @Override
  public void onCreate(SQLiteDatabase db) {
    db.execSQL("CREATE TABLE restaurants (_id INTEGER PRIMARY KEY AUTOINCREMENT,
name TEXT, address TEXT, type TEXT, notes TEXT, feed TEXT, lat REAL, lon REAL,
phone TEXT);");
  }

  @Override
  public void onUpgrade(SQLiteDatabase db, int oldVersion, int newVersion) {
    if (oldVersion<2) {
      db.execSQL("ALTER TABLE restaurants ADD COLUMN feed TEXT");
    }

    if (oldVersion<3) {
      db.execSQL("ALTER TABLE restaurants ADD COLUMN lat REAL");
      db.execSQL("ALTER TABLE restaurants ADD COLUMN lon REAL");
    }

    if (oldVersion<4) {
      db.execSQL("ALTER TABLE restaurants ADD COLUMN phone TEXT");
    }
```

```
  }

  public Cursor getAll(String orderBy) {
    return(getReadableDatabase()
              .rawQuery("SELECT _id, name, address, type, notes, lat, lon, phone
FROM restaurants ORDER BY "+orderBy,
                      null));
  }

  public Cursor getById(String id) {
    String[] args={id};

    return(getReadableDatabase()
              .rawQuery("SELECT _id, name, address, type, notes, feed, lat, lon,
phone FROM restaurants WHERE _ID=?",
                      args));
  }

  public void insert(String name, String address,
                     String type, String notes,
                     String feed, String phone) {
    ContentValues cv=new ContentValues();

    cv.put("name", name);
    cv.put("address", address);
    cv.put("type", type);
    cv.put("notes", notes);
    cv.put("feed", feed);
    cv.put("phone", phone);

    getWritableDatabase().insert("restaurants", "name", cv);
  }

  public void update(String id, String name, String address,
                     String type, String notes, String feed,
                     String phone) {
    ContentValues cv=new ContentValues();
    String[] args={id};

    cv.put("name", name);
    cv.put("address", address);
    cv.put("type", type);
    cv.put("notes", notes);
    cv.put("feed", feed);
    cv.put("phone", phone);

    getWritableDatabase().update("restaurants", cv, "_ID=?",
                                 args);
  }

  public void updateLocation(String id, double lat, double lon) {
    ContentValues cv=new ContentValues();
    String[] args={id};
```

```
    cv.put("lat", lat);
    cv.put("lon", lon);

    getWritableDatabase().update("restaurants", cv, "_ID=?",
                                 args);
  }

  public String getName(Cursor c) {
    return(c.getString(1));
  }

  public String getAddress(Cursor c) {
    return(c.getString(2));
  }

  public String getType(Cursor c) {
    return(c.getString(3));
  }

  public String getNotes(Cursor c) {
    return(c.getString(4));
  }

  public String getFeed(Cursor c) {
    return(c.getString(5));
  }

  public double getLatitude(Cursor c) {
    return(c.getDouble(6));
  }

  public double getLongitude(Cursor c) {
    return(c.getDouble(7));
  }

  public String getPhone(Cursor c) {
    return(c.getString(8));
  }
}
```

Step #4: Collect the Phone Number on the Detail Form

If we actually want to have phone numbers, though, we need to actually collect them on DetailFragment.

First, update LunchList/res/layout/detail_form.xml to add the following after the address row in our TableLayout:

```
<TableRow>
  <TextView android:text="Phone:" />
  <EditText android:id="@+id/phone" android:inputType="phone" />
</TableRow>
```

Notice that we are using `android:inputType="phone"` on the new `EditText` widget. This will cause Android to use a soft keyboard set up for entering a phone number (where available), rather than a standard keyboard layout.

Similarly, add the following after the `address` row in `LunchList/res/layout-land/detail_form.xml`:

```
<TableRow>
  <TextView android:text="Phone:" />
  <EditText android:id="@+id/phone"
    android:layout_span="2"
  />
</TableRow>
```

Then, as in the previous section, clone all references to `address` in `DetailFragment` to make references to our `phone` widgets, such as:

```
EditText address=null;
EditText phone=null;
```

and:

```
address=(EditText)getView().findViewById(R.id.addr);
phone=(EditText)getView().findViewById(R.id.phone);
```

At this point, you can recompile and reinstall the application. When you first run it, there will be a tiny pause as the database is updated. After that point, you can use the new field to add phone numbers to whichever restaurants you want:

Figure 108. The new DetailForm layout

Step #5: Ask for Permission to Make Calls

Then, we can update AndroidManifest.xml to put in a permission request to be able to place phone calls.

But, there's a catch.

We could just pop in another <uses-permission> element, this time asking for the CALL_PHONE permission. However, asking for this permission implies that we need the device to be a phone. In this case, we do not want to limit the application to only run on phones – we can use techniques to determine if a device is a phone at runtime. That way, we can offer integrated calling on phones, yet still work on tablets, televisions, etc. But to do that, we need to indicate to Android that we want to be able to call phones, but if the device is not a phone, that is fine as well.

With that in mind, add the CALL_PHONE permission and subsequent ‹uses-feature› element as shown below

```xml
<?xml version="1.0" encoding="utf-8"?>
<manifest android:versionCode="1"
          android:versionName="1.0"
          package="apt.tutorial"
          xmlns:android="http://schemas.android.com/apk/res/android">

    <uses-sdk android:minSdkVersion="4" android:targetSdkVersion="11" />
    <uses-permission android:name="android.permission.INTERNET" />
    <uses-permission android:name="android.permission.ACCESS_NETWORK_STATE" />
    <uses-permission android:name="android.permission.ACCESS_FINE_LOCATION" />
    <uses-permission android:name="android.permission.RECEIVE_BOOT_COMPLETED" />
    <uses-permission android:name="android.permission.CALL_PHONE" />
    <uses-feature android:name="android.hardware.telephony"
                  android:required="false" />
    <supports-screens android:largeScreens="true"
                      android:normalScreens="true"
                      android:smallScreens="false" />
    <application android:label="@string/app_name">
      <uses-library android:name="com.google.android.maps" />
      <activity android:label="@string/app_name"
                android:name=".LunchList">
        <intent-filter>
          <action android:name="android.intent.action.MAIN" />
          <category android:name="android.intent.category.LAUNCHER" />
        </intent-filter>
      </activity>
      <activity android:name=".DetailForm"></activity>
      <activity android:name=".EditPreferences"></activity>
      <activity android:name=".FeedActivity"></activity>
      <activity android:name=".RestaurantMap"></activity>
      <activity android:name=".AlarmActivity"></activity>
      <activity android:name=".HelpPage"></activity>
      <service android:name=".FeedService"></service>
      <service android:name=".WidgetService"></service>
      <service android:name=".ListWidgetService"
               android:permission="android.permission.BIND_REMOTEVIEWS">
      </service>
      <receiver android:enabled="false"
                android:name=".OnBootReceiver">
        <intent-filter>
          <action android:name="android.intent.action.BOOT_COMPLETED" />
        </intent-filter>
      </receiver>
      <receiver android:name=".OnAlarmReceiver"></receiver>
      <receiver android:icon="@drawable/icon"
                android:label="@string/app_name"
                android:name=".AppWidget">
        <intent-filter>
          <action android:name="android.appwidget.action.APPWIDGET_UPDATE" />
        </intent-filter>
```

```
        <meta-data android:name="android.appwidget.provider"
                android:resource="@xml/widget_provider" />
    </receiver>
  </application>
</manifest>
```

Here, the `<uses-feature>` element says that it would be nice if the device were a phone (`android.hardware.telephony`) but that it is not required (`android:required="false"`). If we were to leave out this element, Android would assume, based on the `CALL_PHONE` permission, that `android.hardware.telephony` *was* required, and our application would not install on non-phones.

Step #6: See If We Have Telephony

However, this means that we need to determine, at runtime, if we are on a phone or not. The best way to do that is to use `PackageManager` and the `hasSystemFeature()` method. This takes the name of a hardware feature (e.g., `android.hardware.telephony`) and tells us if the device has it or not. For features we request but do not make mandatory, this is how we can find out what is possible so we can update our UI to match.

With that in mind, on `DetailFragment`, add an `isTelephonyAvailable()` method as follows:

```
private boolean isTelephonyAvailable() {
  return(getActivity()
        .getPackageManager()
        .hasSystemFeature("android.hardware.telephony"));
}
```

Step #7: Dial the Number

Next, let us set up `DetailForm` with its own option menu that contains a Call item. When chosen, we dial the phone number, assuming there is one.

First, update `LunchList/res/menu/details_option.xml` to include a call menu choice:

```
<?xml version="1.0" encoding="utf-8"?>
<menu xmlns:android="http://schemas.android.com/apk/res/android">
  <item android:id="@+id/feed"
    android:title="RSS Feed"
    android:icon="@drawable/ic_menu_friendslist"
  />
  <item android:id="@+id/location"
    android:title="Save Location"
    android:icon="@drawable/ic_menu_compass"
  />
  <item android:id="@+id/map"
    android:title="Show on Map"
    android:icon="@drawable/ic_menu_mapmode"
  />
  <item android:id="@+id/call"
    android:title="Call"
    android:icon="@drawable/ic_menu_call"
    android:enabled="false"
  />
  <item android:id="@+id/help"
    android:title="Help"
    android:icon="@drawable/ic_menu_help"
  />
</menu>
```

You will note that the above code makes the menu item disabled by default. We need to update onPrepareOptionsMenu() in DetailFragment to enable it if telephony is available:

```
@Override
public void onPrepareOptionsMenu(Menu menu) {
  if (restaurantId==null) {
    menu.findItem(R.id.location).setEnabled(false);
    menu.findItem(R.id.map).setEnabled(false);
  }

  if (isTelephonyAvailable()) {
    menu.findItem(R.id.call).setEnabled(true);
  }
}
```

Then, update onOptionsItemSelected() in DetailFragment to include code for the R.id.call case:

```
@Override
public boolean onOptionsItemSelected(MenuItem item) {
  if (item.getItemId()==R.id.feed) {
    if (isNetworkAvailable()) {
      Intent i=new Intent(getActivity(), FeedActivity.class);
```

```
      i.putExtra(FeedActivity.FEED_URL, feed.getText().toString());
      startActivity(i);
    }
    else {
      Toast
        .makeText(getActivity(), "Sorry, the Internet is not available",
                  Toast.LENGTH_LONG)
        .show();
    }

    return(true);
  }
  else if (item.getItemId()==R.id.location) {
    locMgr.requestLocationUpdates(LocationManager.GPS_PROVIDER,
                                  0, 0, onLocationChange);

    return(true);
  }
  else if (item.getItemId()==R.id.map) {
    Intent i=new Intent(getActivity(), RestaurantMap.class);

    i.putExtra(RestaurantMap.EXTRA_LATITUDE, latitude);
    i.putExtra(RestaurantMap.EXTRA_LONGITUDE, longitude);
    i.putExtra(RestaurantMap.EXTRA_NAME, name.getText().toString());

    startActivity(i);

    return(true);
  }
  else if (item.getItemId()==R.id.call) {
    String toDial="tel:"+phone.getText().toString();

    if (toDial.length()>4) {
      startActivity(new Intent(Intent.ACTION_CALL,
                               Uri.parse(toDial)));
    }
  }
  else if (item.getItemId()==R.id.help) {
    startActivity(new Intent(getActivity(), HelpPage.class));
  }

  return(super.onOptionsItemSelected(item));
}
```

Note that you will need to add an import to android.net.Uri to get this to compile cleanly.

In the new code, we check to see if there is a phone number. If so, we wrap the phone number in a tel: Uri, then put that in an ACTION_DIAL Intent and start an activity on that Intent. This puts the phone number in the dialer.

If you rebuild and reinstall the application *on a device* and try out the new menu choice on some restaurant with a phone number, you will see the Dialer appear:

Figure 109. The Dialer

Step #8: Make the Call

Suppose we want to take advantage of the CALL_PHONE permission we requested earlier in this tutorial. Simply switch your Intent from ACTION_DIAL to ACTION_CALL. Now, if you rebuild and reinstall the application, and try choosing the Call option menu item, you will immediately "call" the phone number...which will actually place a phone call if you are trying this on a device. The emulator, of course, cannot place phone calls.

The DetailFragment implementation you should wind up with, in the end, should look a bit like:

```
package apt.tutorial;
```

```java
import android.content.Context;
import android.content.Intent;
import android.database.Cursor;
import android.location.Location;
import android.location.LocationListener;
import android.location.LocationManager;
import android.net.ConnectivityManager;
import android.net.NetworkInfo;
import android.net.Uri;
import android.os.Bundle;
import android.support.v4.app.Fragment;
import android.view.LayoutInflater;
import android.view.Menu;
import android.view.MenuInflater;
import android.view.MenuItem;
import android.view.View;
import android.view.ViewGroup;
import android.widget.EditText;
import android.widget.RadioGroup;
import android.widget.TextView;
import android.widget.Toast;

public class DetailFragment extends Fragment {
  private static final String ARG_REST_ID="apt.tutorial.ARG_REST_ID";
  EditText name=null;
  EditText address=null;
  EditText phone=null;
  EditText notes=null;
  EditText feed=null;
  RadioGroup types=null;
  RestaurantHelper helper=null;
  String restaurantId=null;
  TextView location=null;
  LocationManager locMgr=null;
  double latitude=0.0d;
  double longitude=0.0d;

  public static DetailFragment newInstance(long id) {
    DetailFragment result=new DetailFragment();
    Bundle args=new Bundle();

    args.putString(ARG_REST_ID, String.valueOf(id));
    result.setArguments(args);

    return(result);
  }

  @Override
  public void onCreate(Bundle state) {
    super.onCreate(state);

    setHasOptionsMenu(true);
  }
```

```java
@Override
public View onCreateView(LayoutInflater inflater, ViewGroup container,
                         Bundle savedInstanceState) {
  return(inflater.inflate(R.layout.detail_form, container, false));
}

@Override
public void onActivityCreated(Bundle savedInstanceState) {
  super.onActivityCreated(savedInstanceState);

  locMgr=(LocationManager)getActivity().
                          getSystemService(Context.LOCATION_SERVICE);

  name=(EditText)getView().findViewById(R.id.name);
  address=(EditText)getView().findViewById(R.id.addr);
  phone=(EditText)getView().findViewById(R.id.phone);
  notes=(EditText)getView().findViewById(R.id.notes);
  types=(RadioGroup)getView().findViewById(R.id.types);
  feed=(EditText)getView().findViewById(R.id.feed);
  location=(TextView)getView().findViewById(R.id.location);

  Bundle args=getArguments();

  if (args!=null) {
    loadRestaurant(args.getString(ARG_REST_ID));
  }
}

@Override
public void onPause() {
  save();
  getHelper().close();
  locMgr.removeUpdates(onLocationChange);

  super.onPause();
}

@Override
public void onCreateOptionsMenu(Menu menu, MenuInflater inflater) {
  inflater.inflate(R.menu.details_option, menu);
}

@Override
public void onPrepareOptionsMenu(Menu menu) {
  if (restaurantId==null) {
    menu.findItem(R.id.location).setEnabled(false);
    menu.findItem(R.id.map).setEnabled(false);
  }

  if (isTelephonyAvailable()) {
    menu.findItem(R.id.call).setEnabled(true);
  }
}
```

```
@Override
public boolean onOptionsItemSelected(MenuItem item) {
  if (item.getItemId()==R.id.feed) {
    if (isNetworkAvailable()) {
      Intent i=new Intent(getActivity(), FeedActivity.class);

      i.putExtra(FeedActivity.FEED_URL, feed.getText().toString());
      startActivity(i);
    }
    else {
      Toast
        .makeText(getActivity(), "Sorry, the Internet is not available",
                 Toast.LENGTH_LONG)
        .show();
    }

    return(true);
  }
  else if (item.getItemId()==R.id.location) {
    locMgr.requestLocationUpdates(LocationManager.GPS_PROVIDER,
                                  0, 0, onLocationChange);

    return(true);
  }
  else if (item.getItemId()==R.id.map) {
    Intent i=new Intent(getActivity(), RestaurantMap.class);

    i.putExtra(RestaurantMap.EXTRA_LATITUDE, latitude);
    i.putExtra(RestaurantMap.EXTRA_LONGITUDE, longitude);
    i.putExtra(RestaurantMap.EXTRA_NAME, name.getText().toString());

    startActivity(i);

    return(true);
  }
  else if (item.getItemId()==R.id.call) {
    String toDial="tel:"+phone.getText().toString();

    if (toDial.length()>4) {
      startActivity(new Intent(Intent.ACTION_DIAL,
                               Uri.parse(toDial)));
    }
  }
  else if (item.getItemId()==R.id.help) {
    startActivity(new Intent(getActivity(), HelpPage.class));
  }

  return(super.onOptionsItemSelected(item));
}

public void loadRestaurant(String restaurantId) {
  this.restaurantId=restaurantId;

  if (restaurantId!=null) {
```

```
    load();
  }
}

private boolean isNetworkAvailable() {
  ConnectivityManager cm=(ConnectivityManager)getActivity().
                                             getSystemService(Context.CONNECT
IVITY_SERVICE);
  NetworkInfo info=cm.getActiveNetworkInfo();

  return(info!=null);
}

private boolean isTelephonyAvailable() {
  return(getActivity()
          .getPackageManager()
          .hasSystemFeature("android.hardware.telephony"));
}

private RestaurantHelper getHelper() {
  if (helper==null) {
    helper=new RestaurantHelper(getActivity());
  }

  return(helper);
}

private void load() {
  Cursor c=getHelper().getById(restaurantId);

  c.moveToFirst();
  name.setText(getHelper().getName(c));
  address.setText(getHelper().getAddress(c));
  phone.setText(getHelper().getPhone(c));
  notes.setText(getHelper().getNotes(c));
  feed.setText(getHelper().getFeed(c));

  if (getHelper().getType(c).equals("sit_down")) {
    types.check(R.id.sit_down);
  }
  else if (getHelper().getType(c).equals("take_out")) {
    types.check(R.id.take_out);
  }
  else {
    types.check(R.id.delivery);
  }

  latitude=getHelper().getLatitude(c);
  longitude=getHelper().getLongitude(c);

  location.setText(String.valueOf(latitude)
                    +", "
                    +String.valueOf(longitude));
```

```
    c.close();
  }

  private void save() {
    if (name.getText().toString().length()>0) {
      String type=null;

      switch (types.getCheckedRadioButtonId()) {
        case R.id.sit_down:
          type="sit_down";
          break;
        case R.id.take_out:
          type="take_out";
          break;
        default:
          type="delivery";
          break;
      }

      if (restaurantId==null) {
        getHelper().insert(name.getText().toString(),
                      address.getText().toString(), type,
                      notes.getText().toString(),
                      feed.getText().toString(),
                      phone.getText().toString());
      }
      else {
        getHelper().update(restaurantId, name.getText().toString(),
                      address.getText().toString(), type,
                      notes.getText().toString(),
                      feed.getText().toString(),
                      phone.getText().toString());
      }
    }
  }

  LocationListener onLocationChange=new LocationListener() {
    public void onLocationChanged(Location fix) {
      getHelper().updateLocation(restaurantId, fix.getLatitude(),
                        fix.getLongitude());
      location.setText(String.valueOf(fix.getLatitude())
                  +", "
                  +String.valueOf(fix.getLongitude())));
      locMgr.removeUpdates(onLocationChange);

      Toast
        .makeText(getActivity(), "Location saved",
                Toast.LENGTH_LONG)
        .show();
    }

    public void onProviderDisabled(String provider) {
      // required for interface, not used
    }
```

```
    public void onProviderEnabled(String provider) {
      // required for interface, not used
    }

    public void onStatusChanged(String provider, int status,
                                Bundle extras) {
      // required for interface, not used
    }
  };
}
```

Extra Credit

Here are some things you can try beyond those step-by-step instructions:

- Add a preference to display the phone number instead of the address in the restaurant list. Have the list detect the preference and fill in the second line of the restaurant rows accordingly.

- Push your APK file to a Web site that is configured to support the proper MIME type for Android application downloads (e.g., Amazon S3). Try installing your APK onto a device from the published location, to see how your requested permission appears to end users at install time.

Further Reading

Permissions in general are covered in the "Requesting and Requiring Permissions" chapter of The Busy Coder's Guide to Android Development[71]. Working with the telephony features of Android is briefly covered in the "Handling Telephone Calls" chapter of the same book.

---

71   http://commonsware.com/Android

How To Get Started

Let us get you set up with the pieces and parts necessary to build an Android app.

NOTE: the instructions presented here are accurate as of the time of this writing. However, the tools change rapidly, and so these instructions may be out of date by the time you read this. Please refer to the Android Developers Web site[72] for current instructions, using this as a base guideline of what to expect.

Java

When you write Android applications, you typically write them in Java source code. That Java source code is then turned into the stuff that Android actually runs (Dalvik bytecode in an APK file).

Hence, the first thing you need to do is get set up with a Java development environment and be ready to start writing Java classes.

---

72 http://developer.android.com

Step #1: Install the JDK

You need to obtain and install the official Sun/Oracle Java SE SDK (JDK). You can obtain this from the Oracle Java Web site[73] for Windows and Linux, and presumably from Apple for OS X. The plain JDK (sans any "bundles") should suffice. Follow the instructions supplied by Oracle or Apple for installing it on your machine. At the time of this writing, Android supports Java 5 and Java 6. Note that Android does not support Java 7.

Alternative Java Compilers

In principle, you are supposed to use the official Sun/Oracle Java SE SDK. In practice, it appears that OpenJDK also works, at least on Ubuntu. However, the further removed you get from the official Sun/Oracle implementation, the less likely it is that it will work. For example, the GNU Compiler for Java (GCJ) may not work with Android.

Step #2: Learn Java

This book, like most books and documentation on Android, assumes that you have basic Java programming experience. If you lack this, you really should consider spending a bit of time on Java fundamentals, before you dive into Android. Otherwise, you may find the experience to be frustrating.

If you are in need of a crash course in Java to get involved in Android development, here are the concepts you need to succeed, presented in no particular order:

- Language fundamentals (flow control, etc.)
- Classes and objects
- Methods and data members
- Public, private, and protected

---

73 http://www.oracle.com/technetwork/java/index.html

- Static and instance scope

- Exceptions

- Threads and concurrency control

- Collections

- Generics

- File I/O

- Reflection

- Interfaces

Install the Android SDK

The Android SDK gives you all the tools you need to create and test Android applications. It comes in two parts: the base tools, plus version-specific SDKs and related add-ons.

Step #1: Install the Base Tools

The Android developer tools can be found on the Android Developers Web site[74]. Download the ZIP file appropriate for your platform and unZIP it in some likely spot – there is no specific path that is required. Windows users also have the option of running a self-installing EXE file.

Step #2: Install the SDKs and Add-Ons

Inside the `tools/` directory of your Android SDK installation from the previous step, you will see an `android` batch file or shell script. If you run that, you will be presented with the Android SDK and AVD Manager:

---

74 http://developer.android.com/sdk/index.html

Figure 110. Android SDK and AVD Manager

At this point, while you have some of the build tools, you lack the Java files necessary to compile an Android application. You also lack a few additional build tools, plus the files necessary to run an Android emulator.

To address this, click on the Available Packages option on the left. This brings up a tree:

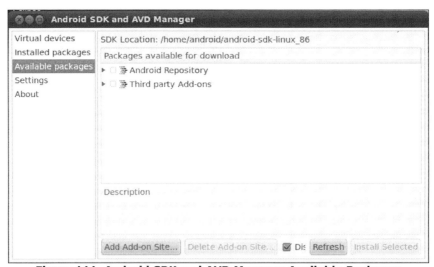

Figure 111. Android SDK and AVD Manager Available Packages

Open the Android Repository branch of the tree. After a short pause, you will see a screen similar to this:

Figure 112. Android SDK and AVD Manager Available Android Packages

You will want to check the following items:

- "SDK Platform" for all Android SDK releases you want to test against – for this book API 8 (Android 2.2) is recommended

- "Documentation for Android SDK" for the latest Android SDK release

- "Samples for SDK" for the latest Android SDK release, and perhaps for older releases if you wish

Then, open the Third-Party Add-Ons branch of the tree. After a short pause, you will see a screen similar to this:

Figure 113. Android SDK and AVD Manager Available Third-Party Add-Ons

Fold open the "Google Inc. add-ons" branch, which will display something like this:

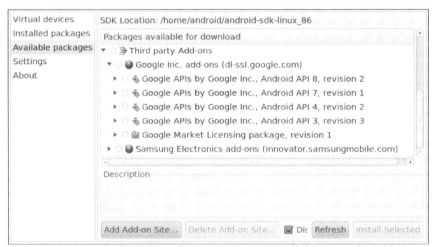

Figure 114. Android SDK and AVD Manager Available Google Add-Ons

Most likely, you will want to check the "Google APIs by Google Inc." items that match up with the SDK versions you selected in the Android Repository branch. The "Google APIs" include support for Google Maps, both from your code and in the Android emulator.

When you have checked all of the items you want to download, click the Install Selected button, which brings up a license confirmation dialog:

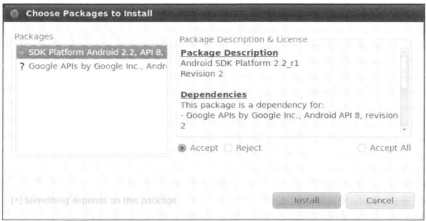

Figure 115. Android SDK and AVD Manger Installing Packages

Review and accept the licenses, then click the Install button. At this point, this is a fine time to go get lunch. Or, perhaps dinner. Unless you have a substantial Internet connection, downloading all of this data and unpacking it will take a fair bit of time.

When the download is complete, you can close up the SDK and AVD Manager if you wish, though we will use it to set up the emulator in a later step of this chapter.

Install the ADT for Eclipse

If you will not be using Eclipse for your Android development, you can skip to the next section.

If you have not yet installed Eclipse, you will need to do that first. Eclipse can be downloaded from the Eclipse Web site[75]. The "Eclipse IDE for Java Developers" package will work fine.

---

75 http://www.eclipse.org/downloads/

Next, you need to install the Android Developer Tools (ADT) plug-in. To do this, go to Help | Install New Software... in the Eclipse main menu. Then, click the Add button to add a new source of plug-ins. Give it some name (e.g., Android) and supply the following URL: `https://dl-ssl.google.com/android/eclipse/`. That should trigger Eclipse to download the roster of plug-ins available from that site:

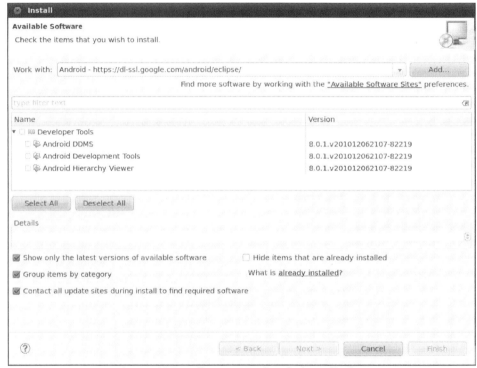

Figure 116. Eclipse ADT plug-in installation

Check the checkbox to the left of "Developer Tools" and click the Next button. Follow the rest of the wizard to review the tools to be downloaded and their respective license agreements. When the Finish button is enabled, click it, and Eclipse will download and install the plug-ins. When done, Eclipse will ask to restart – please let it.

Then, you need to teach ADT where your Android SDK installation is from the preceding section. To do this, choose Window | Preferences from the

Eclipse main menu (or the equivalent Preferences option for OS X). Click on the Android entry in the list on the left:

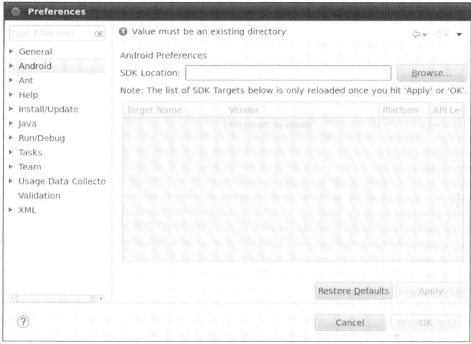

Figure 117. Eclipse ADT configuration

Then, click the Browse... button to find the directory where you installed the SDK. After choosing it, click Apply on the Preferences window, and you should see the Android SDK versions you installed previously. Then, click OK, and the ADT will be ready for use.

You may also wish to read the appendix with tips on working with the tutorials in Eclipse.

Install Apache Ant

If you will be doing all of your development from Eclipse, you can skip to the next section.

If you wish to develop using command-line build tools, you will need to install Apache Ant. You may have this already from previous Java development work, as it is fairly common in Java projects. However, you will need Ant version 1.8.1, so double-check your current copy (e.g., `ant -version`) to ensure you are on the proper edition.

If you do not have Ant, you can obtain it from the Apache Ant Web site[76]. They have full installation instructions[77] in the Ant manual, but the basic steps are:

1. Unpack the ZIP archive wherever it may make sense on your machine

2. Add a `JAVA_HOME` environment variable, pointing to where your JDK is installed, if you do not have one already

3. Add an `ANT_HOME` environment variable, pointing to the directory where you unpacked Ant in the first step above

4. Add `$JAVA_HOME/bin` and `$ANT_HOME/bin` to your `PATH`

5. Run `ant -version` to confirm that Ant is installed properly

Set Up the Emulator

The Android tools include an emulator, a piece of software that pretends to be an Android device. This is very useful for development – not only does it mean you can get started on Android without a device, but the emulator can help test device configurations that you do not own.

The Android emulator can emulate one or several Android devices. Each configuration you want is stored in an "Android Virtual Device", or AVD. The SDK and AVD Manager, which you used to download the SDK components earlier in this chapter, is where you create these AVDs.

If you do not have the SDK and AVD Manager running, you can run it via the android command from your SDK's `tools/` directory, or via Window |

---

76 http://ant.apache.org/bindownload.cgi
77 http://ant.apache.org/manual/installlist.html

SDK and AVD Manager from Eclipse. It starts up on a screen listing the AVDs you have available – initially, the list will be empty:

Figure 118. Android SDK and AVD Manager

Click the New... button to create a new AVD file. This brings up a dialog where you can configure what this AVD should look and work like:

Figure 119. Adding a New AVD

You need to provide the following:

- A name for the AVD. Since the name goes into files on your development machine, you will be limited by filename conventions for your operating system (e.g., no backslashes on Windows).

- The Android version you want the emulator to run (a.k.a., the "target"). Choose one of the SDKs you installed via the drop-down list. Note that in addition to "pure" Android environments, you will have options based on the third-party add-ons you selected. For example, you probably have some options for setting up AVDs containing the Google APIs, and you will need such an AVD for testing an application that uses Google Maps.

- Details about the SD card the emulator should emulate. Since Android devices invariably have some form of "external storage", you probably want to set up an SD card, by supplying a size in the associated field. However, since a file will be created on your development machine of whatever size you specify for the card, you probably do not want to create a 2GB emulated SD card. 32MB is a nice starting point, though you can go larger if needed.

- The "skin" or resolution the emulator should run in. The skin options you have will depend upon what target you chose. The skins let you choose a typical Android screen resolution (e.g., WVGA800 for 800x480). You can also manually specify a resolution when you want to test a non-standard configuration.

You can skip the "Hardware" section for now, as changing those settings is usually only required for advanced configurations.

The resulting dialog might look something like this:

Figure 120. Adding a New AVD (continued)

Click the Create AVD button, and your AVD stub will be created.

To start the emulator, highlight it in the list and click Start... You can skip the launch options for now and just click Launch. The first time you launch a new AVD, it will take a long time to start up. The second and subsequent times you start the AVD, it will come up a bit faster, and usually you only need to start it up once per day (e.g., when you start development). You do not need to stop and restart the emulator every time you want to test your application, in most cases.

The emulator will go through a few startup phases, first with a plain-text "ANDROID" label:

Figure 121. Android emulator, initial startup segment

...then a graphical Android logo:

Figure 122. Android emulator, secondary startup segment

before eventually landing at the home screen (the first time you run the AVD, shown below) or the keyguard:

Figure 123. Android home screen

If you get the keyguard (shown below), press the MENU button, or slide the green lock on the screen to the right, to get to the emulator's home screen:

Figure 124. Android keyguard

Set Up the Device

You do not need an Android device to get started in Android application development. Having one is a good idea before you try to ship an application (e.g., upload it to the Android Market). And, perhaps you already have a device – maybe that is what is spurring your interest in developing for Android.

The first step to make your device ready for use with development is to go into the Settings application on the device. From there, choose Applications, then Development. That should give you a set of checkboxes of development-related options to consider:

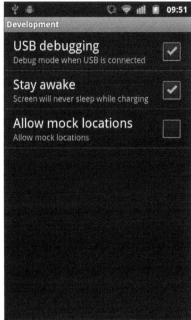

Figure 125. Android device development settings

Generally, you will want to enable USB debugging, so you can use your device with the Android build tools. You can leave the other settings alone for now if you wish, though you may find the "Stay awake" option to be handy, as it saves you from having to unlock your phone all of the time while it is plugged into USB.

Next, you need to get your development machine set up to talk to your device. That process varies by the operating system of your development machine, as is covered in the following sections.

Step #1: Windows

When you first plug in your Android device, Windows will attempt to find a driver for it. It is possible that, by virtue of other software you have installed, that the driver is ready for use. If it finds a driver, you are probably ready to go.

If the driver is not found, here are some options for getting one.

Windows Update

Some versions of Windows (e.g., Vista) will prompt you to search Windows Update for drivers. This is certainly worth a shot, though not every device will have supplied its driver to Microsoft.

Standard Android Driver

In your Android SDK installation, you will find a `google-usb_driver` directory, containing a generic Windows driver for Android devices. You can try pointing the driver wizard at this directory to see if it thinks this driver is suitable for your device.

Manufacturer-Supplied Driver

If you still do not have a driver, search the CD that came with the device (if any) or search the Web site of the device manufacturer. Motorola[78], for example, has drivers available for all of their devices in one spot for download.

Step #2: OS X and Linux

Odds are decent that simply plugging in your device will "just work". You can see if Android recognizes your device via running `adb devices` in a shell (e.g., OS X Terminal), where `adb` is in your `platform-tools/` directory of your SDK. If you get output similar to the following, Android detected your device:

```
List of devices attached
HT9CPP809576  device
```

---

78 http://developer.motorola.com/docstools/USB_Drivers/

If you are running Ubuntu (or perhaps other Linux variants), and this command did not work, you may need to add some udev rules. For example, here is a 51-android.rules file that will handle the devices from a handful of manufacturers:

```
SUBSYSTEM=="usb", SYSFS{idVendor}=="0bb4", MODE="0666"
SUBSYSTEM=="usb", SYSFS{idVendor}=="22b8", MODE="0666"
SUBSYSTEM=="usb", SYSFS{idVendor}=="18d1", MODE="0666"
SUBSYSTEMS=="usb", ATTRS{idVendor}=="18d1", ATTRS{idProduct}=="0c01",
MODE="0666", OWNER="[me]"
SUBSYSTEM=="usb", SYSFS{idVendor}=="19d2", SYSFS{idProduct}=="1354", MODE="0666"
SUBSYSTEM=="usb", SYSFS{idVendor}=="04e8", SYSFS{idProduct}=="681c", MODE="0666"
```

Drop that in your /etc/udev/rules.d directory on Ubuntu, then either reboot the computer or otherwise reload the udev rules (e.g., sudo service udev reload). Then, unplug and re-plug in the device and see if it is detected.

Coping with Eclipse

In addition to the tutorial-specific tips from the main chapters, here are some additional suggestions for how to get the best results when using Eclipse.

How to Import a Non-Eclipse Project

Not all Android projects ship with Eclipse project files, such as the sample projects associated with this book. However, these can still be easily added to your Eclipse workspace, if you wish. Here is how to do it!

First, choose File > New > Project... from the Eclipse main menu:

Figure 126. File menu in Eclipse

Then, choose Android > Android Project from the tree of available project types:

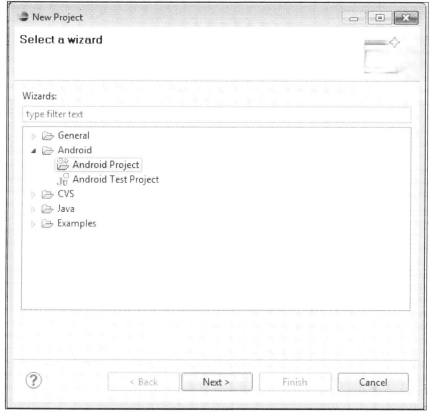

Figure 127. New project wizard in Eclipse

Note: if you do not see this option, you have not installed the Android Developer Tools.

Then, in the next page of the project creation wizard, choose the "Create project from existing source" radio button, click the [Browse...] button, and open the directory containing your project's AndroidManifest.xml file. This will populate most of the rest of this screen, though you may need to also specify a build target from the table:

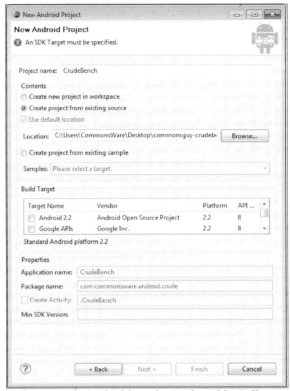

Figure 128. Android project wizard in Eclipse

Then, click [Finish]. This will return you to Eclipse, with the imported project in your workspace:

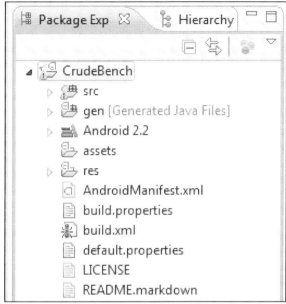

Figure 129. Android project tree in Eclipse

Next, right-click over the project name, and choose Build Path > Configure Build Path from the context menu:

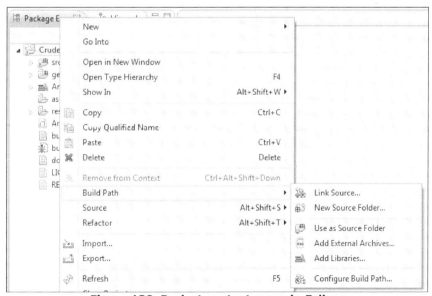

Figure 130. Project context menu in Eclipse

This brings up the build path portion of the project properties window:

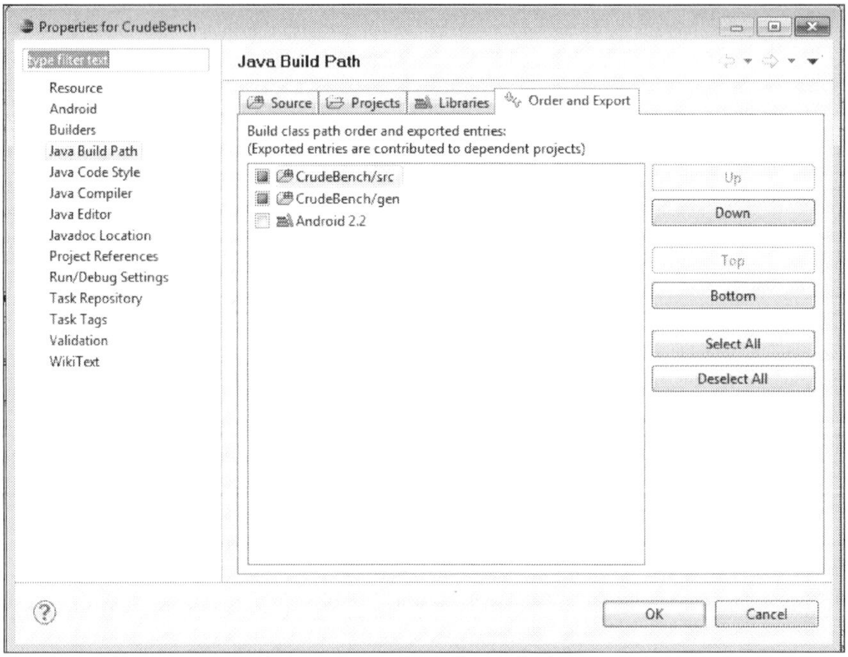

Figure 131. Project properties window in Eclipse

If the Android JAR is not checked (see the Android 2.2 entry in the above image), check it, then close the properties window.

Next, click on the Libraries tab, then click Add JAR. This will bring up a file selection dialog, showing the files in your open projects. In this project's files, go into the libs/ directory and see if there is anything there. If there is, choose it and accept the dialog. Repeat this for every JAR in libs/.

At this point, your project should be ready for use.

How to Get To DDMS

Many times, you will be told to take a look at something in DDMS, such as the LogCat tab to examine Java stack traces. In Eclipse, DDMS is a perspective. To open this perspective in your workspace, choose Window > Open Perspective > Other... from the main menu:

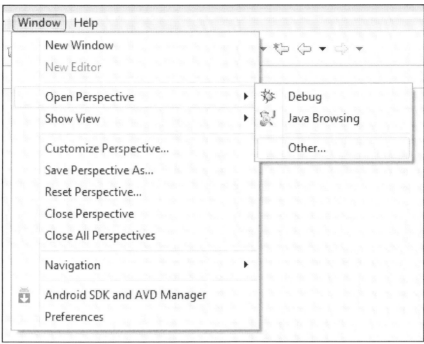

Figure 132. Perspective menu in Eclipse

Then, in the list of perspectives, choose DDMS:

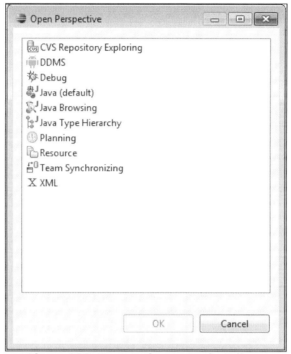

Figure 133. Perspective roster in Eclipse

This will add the DDMS perspective to your workspace and open it in your Eclipse IDE.

How to Create an Emulator

By default, your Eclipse environment has no Android emulators set up. You will need one before you can run your project successfully.

To do this, first choose Window > Android SDK and AVD Manager from the main menu:

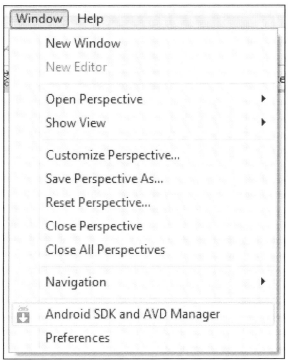

Figure 134. Android AVD Manager menu option in Eclipse

That brings up the same window as you can get by running android from the command line.

How to Run a Project

Given that you have an AVD defined, or that you have a device set up for debugging and connected to your development machine, you can run your project in the emulator.

First, click the Run toolbar button, or choose Project > Run from the main menu. This will bring up the "Run As" dialog the first time you run the project:

Figure 135. Android AVD Manager menu option in Eclipse

Choose Android Application and click OK. If you have more than one AVD or device available, you will be presented with a window where you choose the desired target environment. Then, the emulator will start up to run your application. Note that you will need to unlock the lock screen on the emulator (or device) if it is locked.

Keyword Index

487

Command..

Method...

29126998R00279

Made in the USA
Lexington, KY
14 January 2014